Nashville
Public Library
Foundation

*This book
made possible
through generous gifts
to the
Nashville Public Library
Foundation Book Fund*

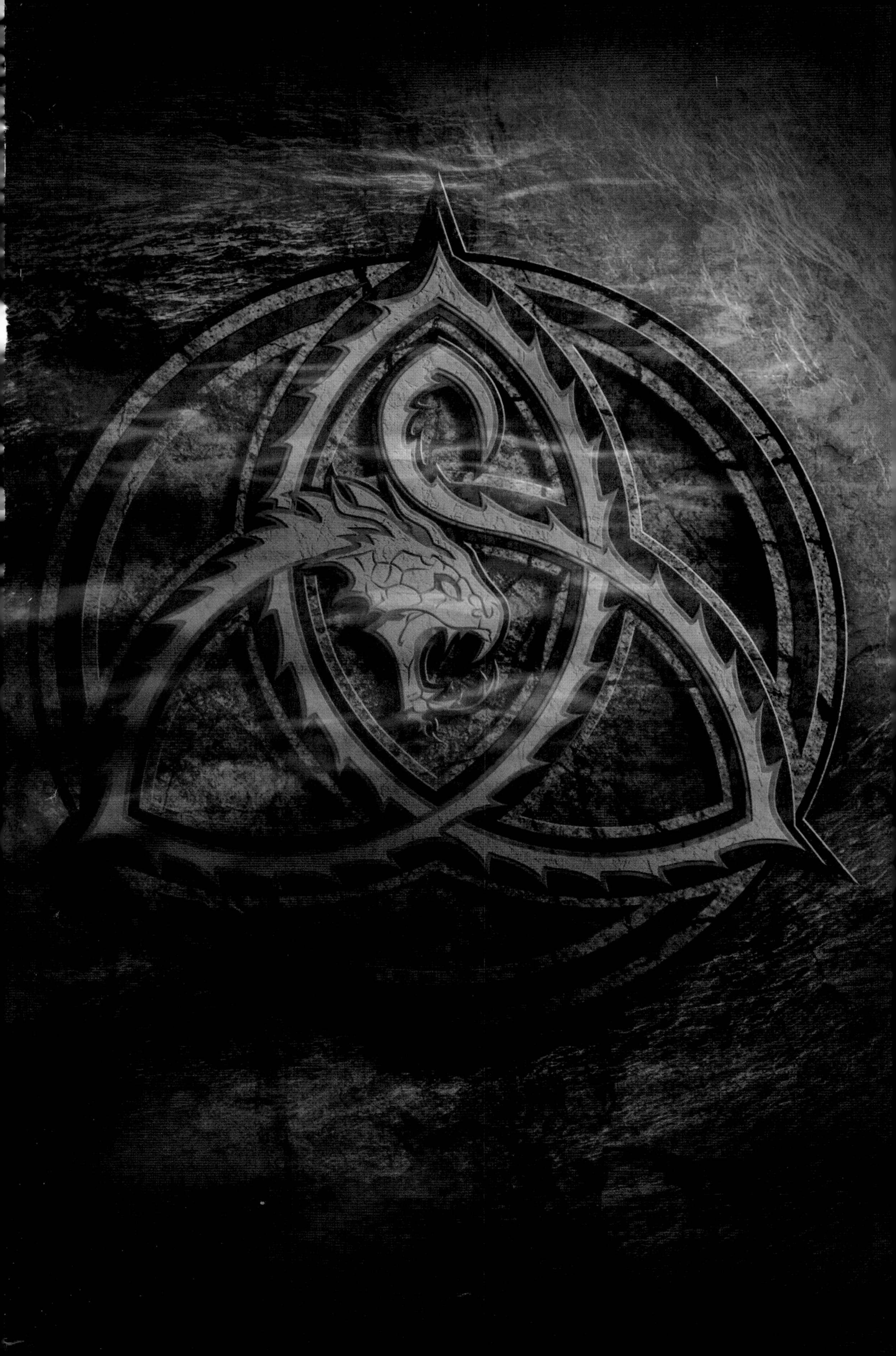

FEAR ITSELF JOURNEY INTO MYSTERY

WRITER
KIERON GILLEN

PENCILER
DOUG BRAITHWAITE

COLORIST
ULISES ARREOLA
WITH ANDY TROY (ISSUE #626)

LETTERER
VC'S CLAYTON COWLES

COVER ARTIST
STEPHANIE HANS

ASSISTANT EDITORS
CHARLIE BECKERMAN & JOHN DENNING

SENIOR EDITOR
RALPH MACCHIO

COLLECTION EDITOR: CORY LEVINE
ASSISTANT EDITORS: ALEX STARBUCK & NELSON RIBEIRO
EDITORS, SPECIAL PROJECTS: JENNIFER GRÜNWALD & MARK D. BEAZLEY
SENIOR EDITOR, SPECIAL PROJECTS: JEFF YOUNGQUIST
SENIOR VICE PRESIDENT OF SALES: DAVID GABRIEL
SVP OF BRAND PLANNING & COMMUNICATIONS: MICHAEL PASCIULLO
BOOK DESIGN: JEFF POWELL

EDITOR IN CHIEF: AXEL ALONSO
CHIEF CREATIVE OFFICER: JOE QUESADA
PUBLISHER: DAN BUCKLEY
EXECUTIVE PRODUCER: ALAN FINE

FEAR ITSELF: JOURNEY INTO MYSTERY. Contains material originally published in magazine form as JOURNEY INTO MYSTERY #622-626, THOR SPOTLIGHT and FEAR ITSELF SPOTLIGHT. First printing 2011. Hardcover ISBN# 978-0-7851-4840-1. Softcover ISBN# 978-0-7851-4841-8. Published by MARVEL WORLDWIDE, INC., a subsidiary of MARVEL ENTERTAINMENT, LLC. OFFICE OF PUBLICATION: 135 West 50th Street, New York, NY 10020. Hardcover: $19.99 per copy in the U.S. and $21.99 in Canada (GST #R127032852). Softcover: $15.99 per copy in the U.S. and $17.99 in Canada (GST #R127032852). Canadian Agreement #40668537. **Printed in the U.S.A.** ALAN FINE, EVP - Office of the President, Marvel Worldwide, Inc. and EVP & CMO Marvel Characters B.V.; DAN BUCKLEY, Publisher & President - Print, Animation & Digital Divisions; JOE QUESADA, Chief Creative Officer; DAVID BOGART, SVP of Business Affairs & Talent Management; TOM BREVOORT, SVP of Publishing; C.B. CEBULSKI, SVP of Creator & Content Development; DAVID GABRIEL, SVP of Publishing Sales & Circulation; MICHAEL PASCIULLO, SVP of Brand Planning & Communications; JIM O'KEEFE, VP of Operations & Logistics; DAN CARR, Executive Director of Publishing Technology; SUSAN CRESPI, Editorial Operations Manager; ALEX MORALES, Publishing Operations Manager; STAN LEE, Chairman Emeritus. For information regarding advertising in Marvel Comics or on Marvel.com, please contact John Dokes, SVP Integrated Sales and Marketing, at jdokes@marvel.com. For Marvel subscription inquiries, please call 800-217-9158. **Manufactured between 11/28/2011 and 1/2/2012 (hardcover), and 11/28/2011 and 8/13/2012 (softcover), by R.R. DONNELLEY, INC., SALEM, VA, USA.**

10 9 8 7 6 5 4 3 2 1

PREVIOUSLY

IN THE END, MANY OF THE ANSWERS ENDED UP BEING "LOKI."

WHO HELPED PERSUADE NORMAN OSBORN TO INITIATE THE ATTACK ON ASGARD? LOKI.
WHO CRIPPLED ASGARD'S DEFENSES, LEADING TO ITS ULTIMATE FALL? LOKI.

WHO, WHEN THE TIME CAME, TURNED COAT AND RISKED EVERYTHING TO SAVE THE WORLD
FROM THE UNLEASHED POWER OF THE VOID...ONLY TO BE DESTROYED? LOKI.

AND WHO, THROUGH CONTRACTS WITH HELA AND MEPHISTO, HAD HIMSELF STRICKEN
FROM THE BOOKS OF HEL, SO THAT, EVEN THOUGH HE DIED UPON THE BATTLEFIELD, HE
WAS NOT BOUND TO VALHALLA? THIS, TOO, WAS LOKI.

BUT, DESIROUS OF THE COMPANY OF HIS BROTHER, THOR FOUND A REINCARNATED SPIRIT
OF THE GOD OF MISCHIEF IN THE BODY OF A YOUNG STREET RAT. HE BROUGHT HIM BACK
TO ASGARD, MUCH TO THE CHAGRIN OF HIS BRETHREN, WHO STILL VIEWED LOKI—EVEN A
JUVENILE VERSION—AS A TRAITOR.

NOW, YOUNG LOKI ATTEMPTS TO FIT INTO A WORLD WHERE HE IS LARGELY UNWELCOME...

...AND THAT IS WHERE OUR JOURNEY BEGINS.

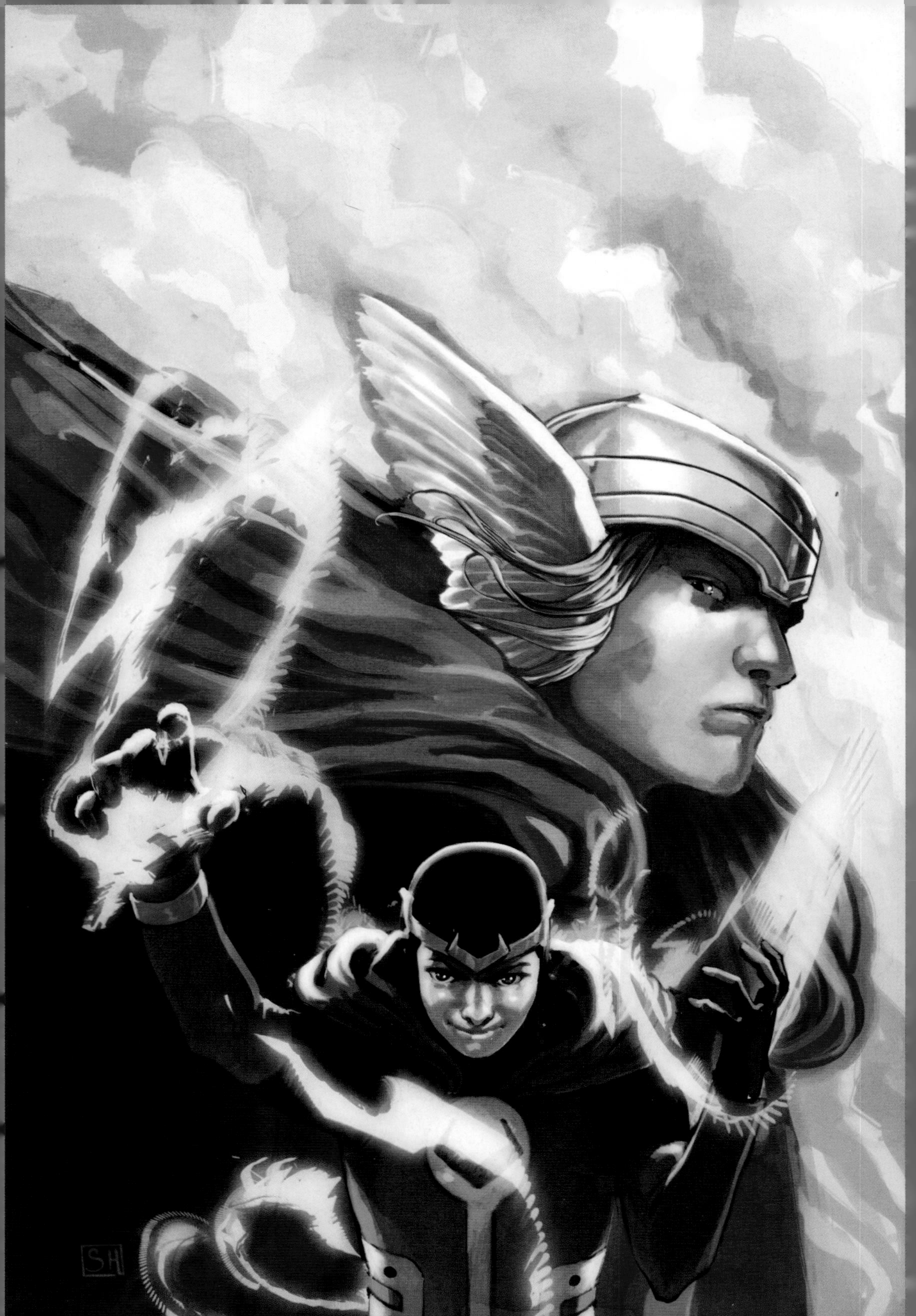
SH

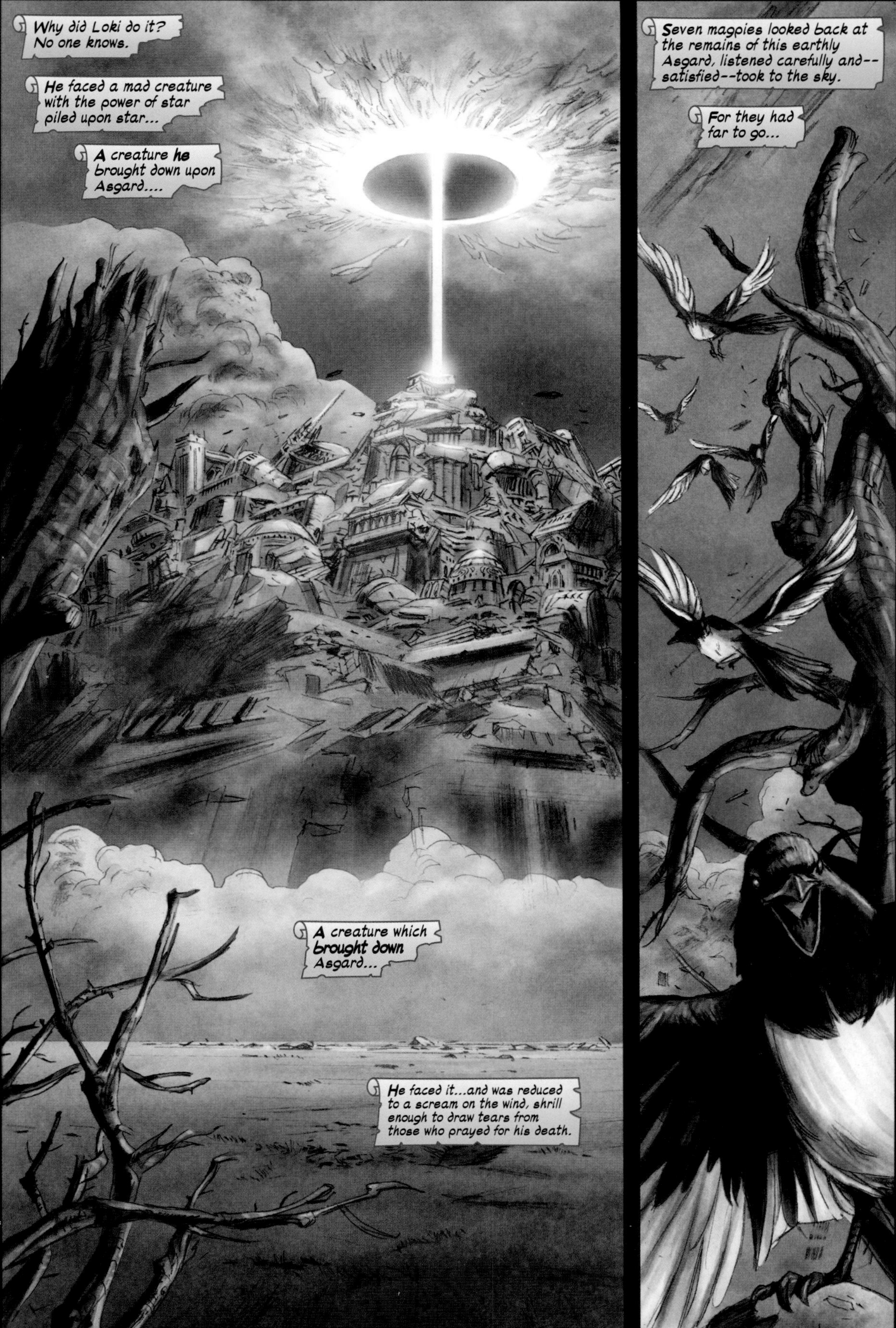
Why did Loki do it? No one knows.
He faced a mad creature with the power of star piled upon star...
A creature he brought down upon Asgard....
A creature which brought down Asgard...
He faced it...and was reduced to a scream on the wind, shrill enough to draw tears from those who prayed for his death.
Seven magpies looked back at the remains of this earthly Asgard, listened carefully and--satisfied--took to the sky.
For they had far to go...

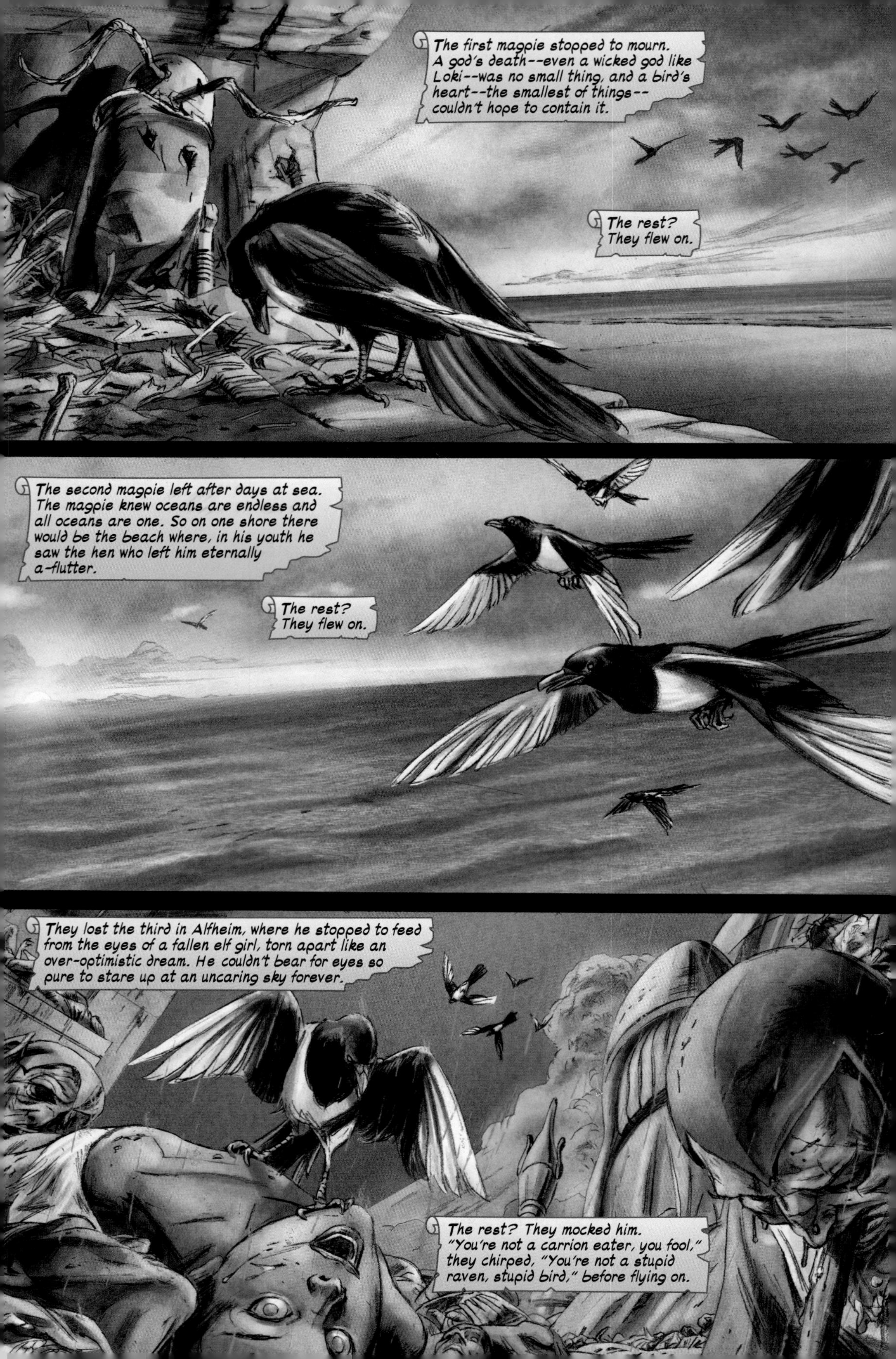
The first magpie stopped to mourn. A god's death--even a wicked god like Loki--was no small thing, and a bird's heart--the smallest of things--couldn't hope to contain it.
The rest? They flew on.
The second magpie left after days at sea. The magpie knew oceans are endless and all oceans are one. So on one shore there would be the beach where, in his youth he saw the hen who left him eternally a-flutter.
The rest? They flew on.
They lost the third in Alfheim, where he stopped to feed from the eyes of a fallen elf girl, torn apart like an over-optimistic dream. He couldn't bear for eyes so pure to stare up at an uncaring sky forever.
The rest? They mocked him. "You're not a carrion eater, you fool," they chirped, "You're not a stupid raven, stupid bird," before flying on.

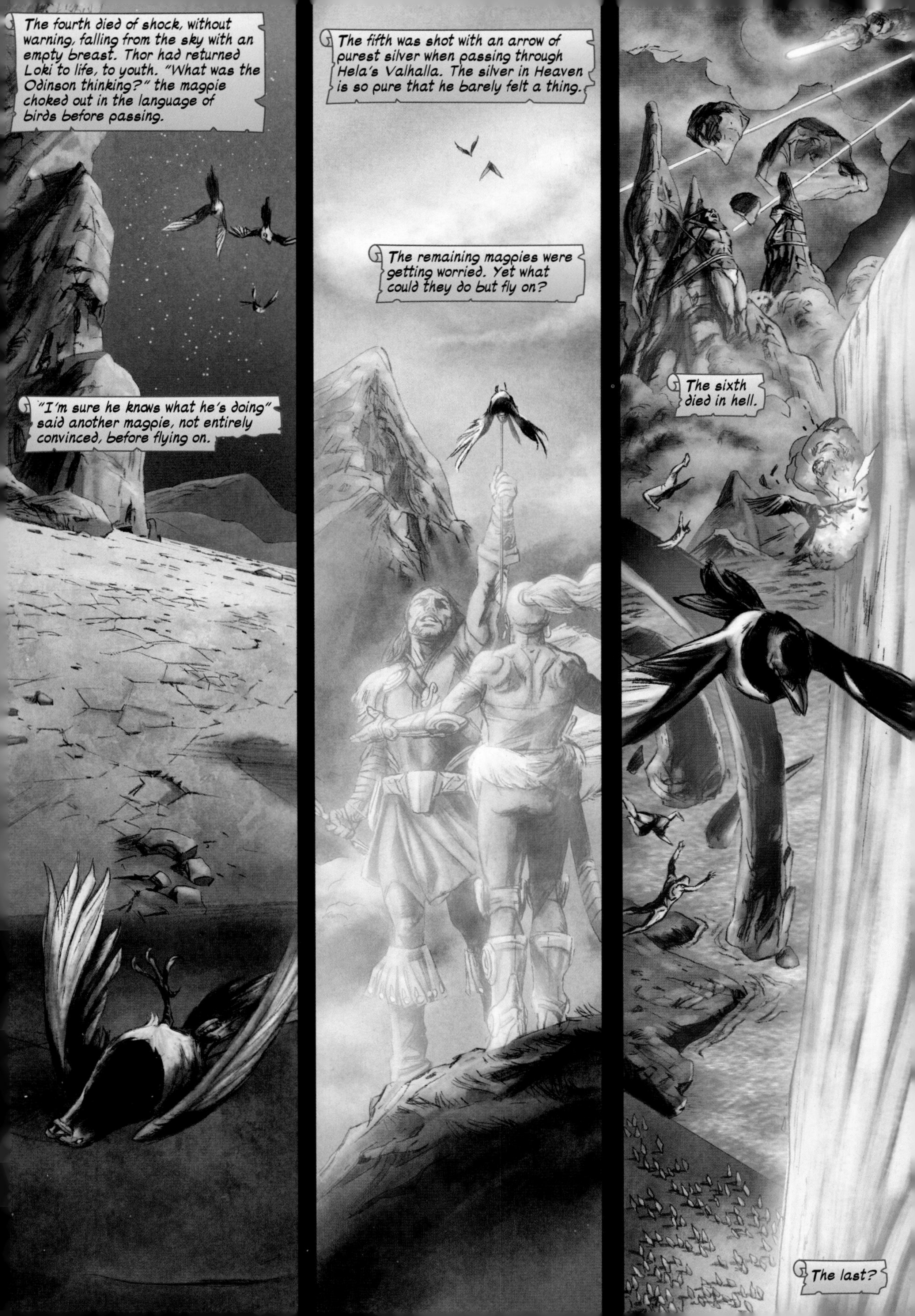
The fourth died of shock, without warning, falling from the sky with an empty breast. Thor had returned Loki to life, to youth. "What was the Odinson thinking?" the magpie choked out in the language of birds before passing.
"I'm sure he knows what he's doing" said another magpie, not entirely convinced, before flying on.
The fifth was shot with an arrow of purest silver when passing through Hela's Valhalla. The silver in Heaven is so pure that he barely felt a thing.
The remaining magpies were getting worried. Yet what could they do but fly on?
The sixth died in hell.
The last?

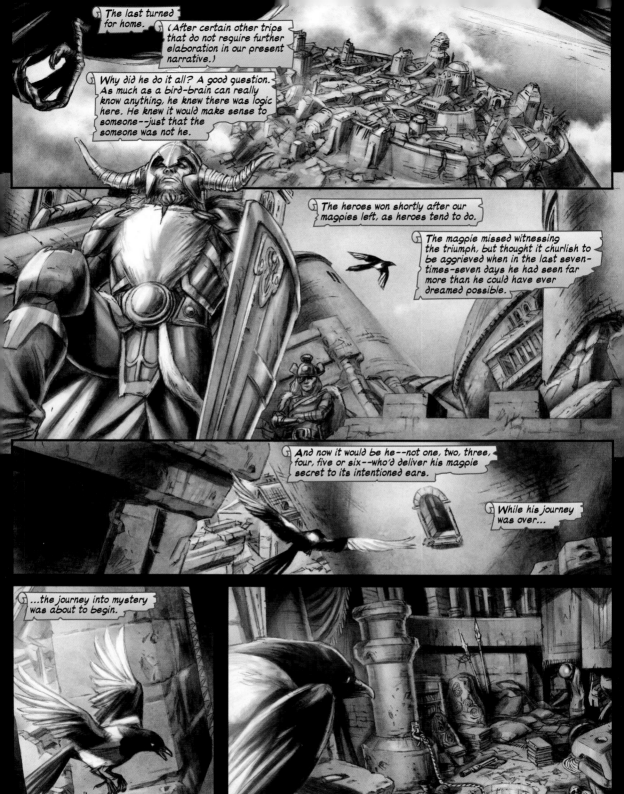

The last turned for home.

(After certain other trips that do not require further elaboration in our present narrative.)

Why did he do it all? A good question. As much as a bird-brain can really know anything, he knew there was logic here. He knew it would make sense to someone--just that the someone was not he.

The heroes won shortly after our magpies left, as heroes tend to do.

The magpie missed witnessing the triumph, but thought it churlish to be aggrieved when in the last seven-times-seven days he had seen far more than he could have ever dreamed possible.

And now it would be he--not one, two, three, four, five or six--who'd deliver his magpie secret to its intentioned ears.

While his journey was over...

...the journey into mystery was about to begin.

Or it could have, if young master Loki was where he was meant to be.

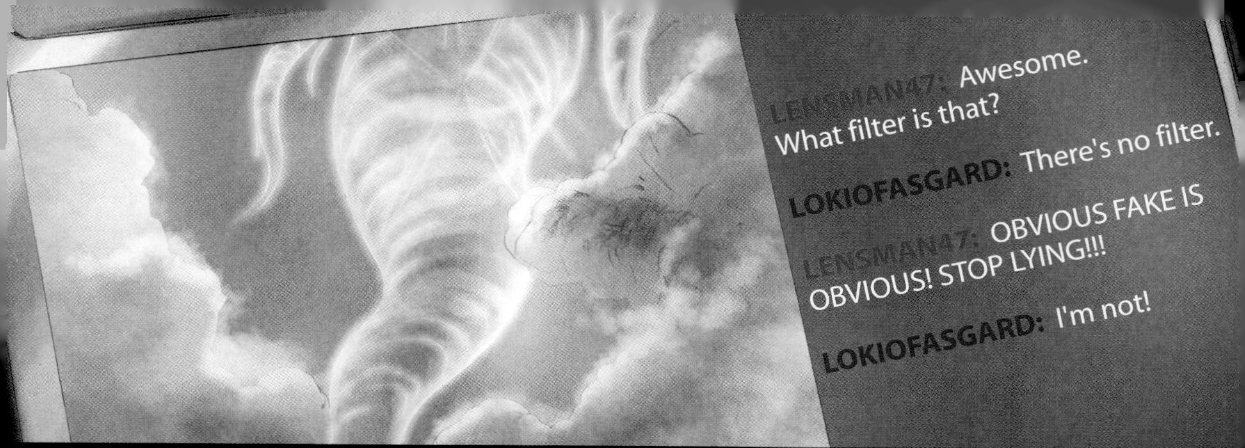
LENSMAN47: Awesome. What filter is that?
LOKIOFASGARD: There's no filter.
LENSMAN47: OBVIOUS FAKE IS OBVIOUS! STOP LYING!!!
LOKIOFASGARD: I'm not!

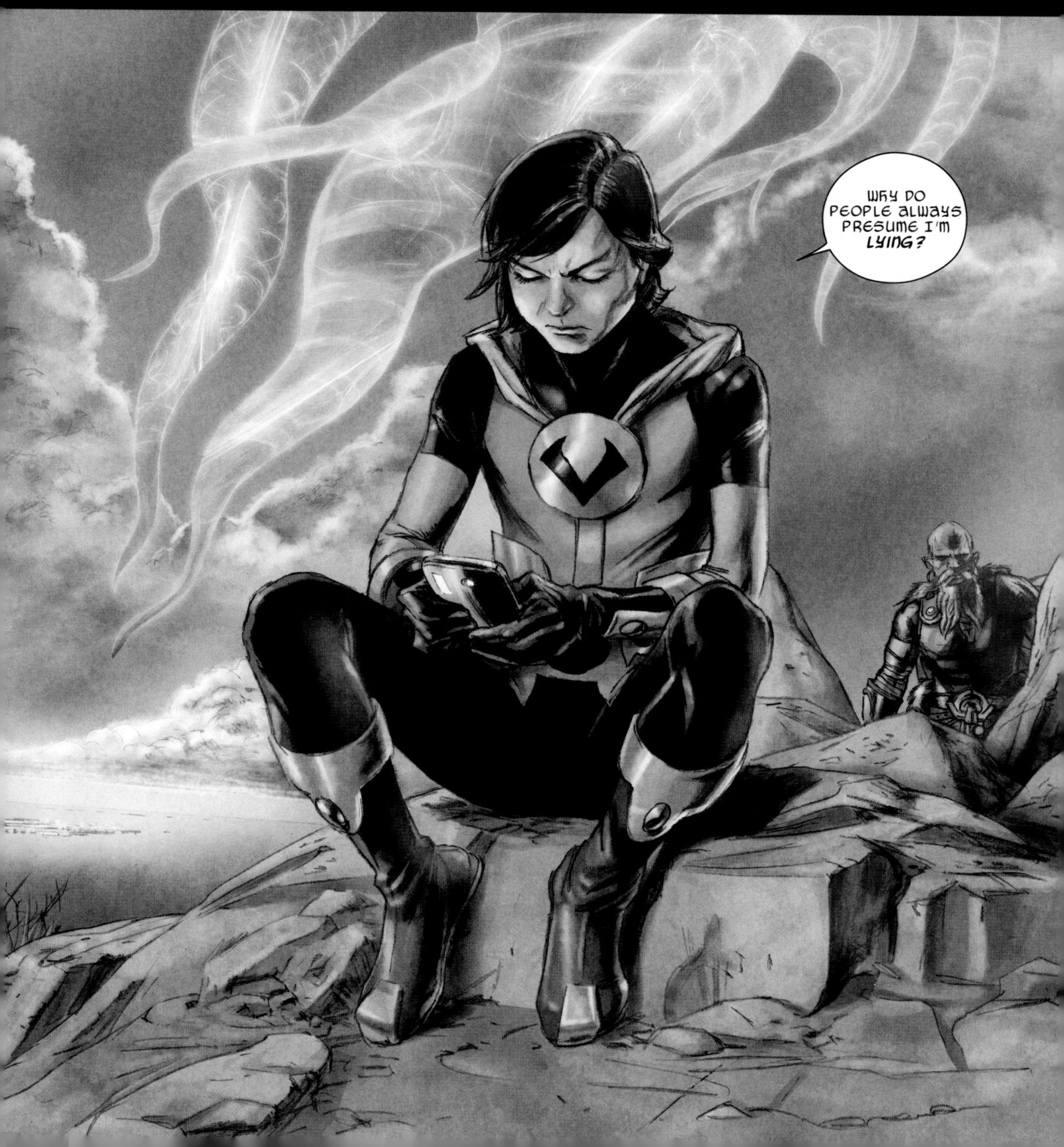
WHY DO PEOPLE ALWAYS PRESUME I'M LYING?

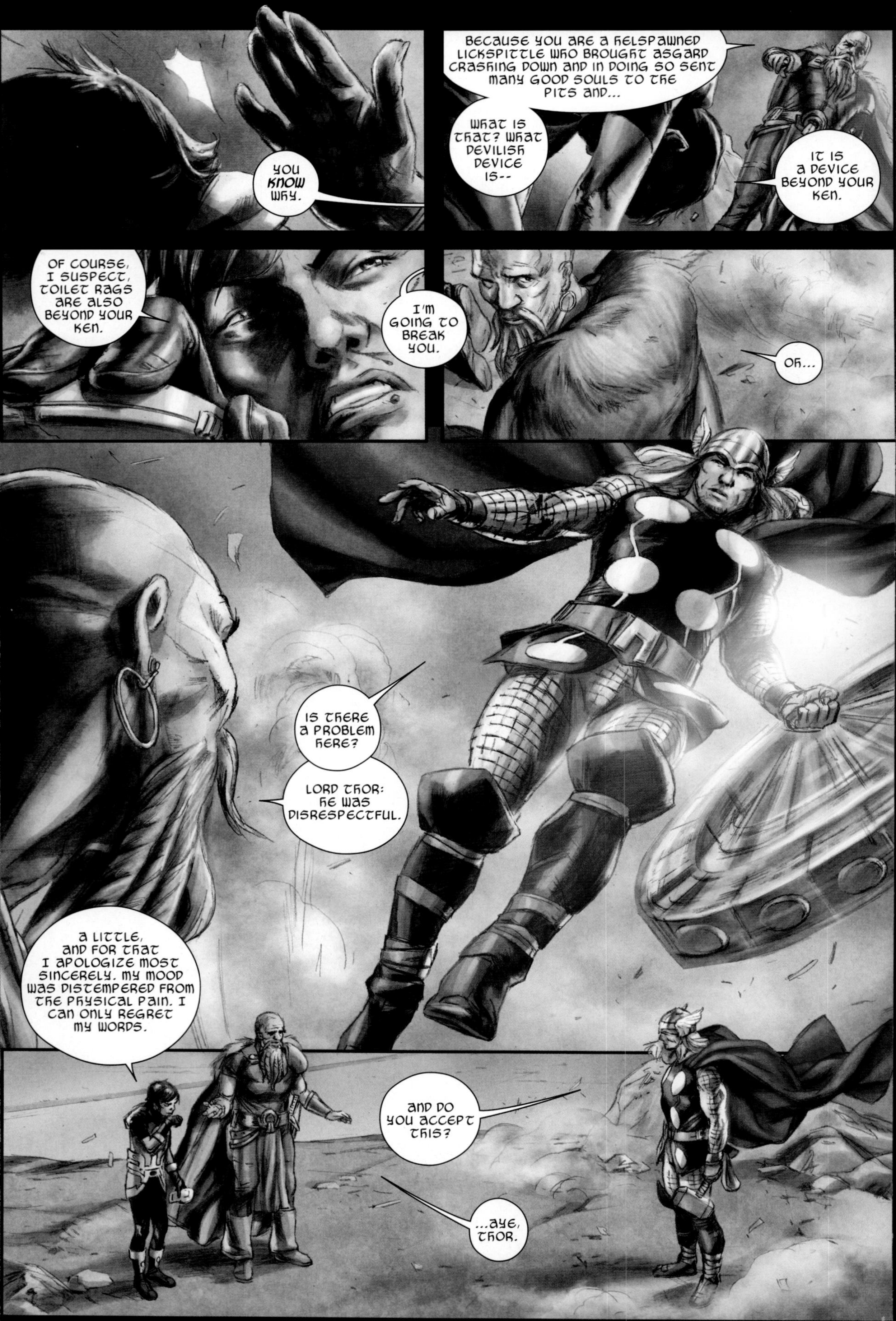

YOU KNOW WHY.
BECAUSE YOU ARE A HELSPAWNED LICKSPITTLE WHO BROUGHT ASGARD CRASHING DOWN AND IN DOING SO SENT MANY GOOD SOULS TO THE PITS AND...
WHAT IS THAT? WHAT DEVILISH DEVICE IS--
IT IS A DEVICE BEYOND YOUR KEN.
OF COURSE, I SUSPECT, TOILET RAGS ARE ALSO BEYOND YOUR KEN.
I'M GOING TO BREAK YOU.
OH...
IS THERE A PROBLEM HERE?
LORD THOR: HE WAS DISRESPECTFUL.
A LITTLE, AND FOR THAT I APOLOGIZE MOST SINCERELY. MY MOOD WAS DISTEMPERED FROM THE PHYSICAL PAIN. I CAN ONLY REGRET MY WORDS.
AND DO YOU ACCEPT THIS?
...AYE, THOR.

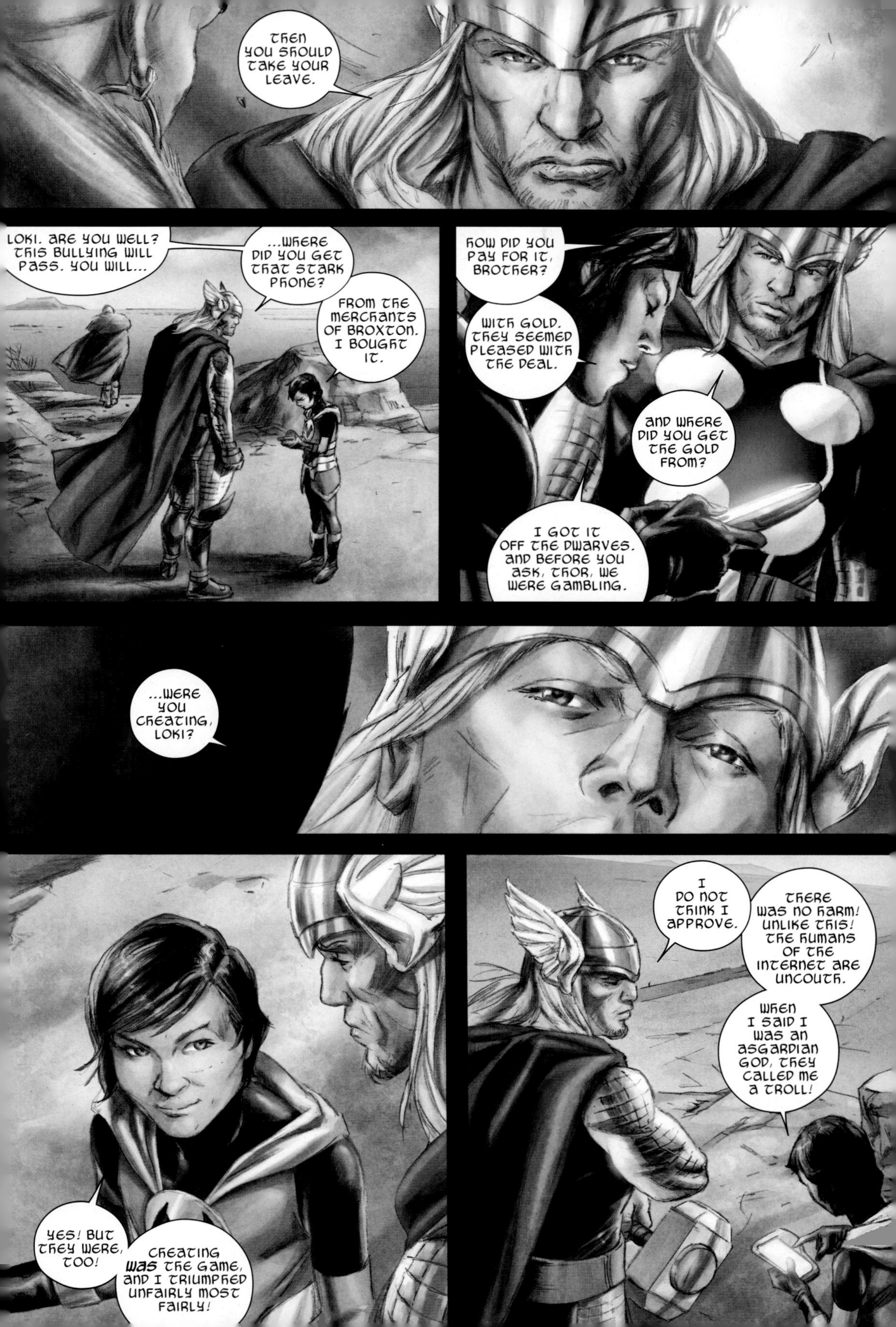
THEN YOU SHOULD TAKE YOUR LEAVE.
LOKI. ARE YOU WELL? THIS BULLYING WILL PASS. YOU WILL...
...WHERE DID YOU GET THAT STARK PHONE?
FROM THE MERCHANTS OF BROXTON. I BOUGHT IT.
HOW DID YOU PAY FOR IT, BROTHER?
WITH GOLD. THEY SEEMED PLEASED WITH THE DEAL.
AND WHERE DID YOU GET THE GOLD FROM?
I GOT IT OFF THE DWARVES. AND BEFORE YOU ASK, THOR, WE WERE GAMBLING.
...WERE YOU CHEATING, LOKI?
YES! BUT THEY WERE, TOO!
CHEATING WAS THE GAME, AND I TRIUMPHED UNFAIRLY MOST FAIRLY!
I DO NOT THINK I APPROVE.
THERE WAS NO HARM! UNLIKE THIS! THE HUMANS OF THE INTERNET ARE UNCOUTH.
WHEN I SAID I WAS AN ASGARDIAN GOD, THEY CALLED ME A TROLL!

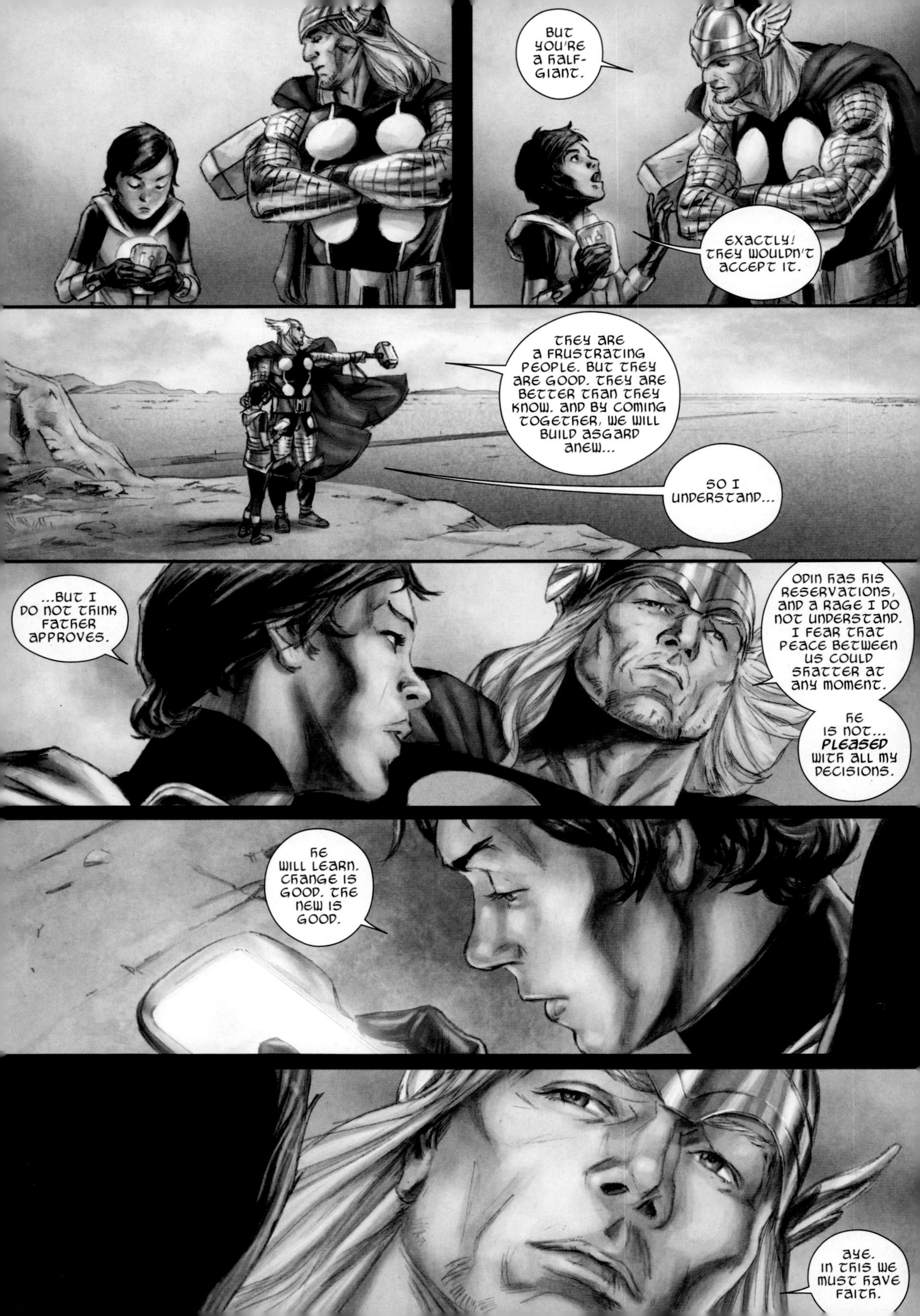
BUT YOU'RE A HALF-GIANT.
EXACTLY! THEY WOULDN'T ACCEPT IT.
THEY ARE A FRUSTRATING PEOPLE. BUT THEY ARE GOOD. THEY ARE BETTER THAN THEY KNOW. AND BY COMING TOGETHER, WE WILL BUILD ASGARD ANEW...
SO I UNDERSTAND...
...BUT I DO NOT THINK FATHER APPROVES.
ODIN HAS HIS RESERVATIONS, AND A RAGE I DO NOT UNDERSTAND. I FEAR THAT PEACE BETWEEN US COULD SHATTER AT ANY MOMENT.
HE IS NOT... **PLEASED** WITH ALL MY DECISIONS.
HE WILL LEARN. CHANGE IS GOOD. THE NEW IS GOOD.
AYE. IN THIS WE MUST HAVE FAITH.

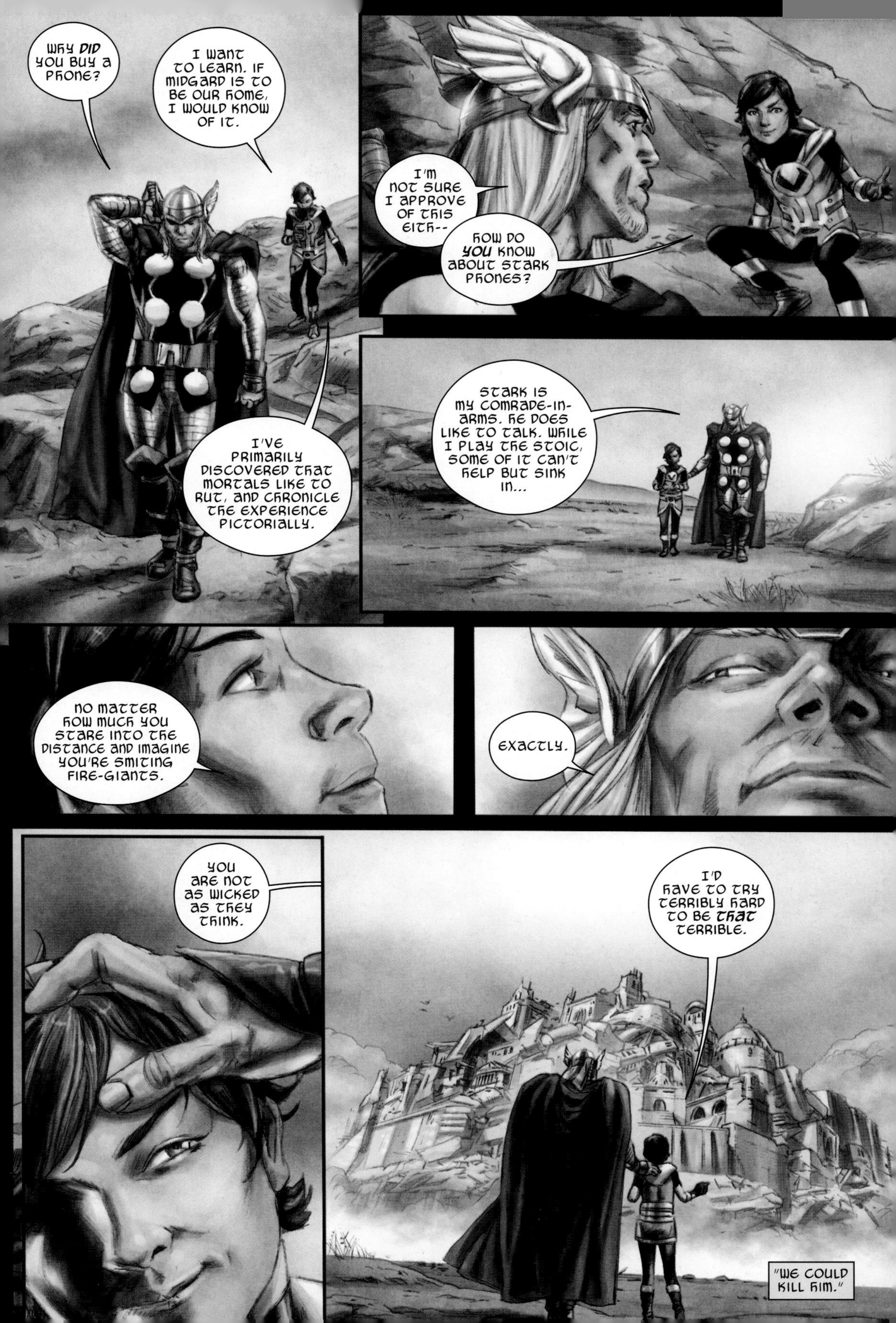
WHY DID YOU BUY A PHONE?
I WANT TO LEARN. IF MIDGARD IS TO BE OUR HOME, I WOULD KNOW OF IT.
I'VE PRIMARILY DISCOVERED THAT MORTALS LIKE TO RUT, AND CHRONICLE THE EXPERIENCE PICTORIALLY.
I'M NOT SURE I APPROVE OF THIS EITH--
HOW DO YOU KNOW ABOUT STARK PHONES?
STARK IS MY COMRADE-IN-ARMS. HE DOES LIKE TO TALK. WHILE I PLAY THE STOIC, SOME OF IT CAN'T HELP BUT SINK IN...
NO MATTER HOW MUCH YOU STARE INTO THE DISTANCE AND IMAGINE YOU'RE SMITING FIRE-GIANTS.
EXACTLY.
YOU ARE NOT AS WICKED AS THEY THINK.
I'D HAVE TO TRY TERRIBLY HARD TO BE THAT TERRIBLE.
"WE COULD KILL HIM."

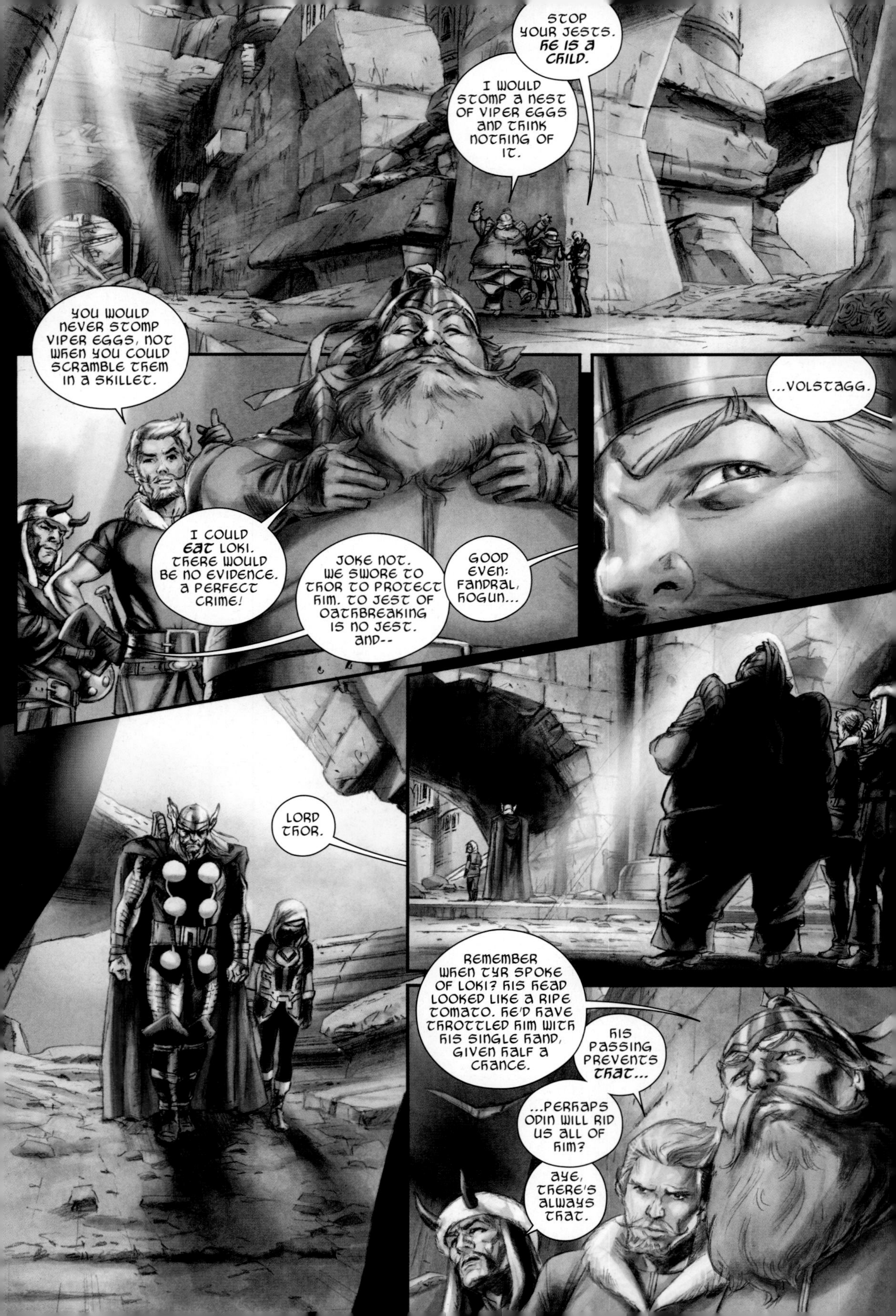
STOP YOUR JESTS. HE IS A CHILD.
I WOULD STOMP A NEST OF VIPER EGGS AND THINK NOTHING OF IT.
YOU WOULD NEVER STOMP VIPER EGGS, NOT WHEN YOU COULD SCRAMBLE THEM IN A SKILLET.
I COULD EAT LOKI. THERE WOULD BE NO EVIDENCE. A PERFECT CRIME!
JOKE NOT. WE SWORE TO THOR TO PROTECT HIM. TO JEST OF OATHBREAKING IS NO JEST. AND--
GOOD EVEN: FANDRAL, HOGUN...
...VOLSTAGG.
LORD THOR.
REMEMBER WHEN TYR SPOKE OF LOKI? HIS HEAD LOOKED LIKE A RIPE TOMATO. HE'D HAVE THROTTLED HIM WITH HIS SINGLE HAND, GIVEN HALF A CHANCE.
HIS PASSING PREVENTS THAT...
...PERHAPS ODIN WILL RID US ALL OF HIM?
AYE, THERE'S ALWAYS THAT.

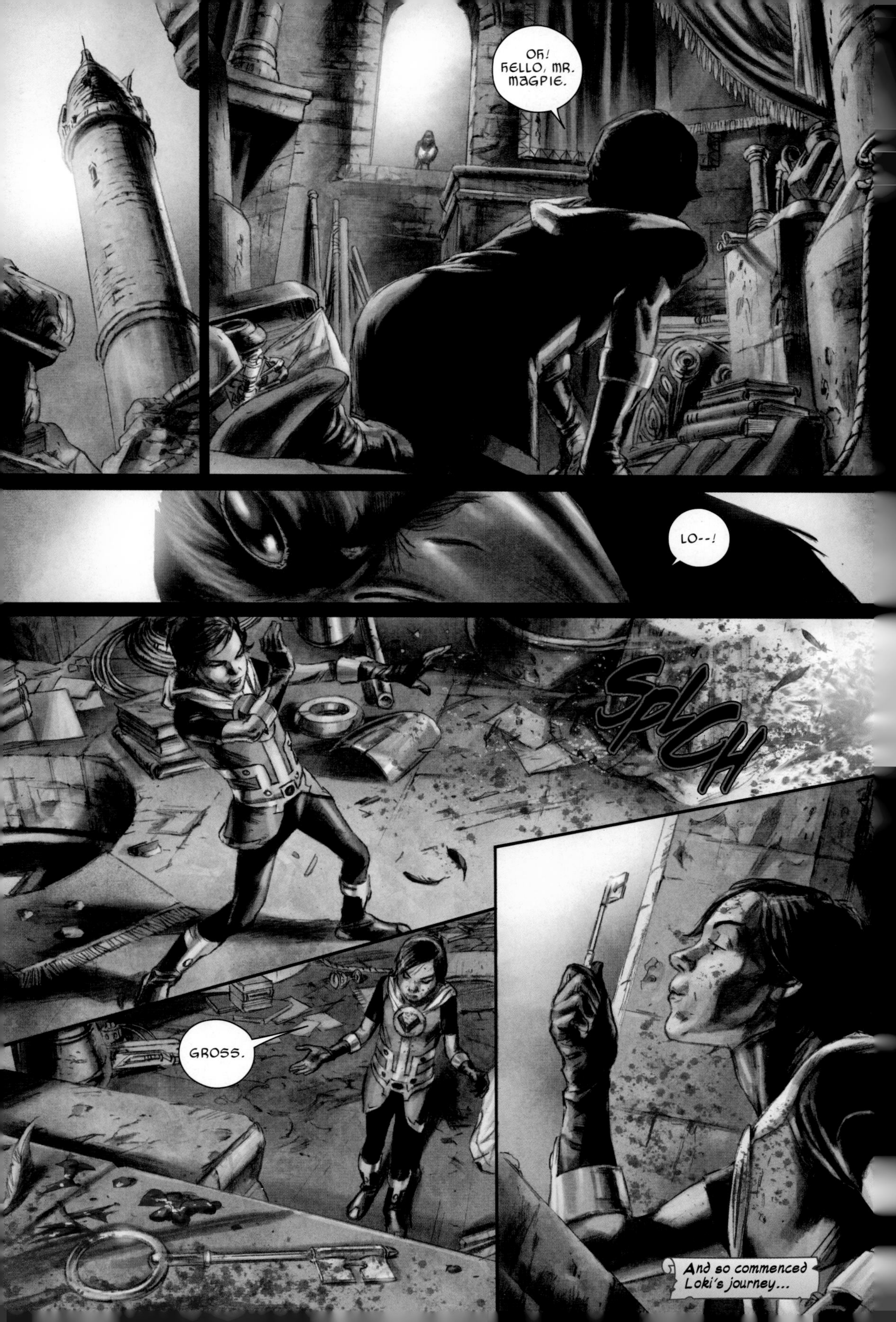
OH! HELLO, MR. MAGPIE.
LO--!
SPLCH
GROSS.
And so commenced Loki's journey...

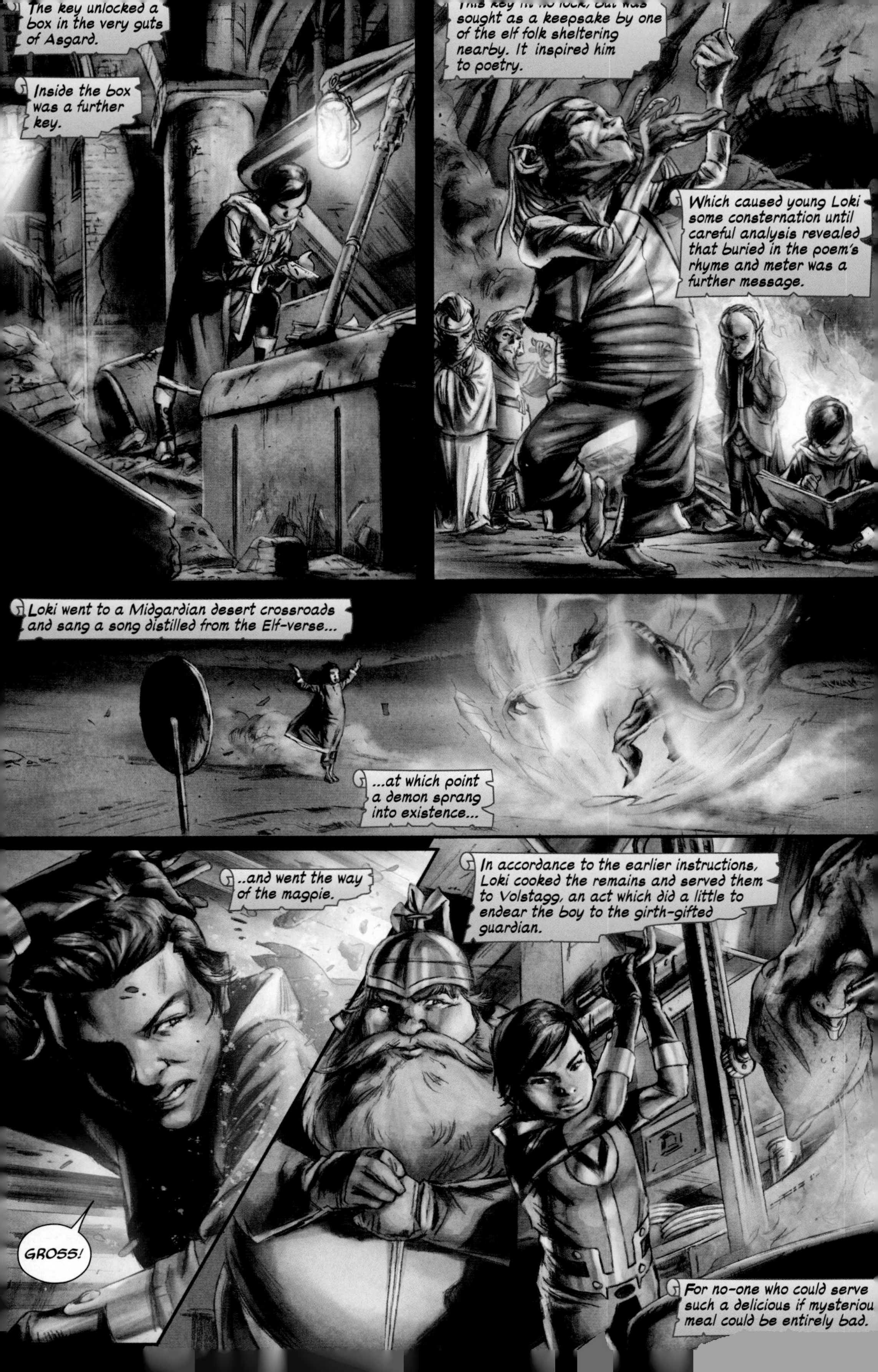

The key unlocked a box in the very guts of Asgard.
Inside the box was a further key.
sought as a keepsake by one of the elf folk sheltering nearby. It inspired him to poetry.
Which caused young Loki some consternation until careful analysis revealed that buried in the poem's rhyme and meter was a further message.
Loki went to a Midgardian desert crossroads and sang a song distilled from the Elf-verse...
...at which point a demon sprang into existence...
..and went the way of the magpie.
In accordance to the earlier instructions, Loki cooked the remains and served them to Volstagg, an act which did a little to endear the boy to the girth-gifted guardian.
GROSS!
For no-one who could serve such a delicious if mysteriou meal could be entirely bad.

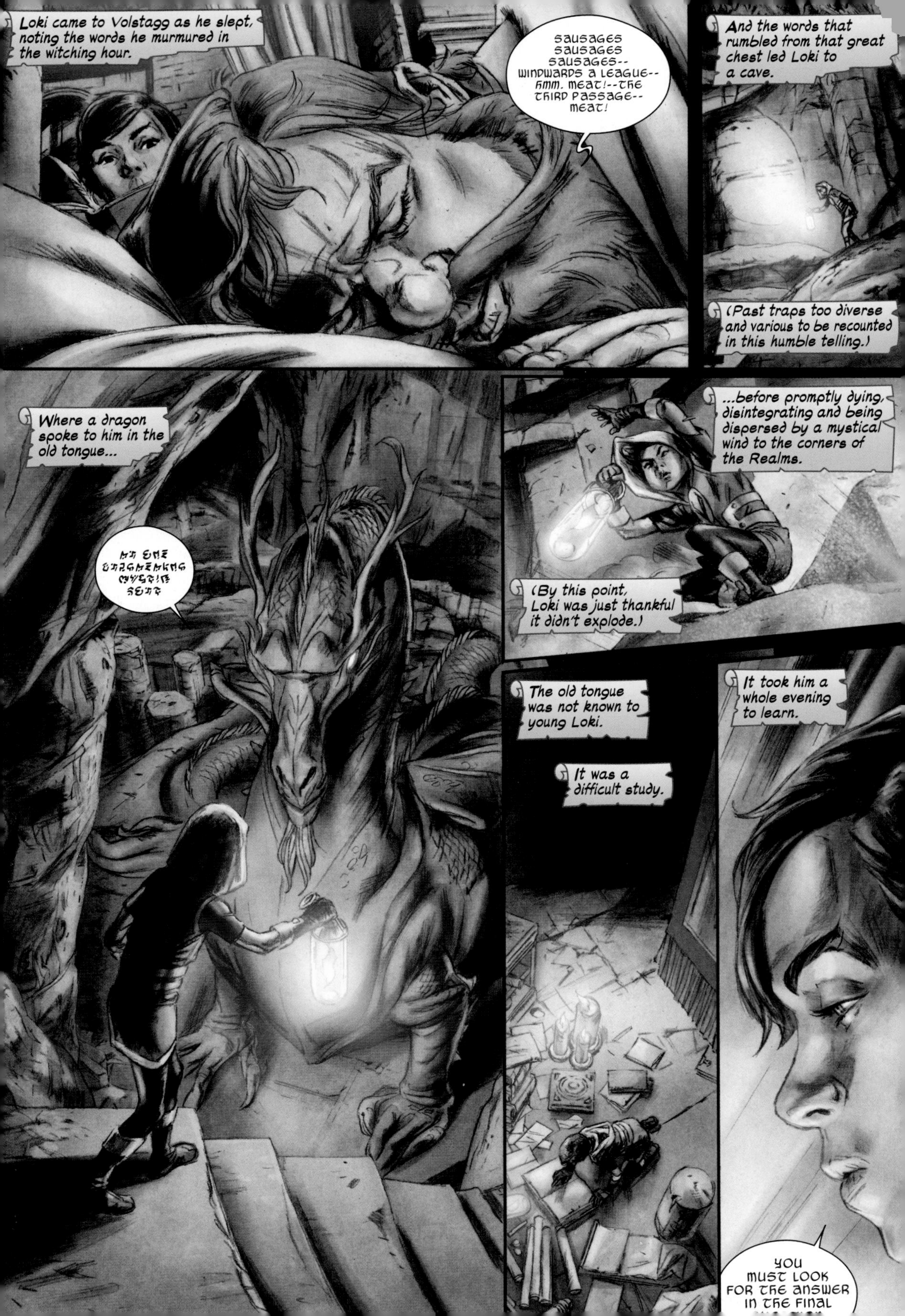
Loki came to Volstagg as he slept, noting the words he murmured in the witching hour.
SAUSAGES SAUSAGES SAUSAGES-- WINDWARDS A LEAGUE-- HMM. MEAT!--THE THIRD PASSAGE-- MEAT!
And the words that rumbled from that great chest led Loki to a cave.
(Past traps too diverse and various to be recounted in this humble telling.)
Where a dragon spoke to him in the old tongue...
...before promptly dying, disintegrating and being dispersed by a mystical wind to the corners of the Realms.
(By this point, Loki was just thankful it didn't explode.)
The old tongue was not known to young Loki.
It was a difficult study.
It took him a whole evening to learn.
YOU MUST LOOK FOR THE ANSWER IN THE FINAL

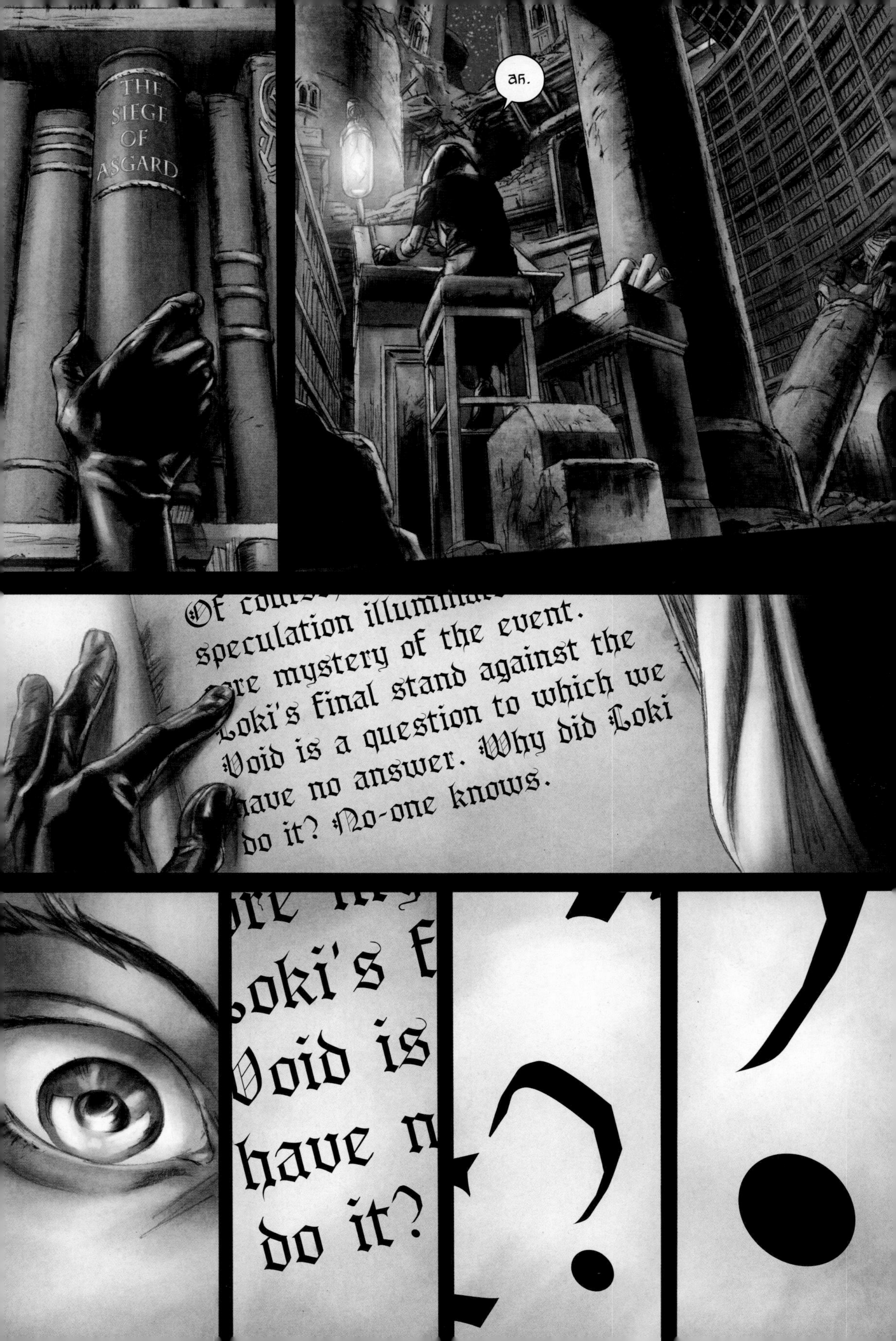
THE SIEGE OF ASGARD
AH.
speculation
mystery of the event.
Loki's final stand against the
Void is a question to which we
have no answer. Why did Loki
do it? No-one knows.
Loki's
Void is
have
do it?

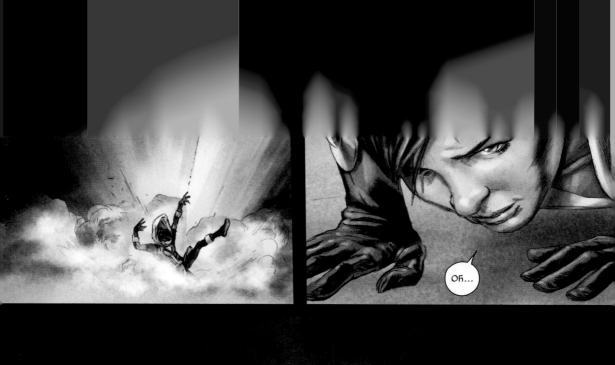

OH...

HELLO, MR. MAGPIE.

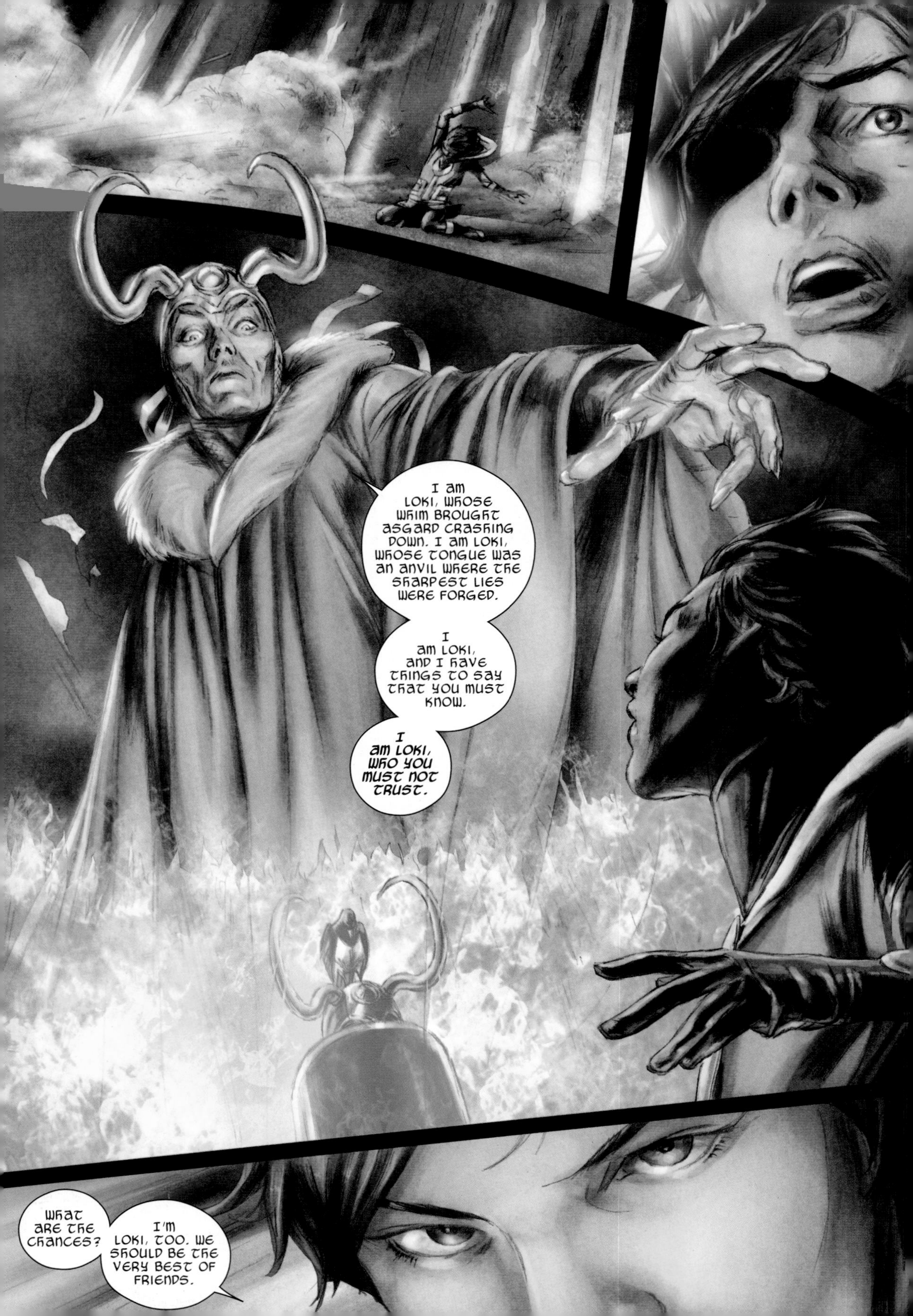
I AM LOKI, WHOSE WHIM BROUGHT ASGARD CRASHING DOWN. I AM LOKI, WHOSE TONGUE WAS AN ANVIL WHERE THE SHARPEST LIES WERE FORGED.
I AM LOKI, AND I HAVE THINGS TO SAY THAT YOU MUST KNOW.
I AM LOKI, WHO YOU MUST NOT TRUST.
WHAT ARE THE CHANCES?
I'M LOKI, TOO. WE SHOULD BE THE VERY BEST OF FRIENDS.

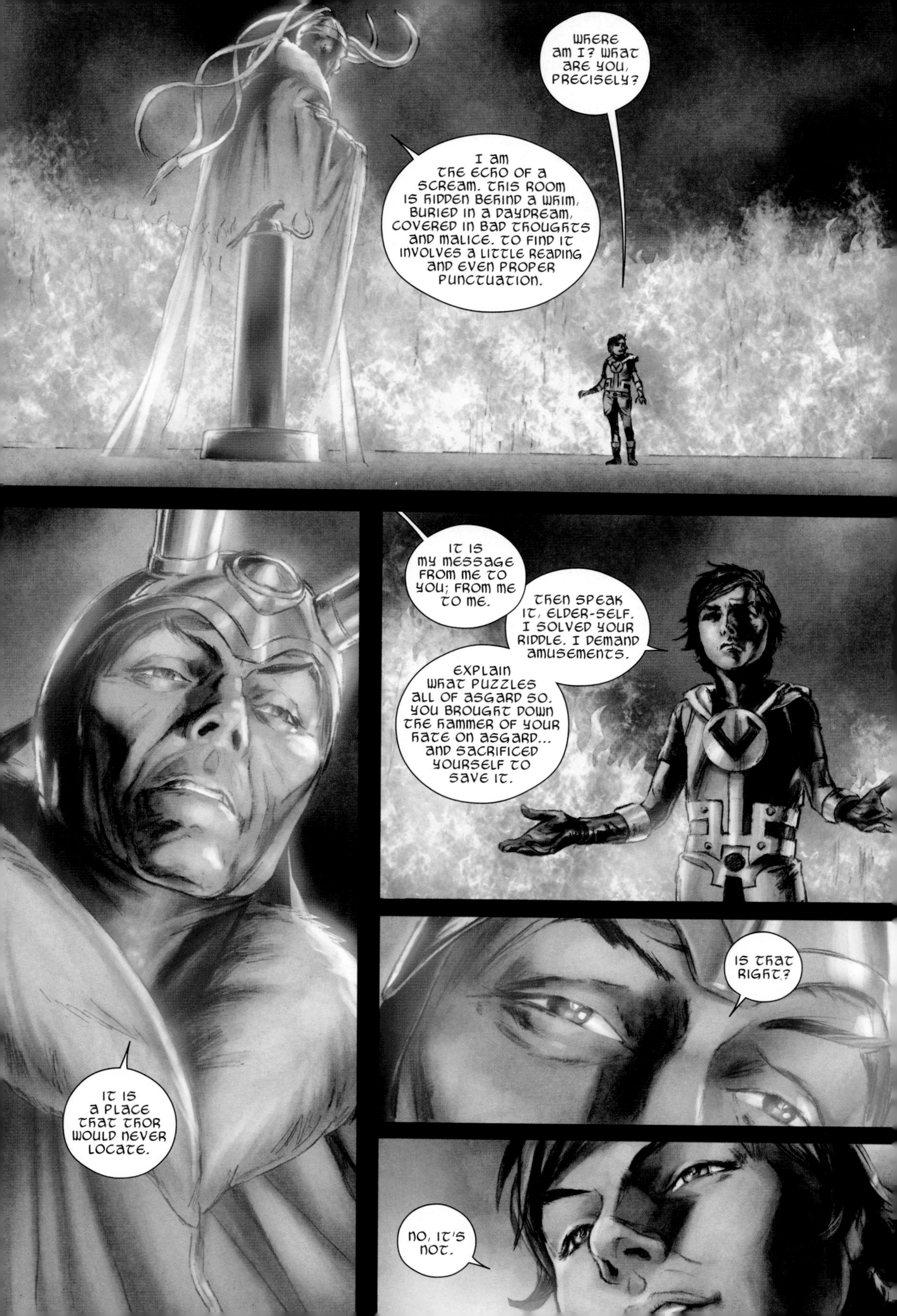
WHERE AM I? WHAT ARE YOU, PRECISELY?
I AM THE ECHO OF A SCREAM. THIS ROOM IS HIDDEN BEHIND A WHIM, BURIED IN A DAYDREAM, COVERED IN BAD THOUGHTS AND MALICE. TO FIND IT INVOLVES A LITTLE READING AND EVEN PROPER PUNCTUATION.
IT IS MY MESSAGE FROM ME TO YOU; FROM ME TO ME.
THEN SPEAK IT, ELDER-SELF. I SOLVED YOUR RIDDLE. I DEMAND AMUSEMENTS.
EXPLAIN WHAT PUZZLES ALL OF ASGARD SO. YOU BROUGHT DOWN THE HAMMER OF YOUR HATE ON ASGARD... AND SACRIFICED YOURSELF TO SAVE IT.
IT IS A PLACE THAT THOR WOULD NEVER LOCATE.
IS THAT RIGHT?
NO, IT'S NOT.

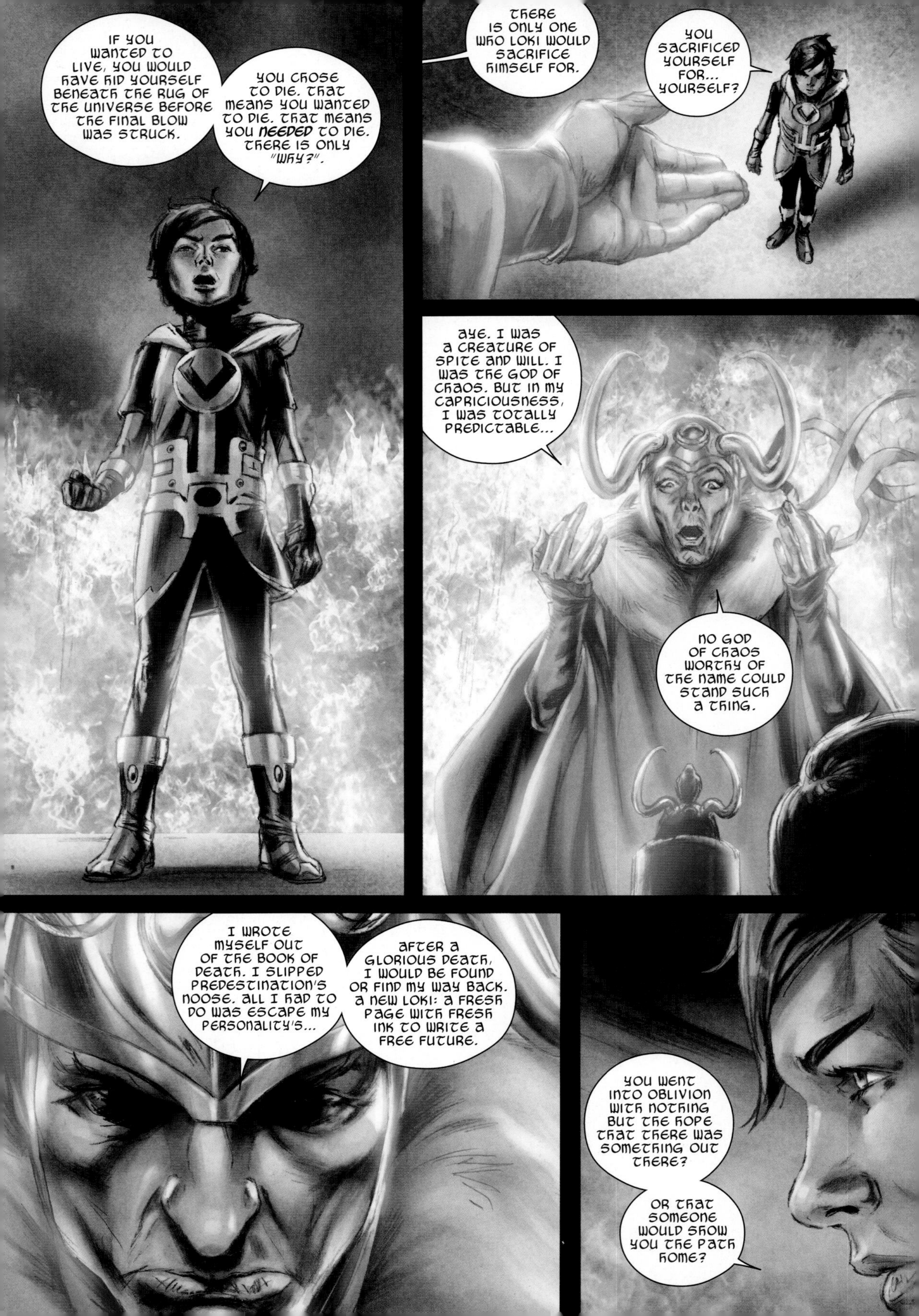
IF YOU WANTED TO LIVE, YOU WOULD HAVE HID YOURSELF BENEATH THE RUG OF THE UNIVERSE BEFORE THE FINAL BLOW WAS STRUCK.
YOU CHOSE TO DIE. THAT MEANS YOU WANTED TO DIE. THAT MEANS YOU *NEEDED* TO DIE. THERE IS ONLY "WHY?".
THERE IS ONLY ONE WHO LOKI WOULD SACRIFICE HIMSELF FOR.
YOU SACRIFICED YOURSELF FOR... YOURSELF?
AYE. I WAS A CREATURE OF SPITE AND WILL. I WAS THE GOD OF CHAOS. BUT IN MY CAPRICIOUSNESS, I WAS TOTALLY PREDICTABLE...
NO GOD OF CHAOS WORTHY OF THE NAME COULD STAND SUCH A THING.
I WROTE MYSELF OUT OF THE BOOK OF DEATH. I SLIPPED PREDESTINATION'S NOOSE. ALL I HAD TO DO WAS ESCAPE MY PERSONALITY'S...
AFTER A GLORIOUS DEATH, I WOULD BE FOUND OR FIND MY WAY BACK. A NEW LOKI: A FRESH PAGE WITH FRESH INK TO WRITE A FREE FUTURE.
YOU WENT INTO OBLIVION WITH NOTHING BUT THE HOPE THAT THERE WAS SOMETHING OUT THERE?
OR THAT SOMEONE WOULD SHOW YOU THE PATH HOME?

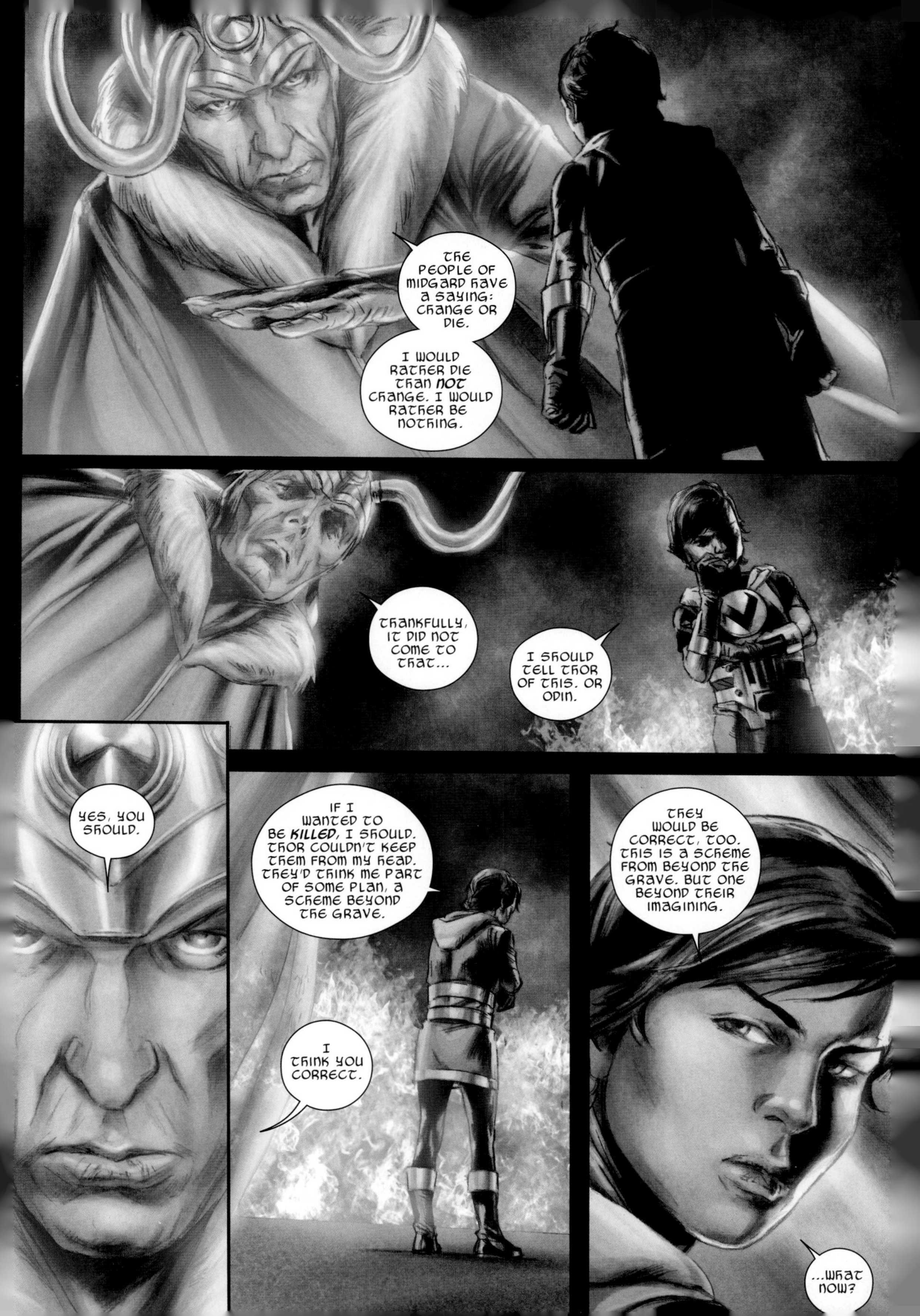
THE PEOPLE OF MIDGARD HAVE A SAYING: CHANGE OR DIE.
I WOULD RATHER DIE THAN NOT CHANGE. I WOULD RATHER BE NOTHING.
THANKFULLY, IT DID NOT COME TO THAT...
I SHOULD TELL THOR OF THIS. OR ODIN.
YES, YOU SHOULD.
IF I WANTED TO BE KILLED, I SHOULD. THOR COULDN'T KEEP THEM FROM MY HEAD. THEY'D THINK ME PART OF SOME PLAN, A SCHEME BEYOND THE GRAVE.
I THINK YOU CORRECT.
THEY WOULD BE CORRECT, TOO. THIS IS A SCHEME FROM BEYOND THE GRAVE. BUT ONE BEYOND THEIR IMAGINING.
...WHAT NOW?

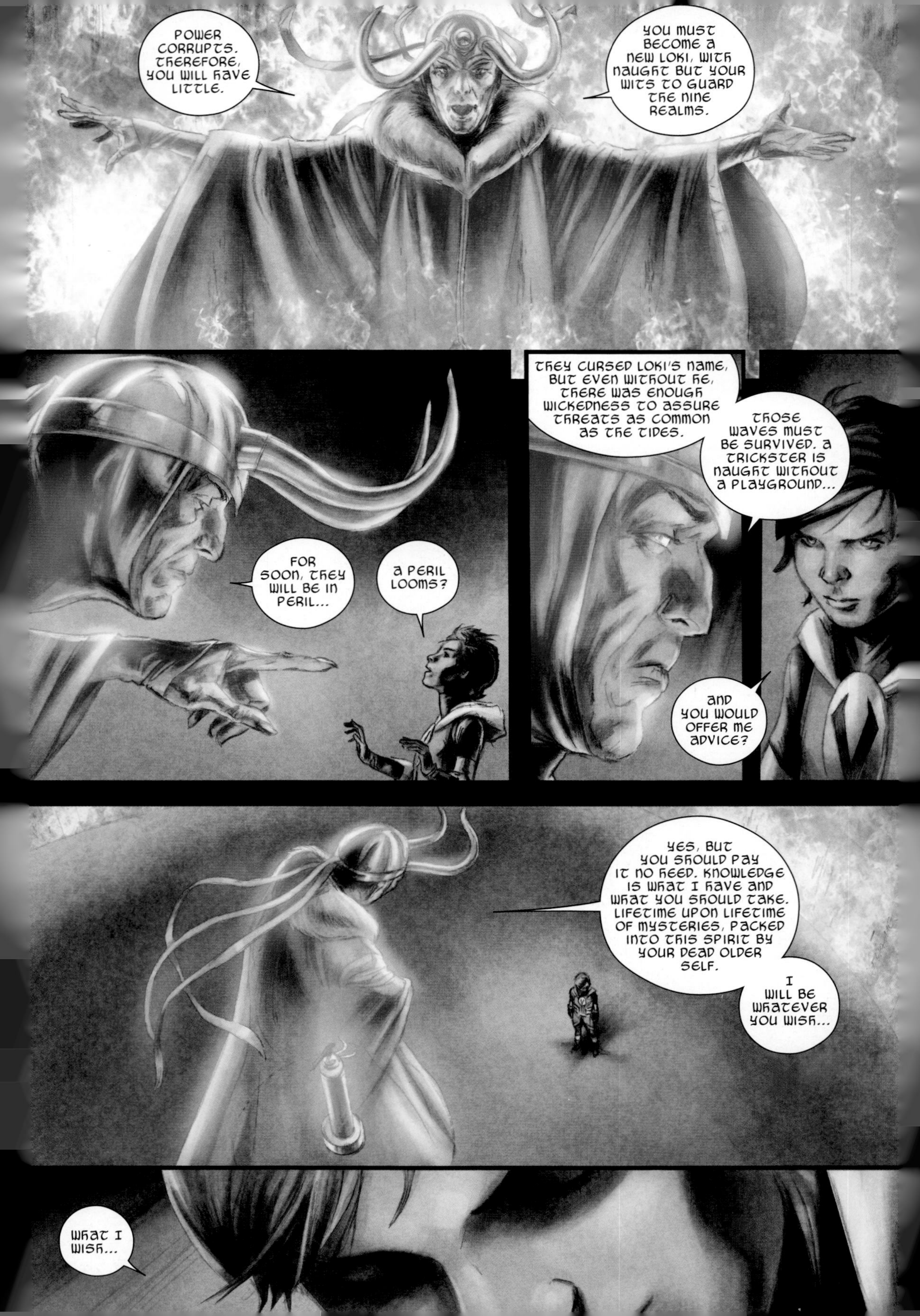
POWER CORRUPTS. THEREFORE, YOU WILL HAVE LITTLE.
YOU MUST BECOME A NEW LOKI, WITH NAUGHT BUT YOUR WITS TO GUARD THE NINE REALMS.
FOR SOON, THEY WILL BE IN PERIL...
A PERIL LOOMS?
THEY CURSED LOKI'S NAME, BUT EVEN WITHOUT HE, THERE WAS ENOUGH WICKEDNESS TO ASSURE THREATS AS COMMON AS THE TIDES.
THOSE WAVES MUST BE SURVIVED. A TRICKSTER IS NAUGHT WITHOUT A PLAYGROUND...
AND YOU WOULD OFFER ME ADVICE?
YES, BUT YOU SHOULD PAY IT NO HEED. KNOWLEDGE IS WHAT I HAVE AND WHAT YOU SHOULD TAKE. LIFETIME UPON LIFETIME OF MYSTERIES, PACKED INTO THIS SPIRIT BY YOUR DEAD OLDER SELF.
I WILL BE WHATEVER YOU WISH...
WHAT I WISH...

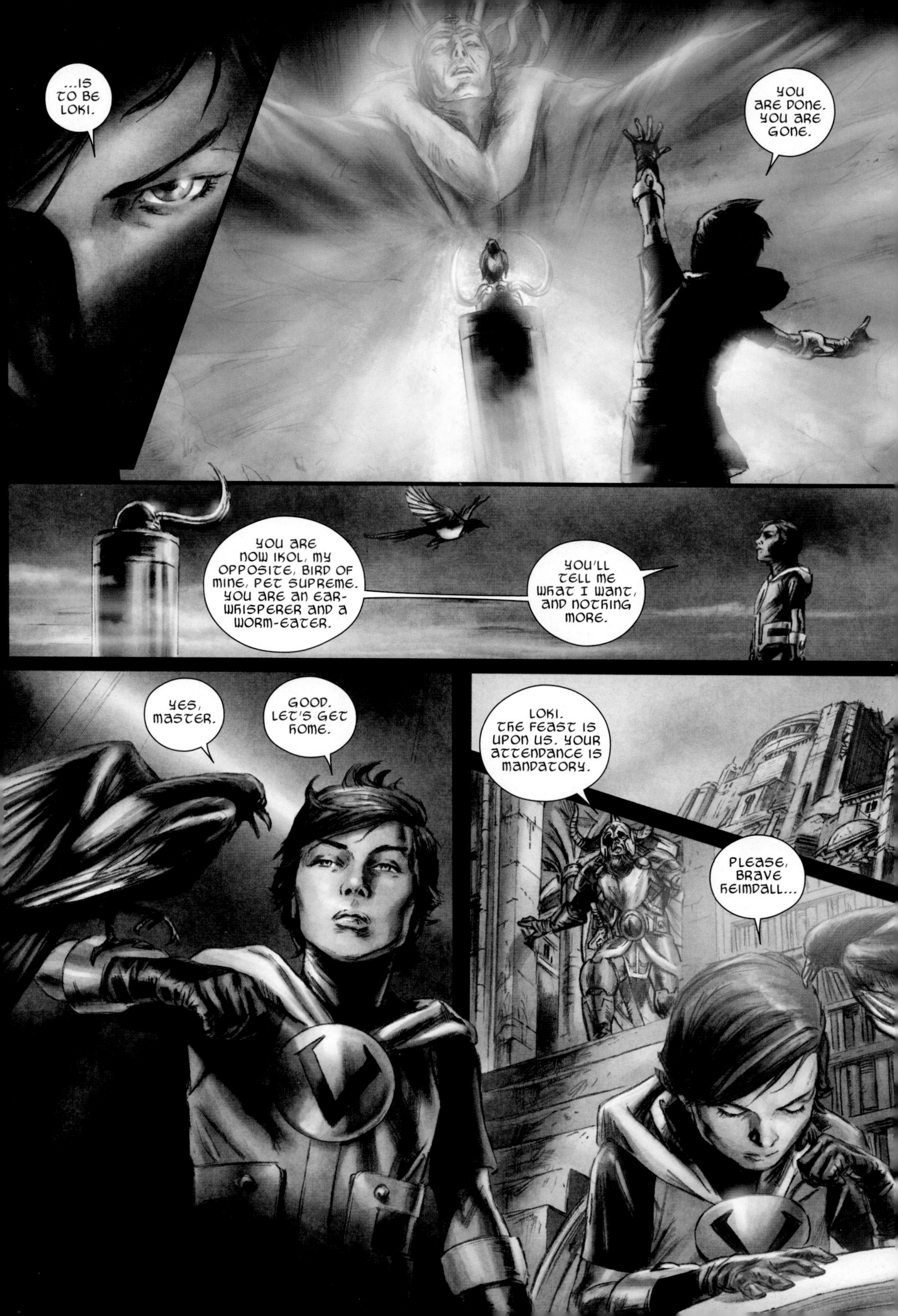
...IS TO BE LOKI.
YOU ARE DONE. YOU ARE GONE.
YOU ARE NOW IKOL, MY OPPOSITE, BIRD OF MINE, PET SUPREME. YOU ARE AN EAR-WHISPERER AND A WORM-EATER.
YOU'LL TELL ME WHAT I WANT, AND NOTHING MORE.
YES, MASTER.
GOOD. LET'S GET HOME.
LOKI. THE FEAST IS UPON US. YOUR ATTENDANCE IS MANDATORY.
PLEASE, BRAVE HEIMDALL...

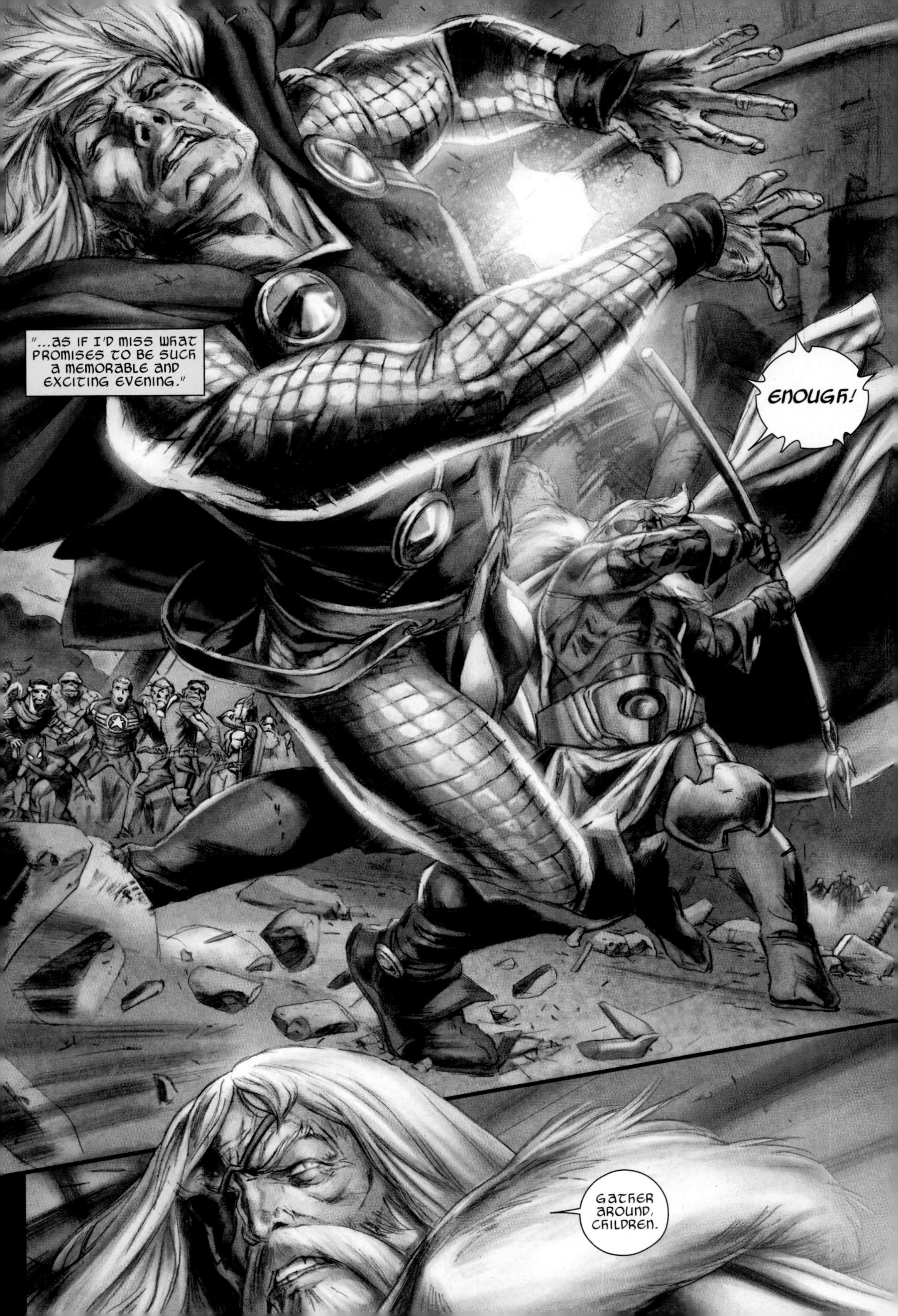
"...AS IF I'D MISS WHAT PROMISES TO BE SUCH A MEMORABLE AND EXCITING EVENING."
ENOUGH!
GATHER AROUND, CHILDREN.

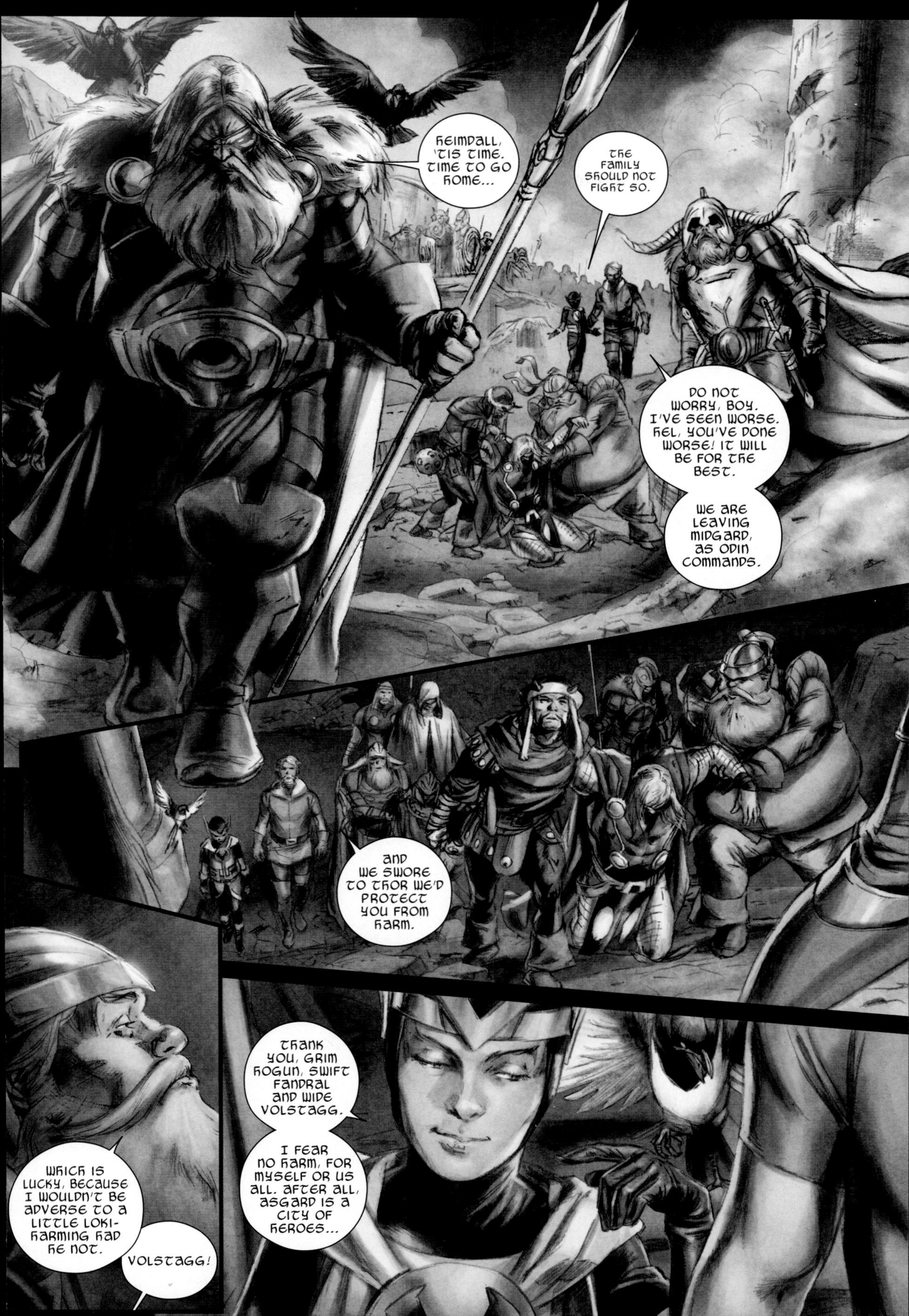
HEIMDALL, 'TIS TIME. TIME TO GO HOME...
THE FAMILY SHOULD NOT FIGHT SO.
DO NOT WORRY, BOY. I'VE SEEN WORSE. HEL, YOU'VE DONE WORSE! IT WILL BE FOR THE BEST.
WE ARE LEAVING MIDGARD, AS ODIN COMMANDS.
AND WE SWORE TO THOR WE'D PROTECT YOU FROM HARM.
THANK YOU, GRIM HOGUN, SWIFT FANDRAL AND WIDE VOLSTAGG.
I FEAR NO HARM, FOR MYSELF OR US ALL. AFTER ALL, ASGARD IS A CITY OF HEROES...
WHICH IS LUCKY, BECAUSE I WOULDN'T BE ADVERSE TO A LITTLE LOKI-HARMING HAD HE NOT.
VOLSTAGG!

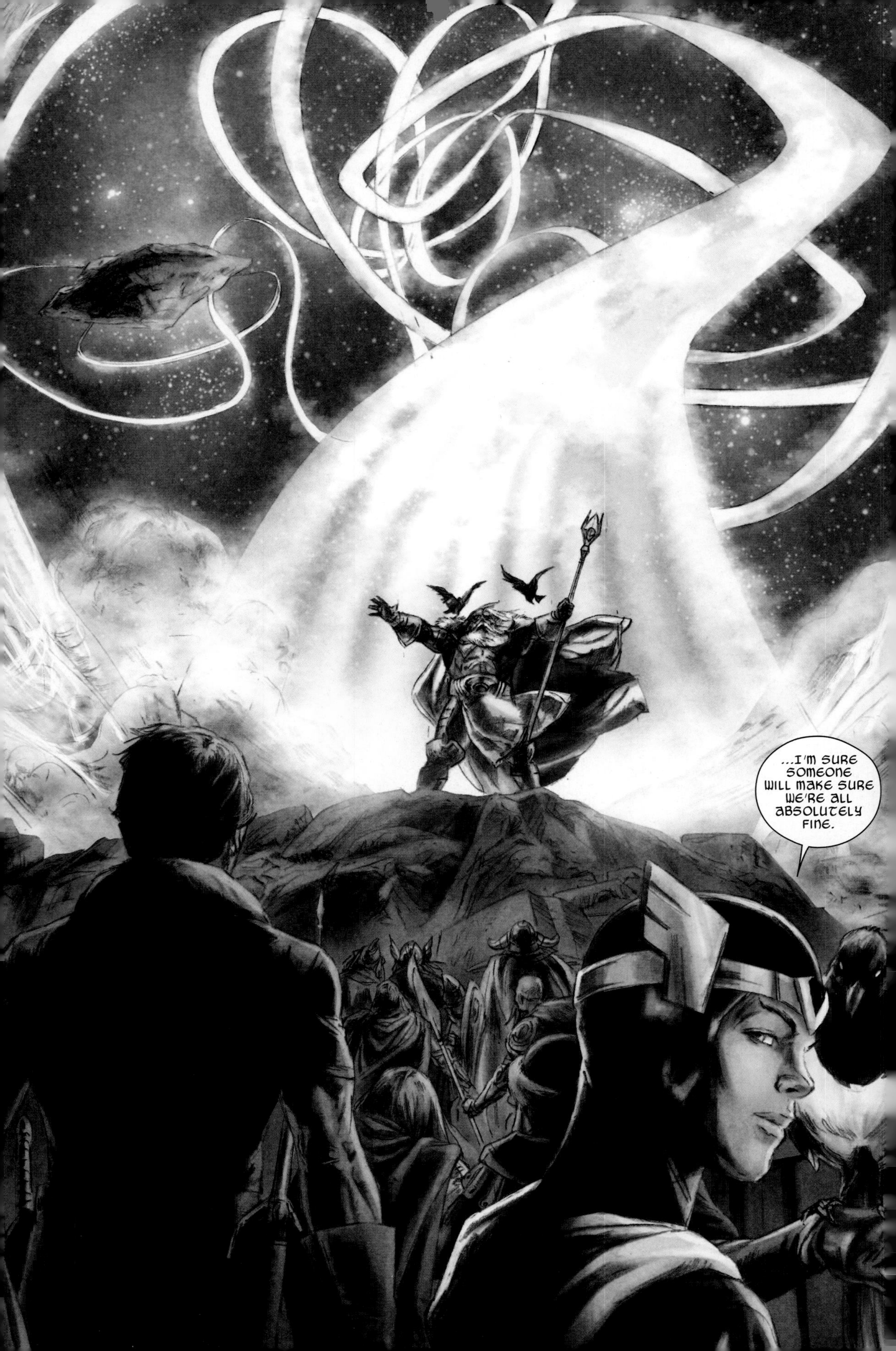
...I'M SURE SOMEONE WILL MAKE SURE WE'RE ALL ABSOLUTELY FINE.

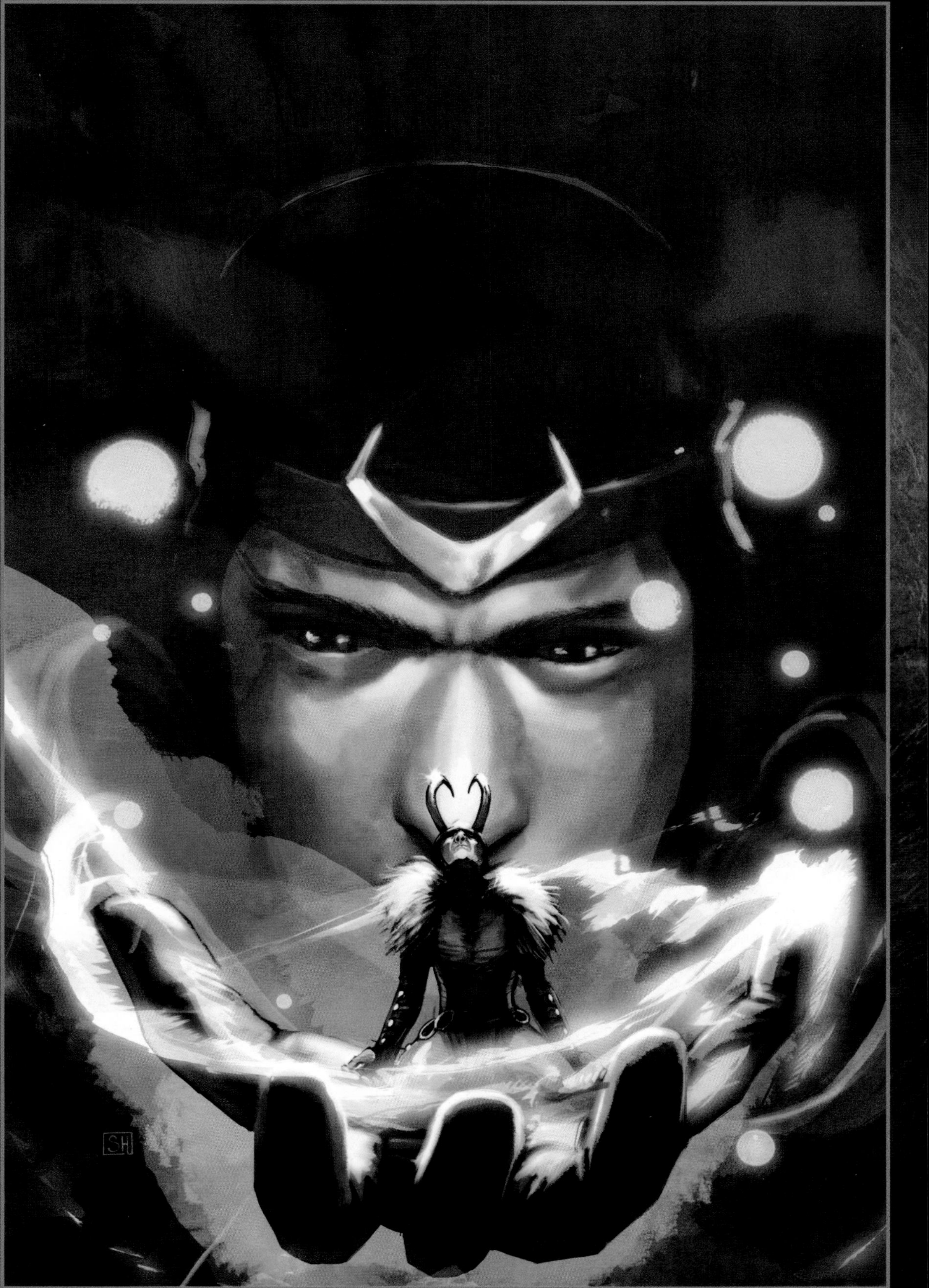
SH

JOURNEY INTO MYSTERY #623

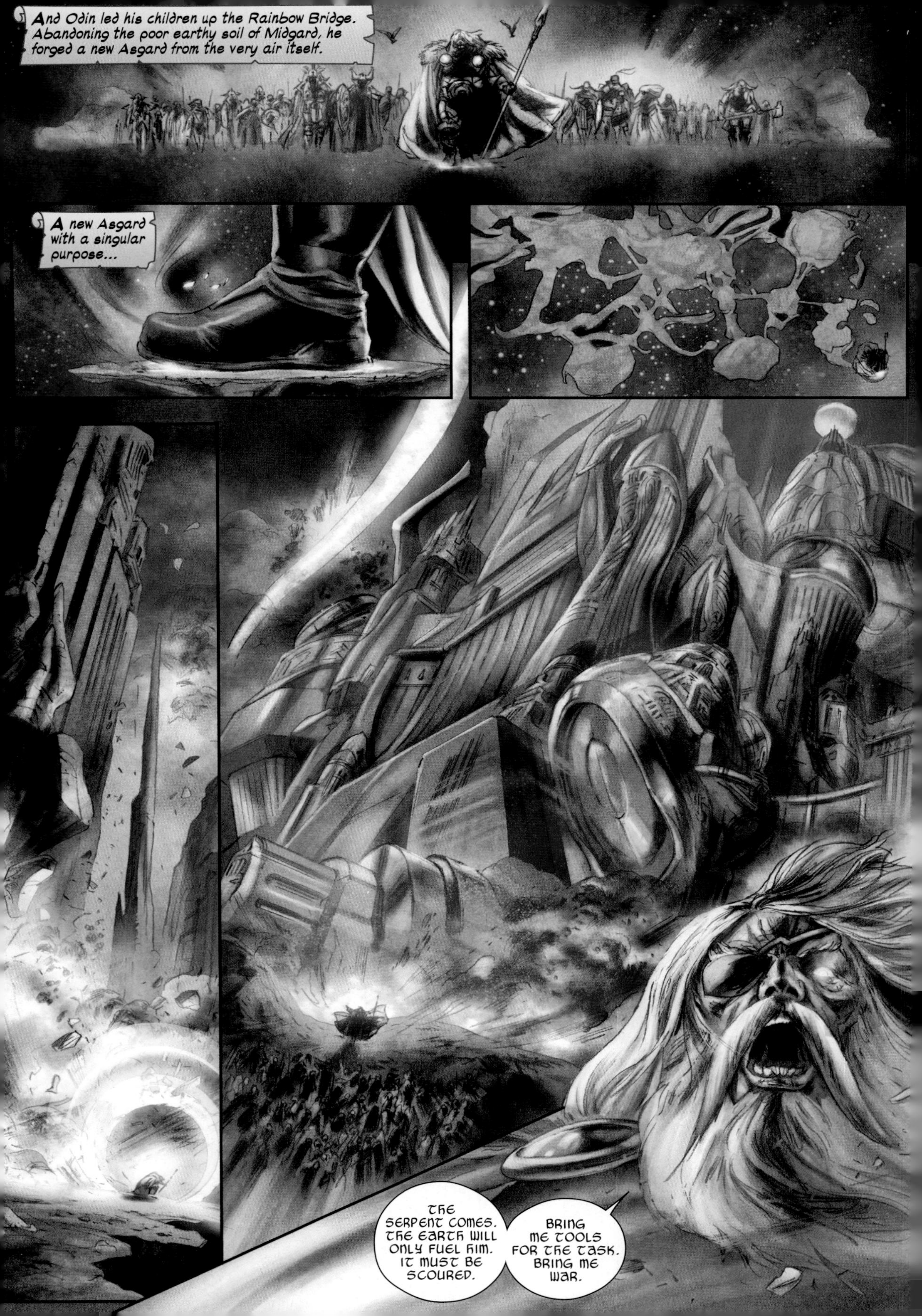
And Odin led his children up the Rainbow Bridge. Abandoning the poor earthy soil of Midgard, he forged a new Asgard from the very air itself.
A new Asgard with a singular purpose...
THE SERPENT COMES. THE EARTH WILL ONLY FUEL HIM. IT MUST BE SCOURED.
BRING ME TOOLS FOR THE TASK. BRING ME WAR.

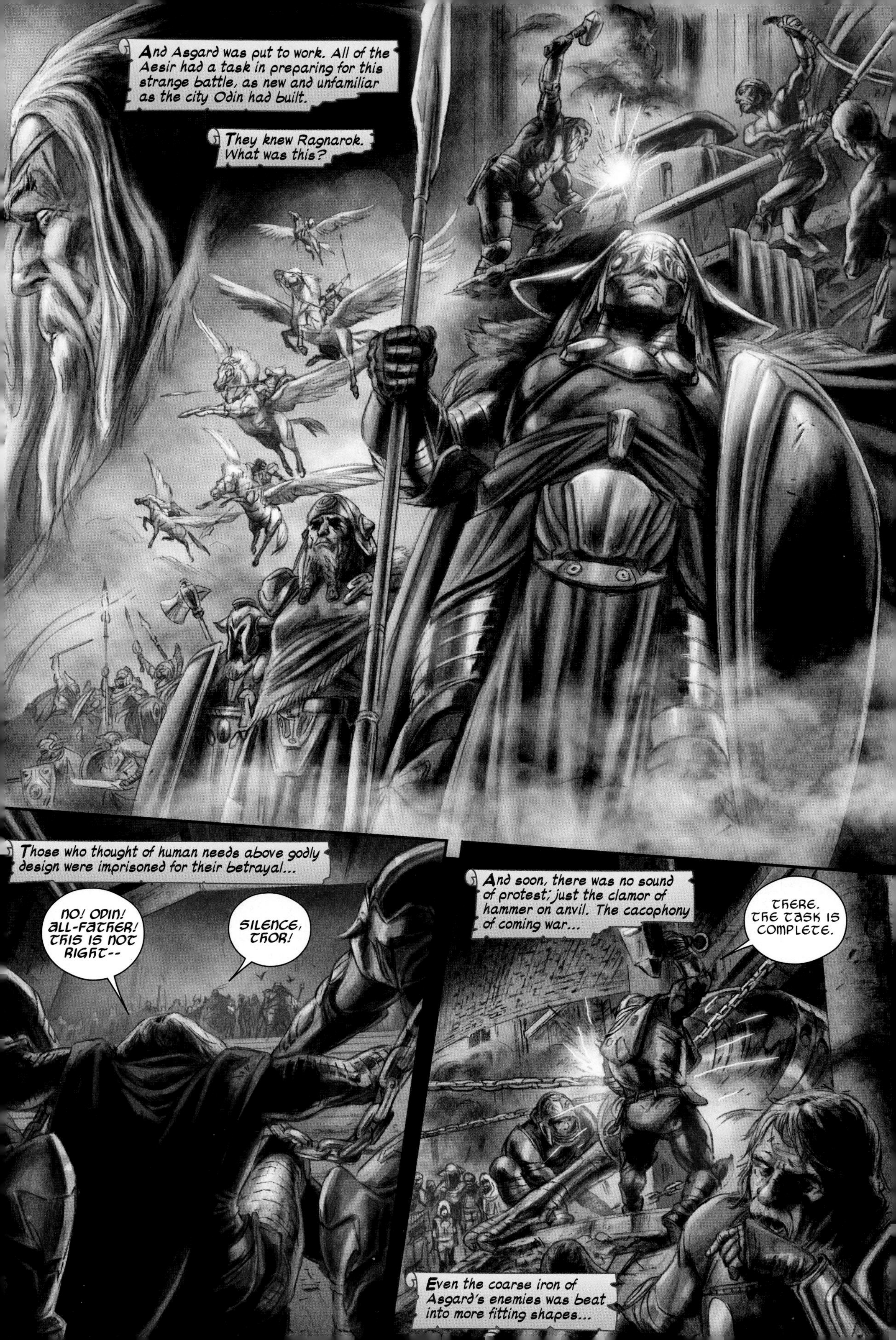
And Asgard was put to work. All of the Aesir had a task in preparing for this strange battle, as new and unfamiliar as the city Odin had built.
They knew Ragnarok. What was this?
Those who thought of human needs above godly design were imprisoned for their betrayal...
NO! ODIN! ALL-FATHER! THIS IS NOT RIGHT--
SILENCE, THOR!
And soon, there was no sound of protest; just the clamor of hammer on anvil. The cacophony of coming war...
THERE. THE TASK IS COMPLETE.
Even the coarse iron of Asgard's enemies was beat into more fitting shapes...

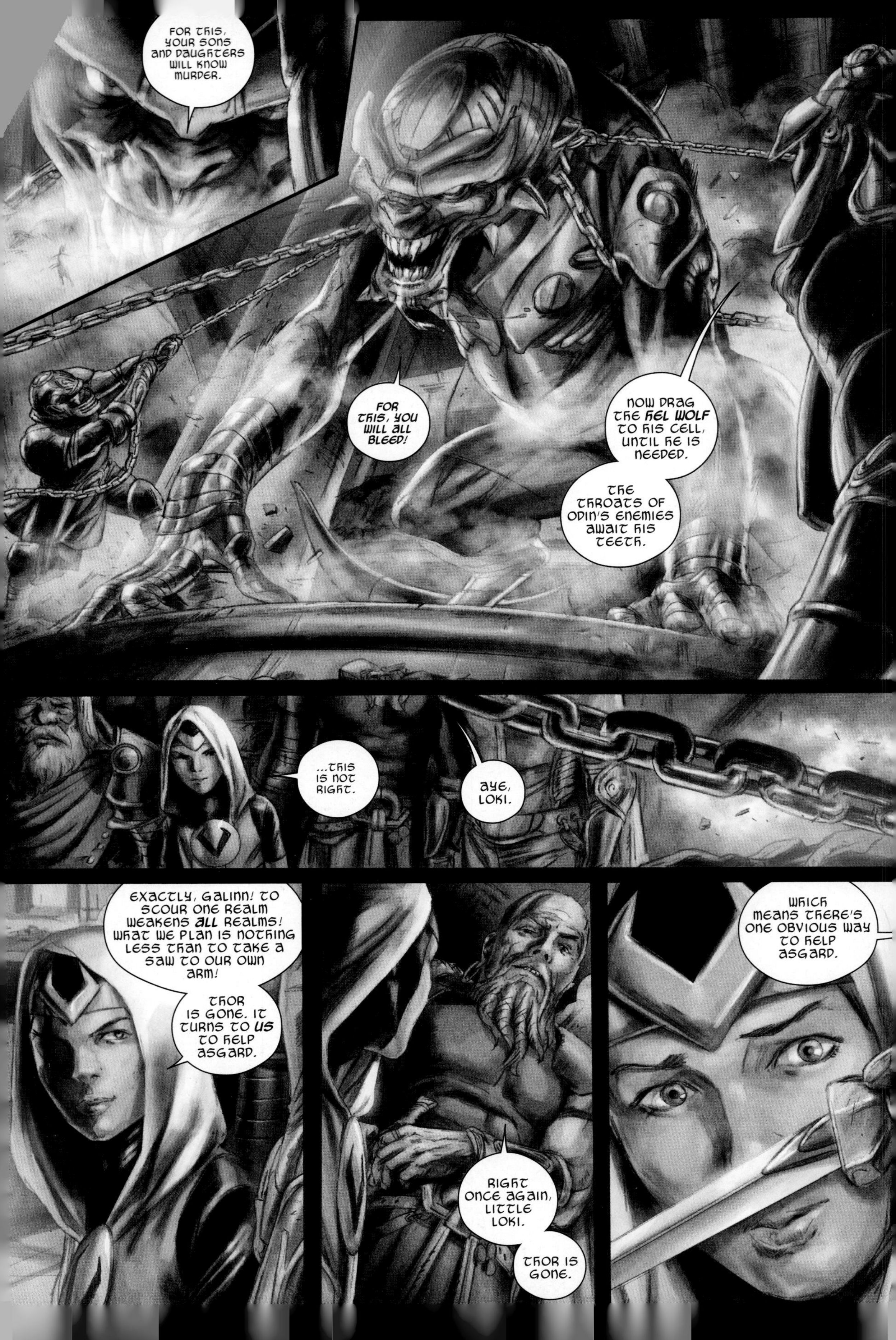

FOR THIS, YOUR SONS AND DAUGHTERS WILL KNOW MURDER.
FOR THIS, YOU WILL ALL BLEED!
NOW DRAG THE HEL WOLF TO HIS CELL, UNTIL HE IS NEEDED.
THE THROATS OF ODIN'S ENEMIES AWAIT HIS TEETH.
...THIS IS NOT RIGHT.
AYE, LOKI.
EXACTLY, GALINN! TO SCOUR ONE REALM WEAKENS ALL REALMS! WHAT WE PLAN IS NOTHING LESS THAN TO TAKE A SAW TO OUR OWN ARM!
THOR IS GONE. IT TURNS TO US TO HELP ASGARD.
RIGHT ONCE AGAIN, LITTLE LOKI.
THOR IS GONE.
WHICH MEANS THERE'S ONE OBVIOUS WAY TO HELP ASGARD.

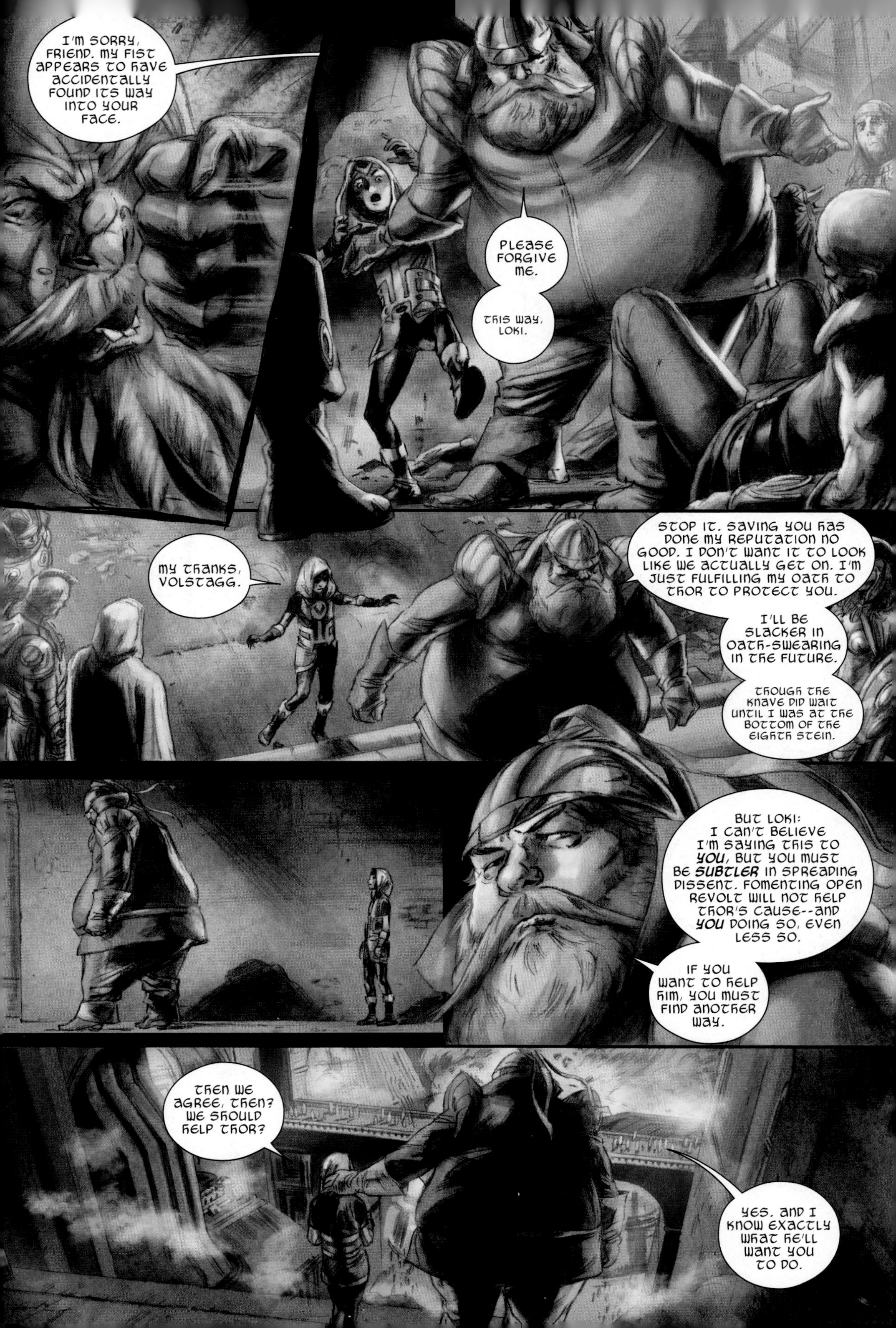
I'M SORRY, FRIEND. MY FIST APPEARS TO HAVE ACCIDENTALLY FOUND ITS WAY INTO YOUR FACE.
PLEASE FORGIVE ME.
THIS WAY, LOKI.
MY THANKS, VOLSTAGG.
STOP IT. SAVING YOU HAS DONE MY REPUTATION NO GOOD. I DON'T WANT IT TO LOOK LIKE WE ACTUALLY GET ON. I'M JUST FULFILLING MY OATH TO THOR TO PROTECT YOU.
I'LL BE SLACKER IN OATH-SWEARING IN THE FUTURE.
THOUGH THE KNAVE DID WAIT UNTIL I WAS AT THE BOTTOM OF THE EIGHTH STEIN.
BUT LOKI: I CAN'T BELIEVE I'M SAYING THIS TO YOU, BUT YOU MUST BE SUBTLER IN SPREADING DISSENT. FOMENTING OPEN REVOLT WILL NOT HELP THOR'S CAUSE--AND YOU DOING SO, EVEN LESS SO.
IF YOU WANT TO HELP HIM, YOU MUST FIND ANOTHER WAY.
THEN WE AGREE, THEN? WE SHOULD HELP THOR?
YES. AND I KNOW EXACTLY WHAT HE'LL WANT YOU TO DO.

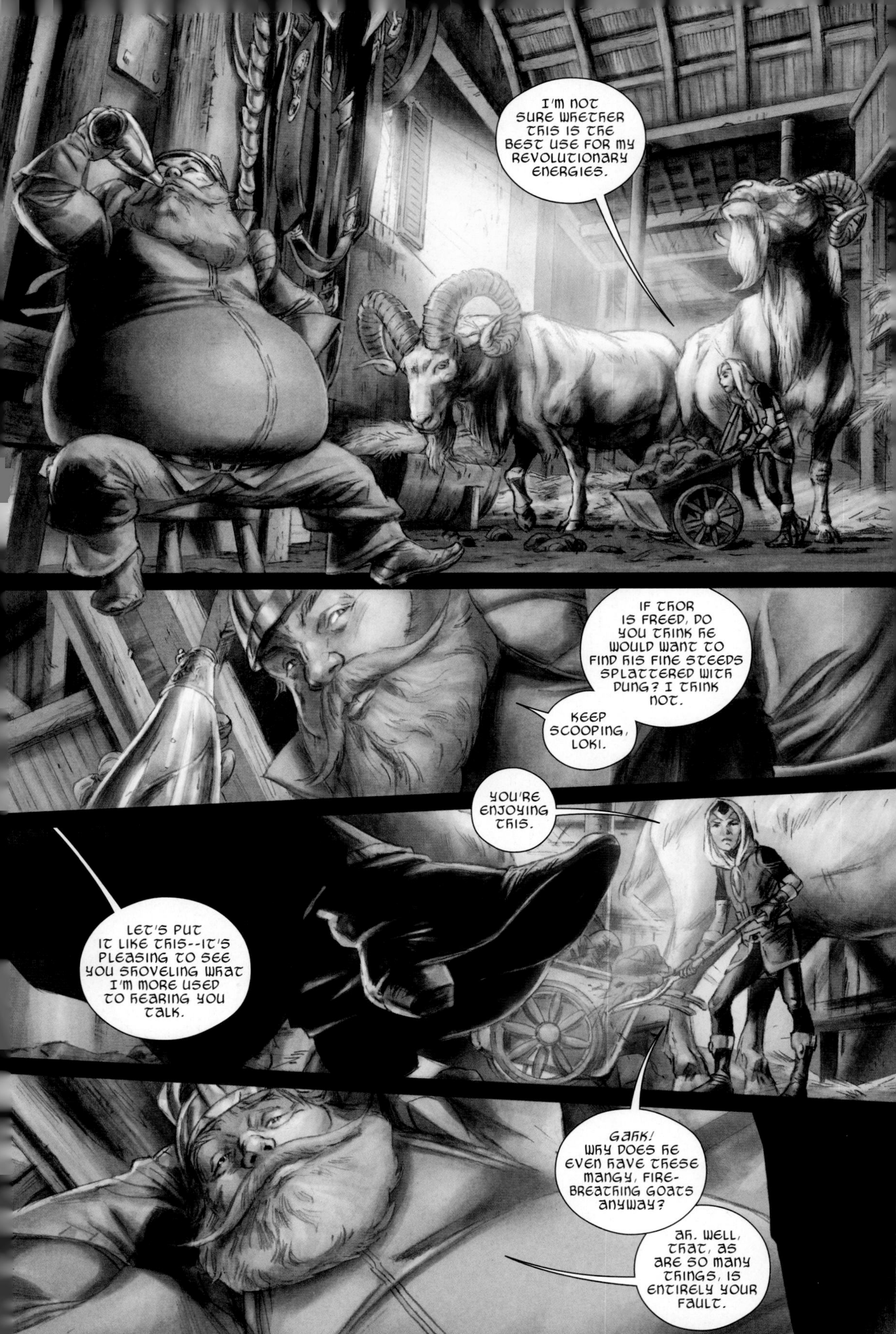
I'M NOT SURE WHETHER THIS IS THE BEST USE FOR MY REVOLUTIONARY ENERGIES.
IF THOR IS FREED, DO YOU THINK HE WOULD WANT TO FIND HIS FINE STEEDS SPLATTERED WITH DUNG? I THINK NOT.
KEEP SCOOPING, LOKI.
YOU'RE ENJOYING THIS.
LET'S PUT IT LIKE THIS--IT'S PLEASING TO SEE YOU SHOVELING WHAT I'M MORE USED TO HEARING YOU TALK.
GAHK! WHY DOES HE EVEN HAVE THESE MANGY, FIRE-BREATHING GOATS ANYWAY?
AH. WELL, THAT, AS ARE SO MANY THINGS, IS ENTIRELY YOUR FAULT.

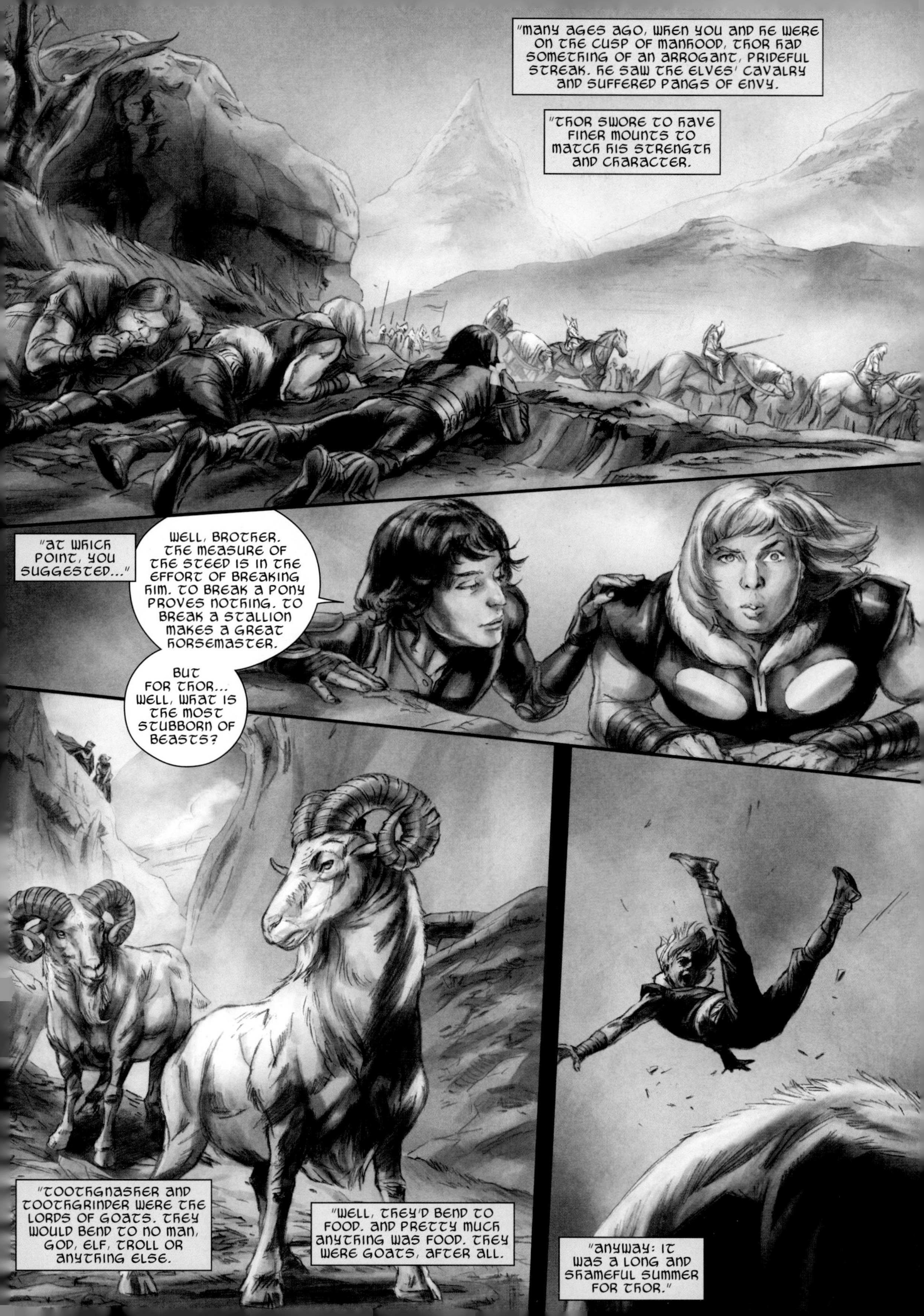
"MANY AGES AGO, WHEN YOU AND HE WERE ON THE CUSP OF MANHOOD, THOR HAD SOMETHING OF AN ARROGANT, PRIDEFUL STREAK. HE SAW THE ELVES' CAVALRY AND SUFFERED PANGS OF ENVY.
"THOR SWORE TO HAVE FINER MOUNTS TO MATCH HIS STRENGTH AND CHARACTER.
"AT WHICH POINT, YOU SUGGESTED..."
WELL, BROTHER. THE MEASURE OF THE STEED IS IN THE EFFORT OF BREAKING HIM. TO BREAK A PONY PROVES NOTHING. TO BREAK A STALLION MAKES A GREAT HORSEMASTER.
BUT FOR THOR... WELL, WHAT IS THE MOST STUBBORN OF BEASTS?
"TOOTHGNASHER AND TOOTHGRINDER WERE THE LORDS OF GOATS. THEY WOULD BEND TO NO MAN, GOD, ELF, TROLL OR ANYTHING ELSE.
"WELL, THEY'D BEND TO FOOD. AND PRETTY MUCH ANYTHING WAS FOOD. THEY WERE GOATS, AFTER ALL.
"ANYWAY: IT WAS A LONG AND SHAMEFUL SUMMER FOR THOR."

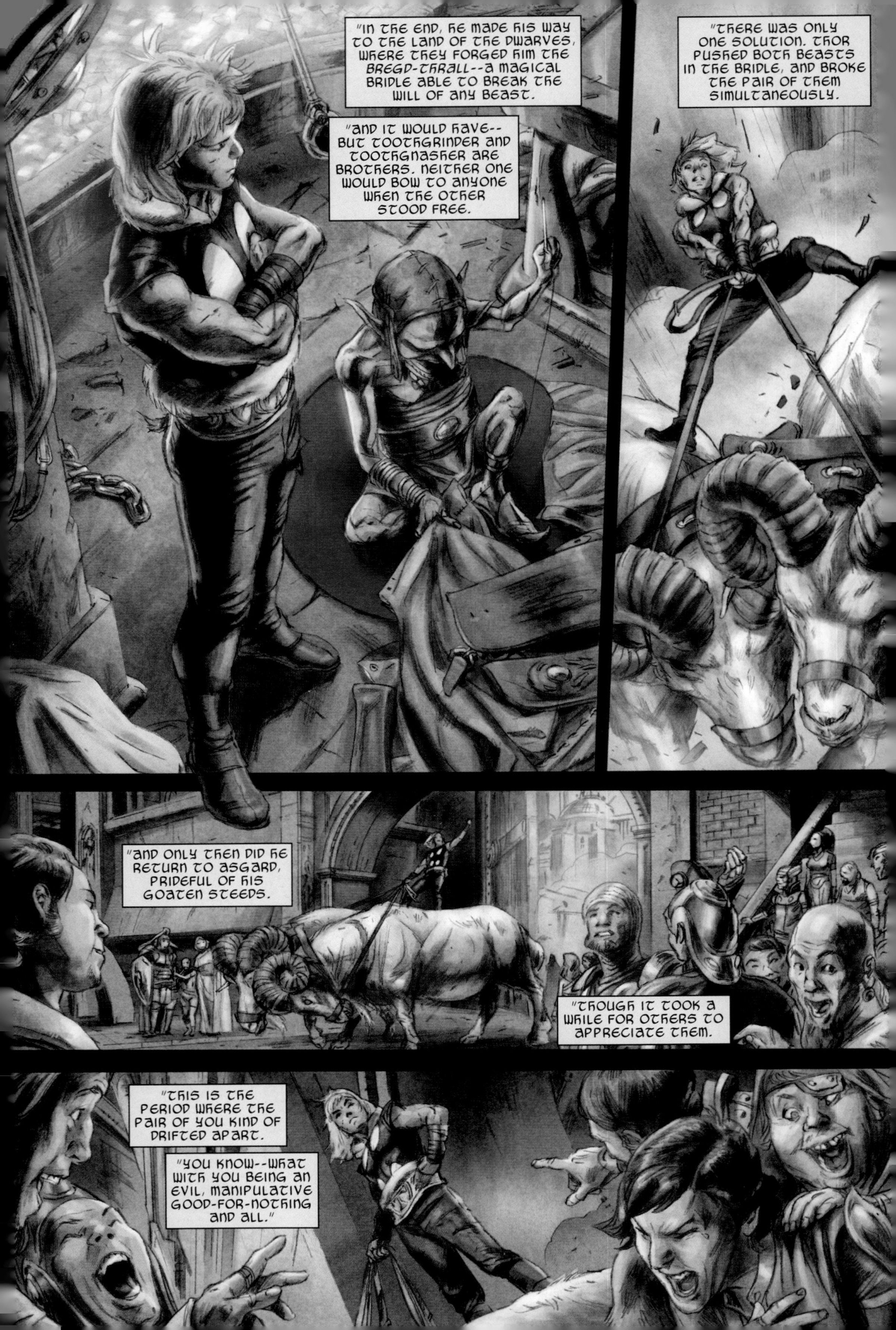
"IN THE END, HE MADE HIS WAY TO THE LAND OF THE DWARVES, WHERE THEY FORGED HIM THE *BREGD-THRALL*--A MAGICAL BRIDLE ABLE TO BREAK THE WILL OF ANY BEAST.
"AND IT WOULD HAVE--BUT TOOTHGRINDER AND TOOTHGNASHER ARE BROTHERS. NEITHER ONE WOULD BOW TO ANYONE WHEN THE OTHER STOOD FREE.
"THERE WAS ONLY ONE SOLUTION. THOR PUSHED BOTH BEASTS IN THE BRIDLE, AND BROKE THE PAIR OF THEM SIMULTANEOUSLY.
"AND ONLY THEN DID HE RETURN TO ASGARD, PRIDEFUL OF HIS GOATEN STEEDS.
"THOUGH IT TOOK A WHILE FOR OTHERS TO APPRECIATE THEM.
"THIS IS THE PERIOD WHERE THE PAIR OF YOU KIND OF DRIFTED APART.
"YOU KNOW--WHAT WITH YOU BEING AN EVIL, MANIPULATIVE GOOD-FOR-NOTHING AND ALL."

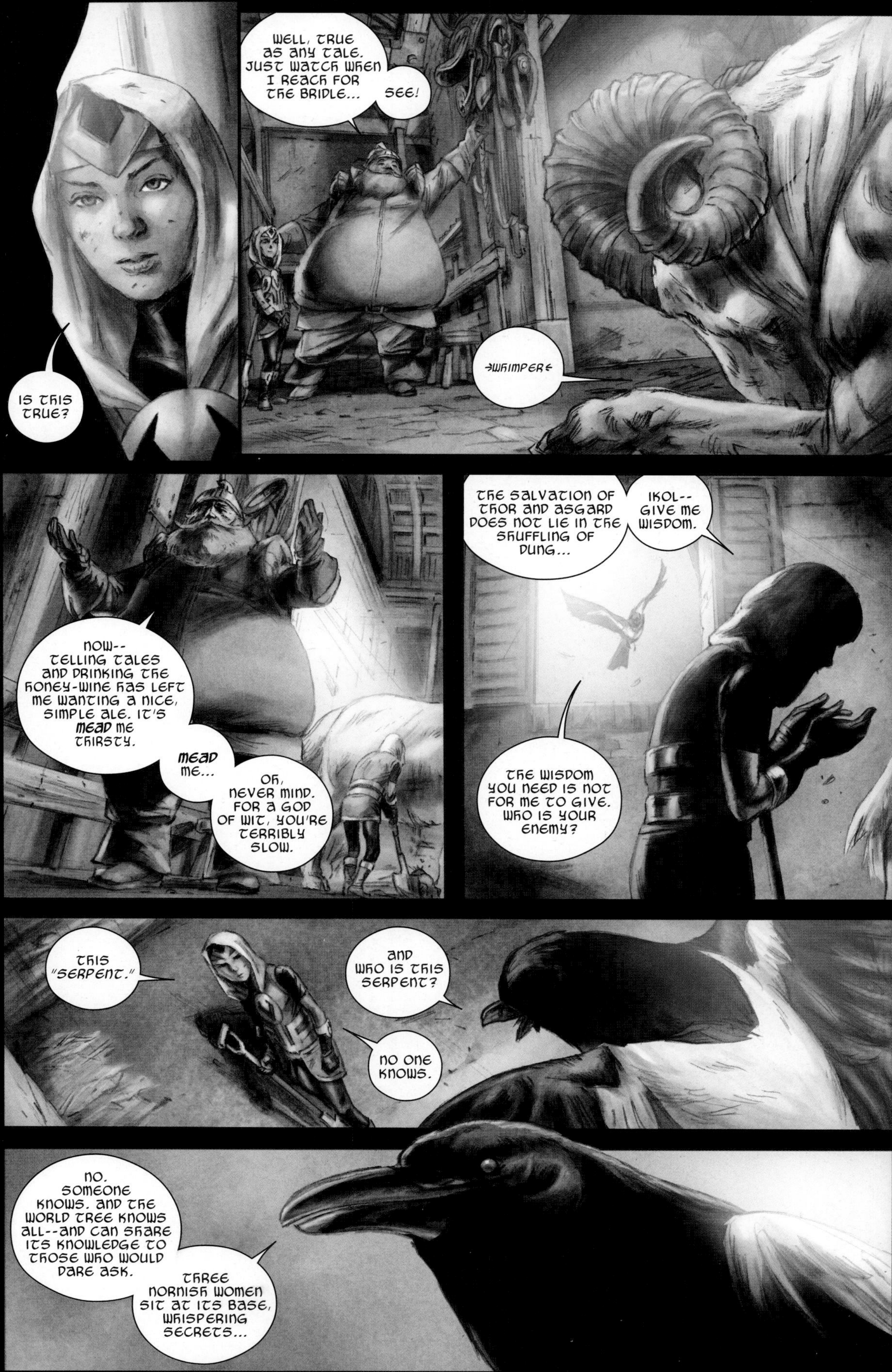

IS THIS TRUE?
WELL, TRUE AS ANY TALE. JUST WATCH WHEN I REACH FOR THE BRIDLE...
SEE!
→WHIMPER←
NOW-- TELLING TALES AND DRINKING THE HONEY-WINE HAS LEFT ME WANTING A NICE, SIMPLE ALE. IT'S MEAD ME THIRSTY.
MEAD ME...
OH, NEVER MIND. FOR A GOD OF WIT, YOU'RE TERRIBLY SLOW.
THE SALVATION OF THOR AND ASGARD DOES NOT LIE IN THE SHUFFLING OF DUNG...
IKOL-- GIVE ME WISDOM.
THE WISDOM YOU NEED IS NOT FOR ME TO GIVE. WHO IS YOUR ENEMY?
THIS "SERPENT."
AND WHO IS THIS SERPENT?
NO ONE KNOWS.
NO. SOMEONE KNOWS. AND THE WORLD TREE KNOWS ALL--AND CAN SHARE ITS KNOWLEDGE TO THOSE WHO WOULD DARE ASK.
THREE NORNISH WOMEN SIT AT ITS BASE, WHISPERING SECRETS...

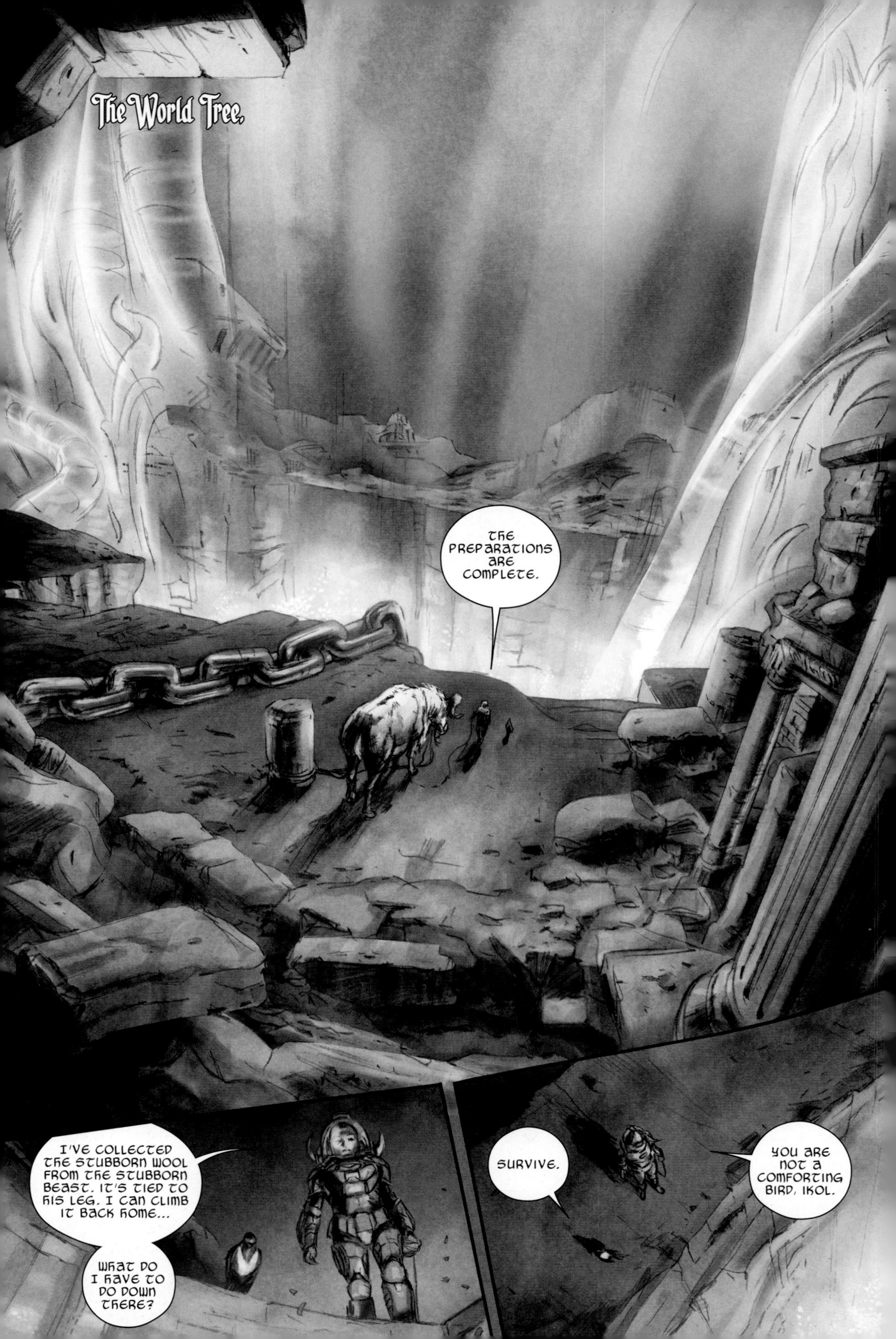
The World Tree.
THE PREPARATIONS ARE COMPLETE.
I'VE COLLECTED THE STUBBORN WOOL FROM THE STUBBORN BEAST. IT'S TIED TO HIS LEG. I CAN CLIMB IT BACK HOME...
WHAT DO I HAVE TO DO DOWN THERE?
SURVIVE.
YOU ARE NOT A COMFORTING BIRD, IKOL.

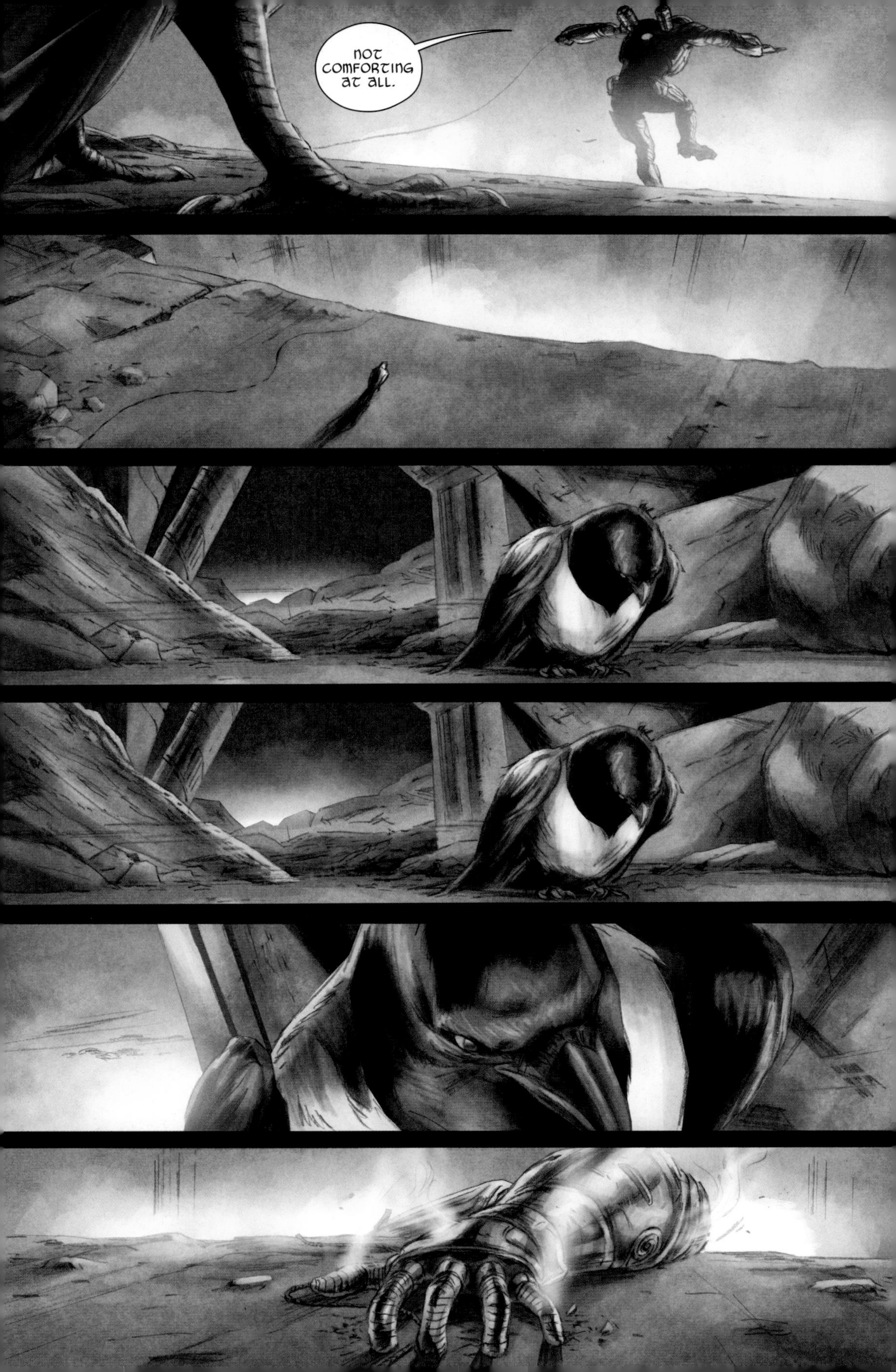
NOT COMFORTING AT ALL.

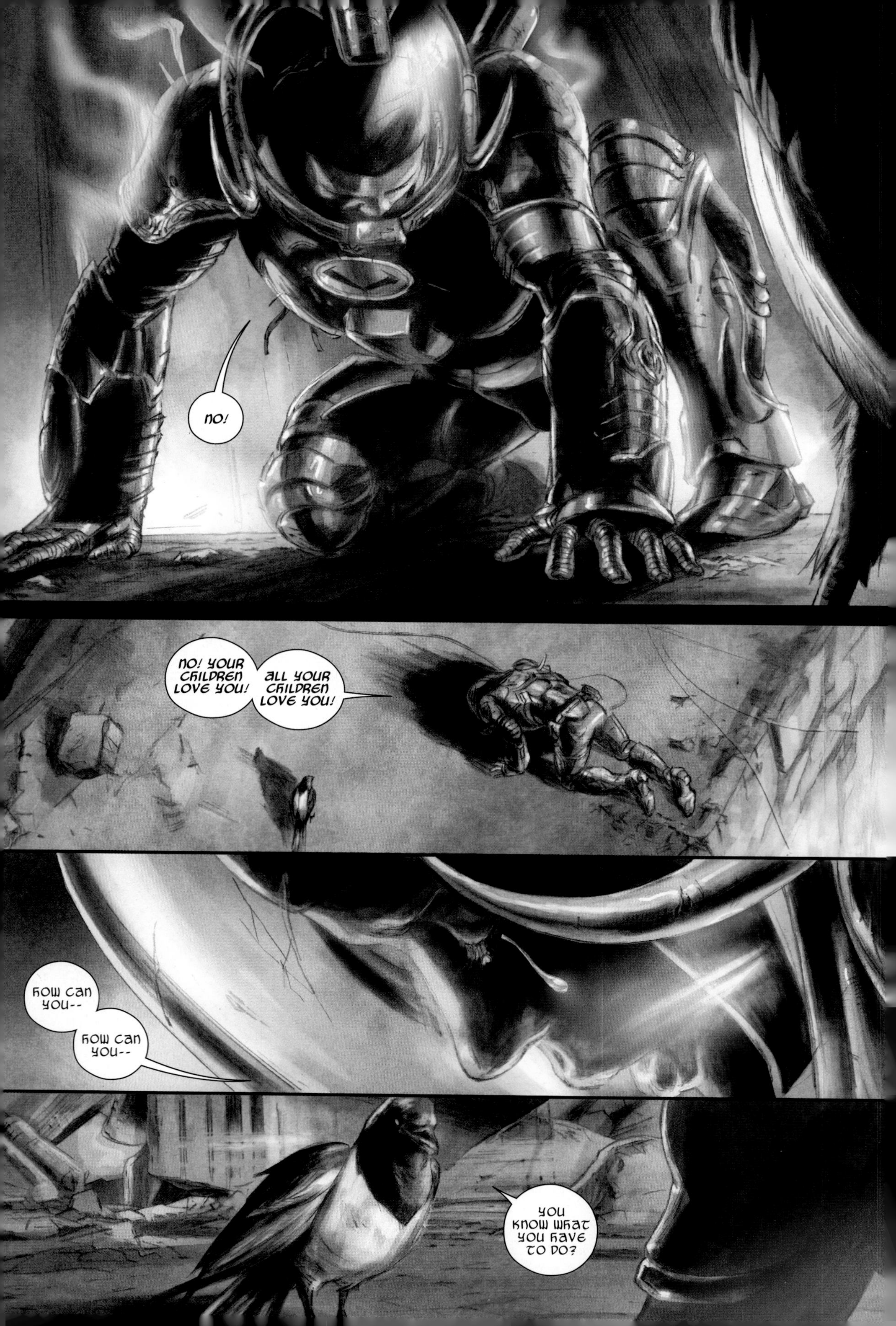
NO!
NO! YOUR CHILDREN LOVE YOU!
ALL YOUR CHILDREN LOVE YOU!
HOW CAN YOU--
HOW CAN YOU--
YOU KNOW WHAT YOU HAVE TO DO?

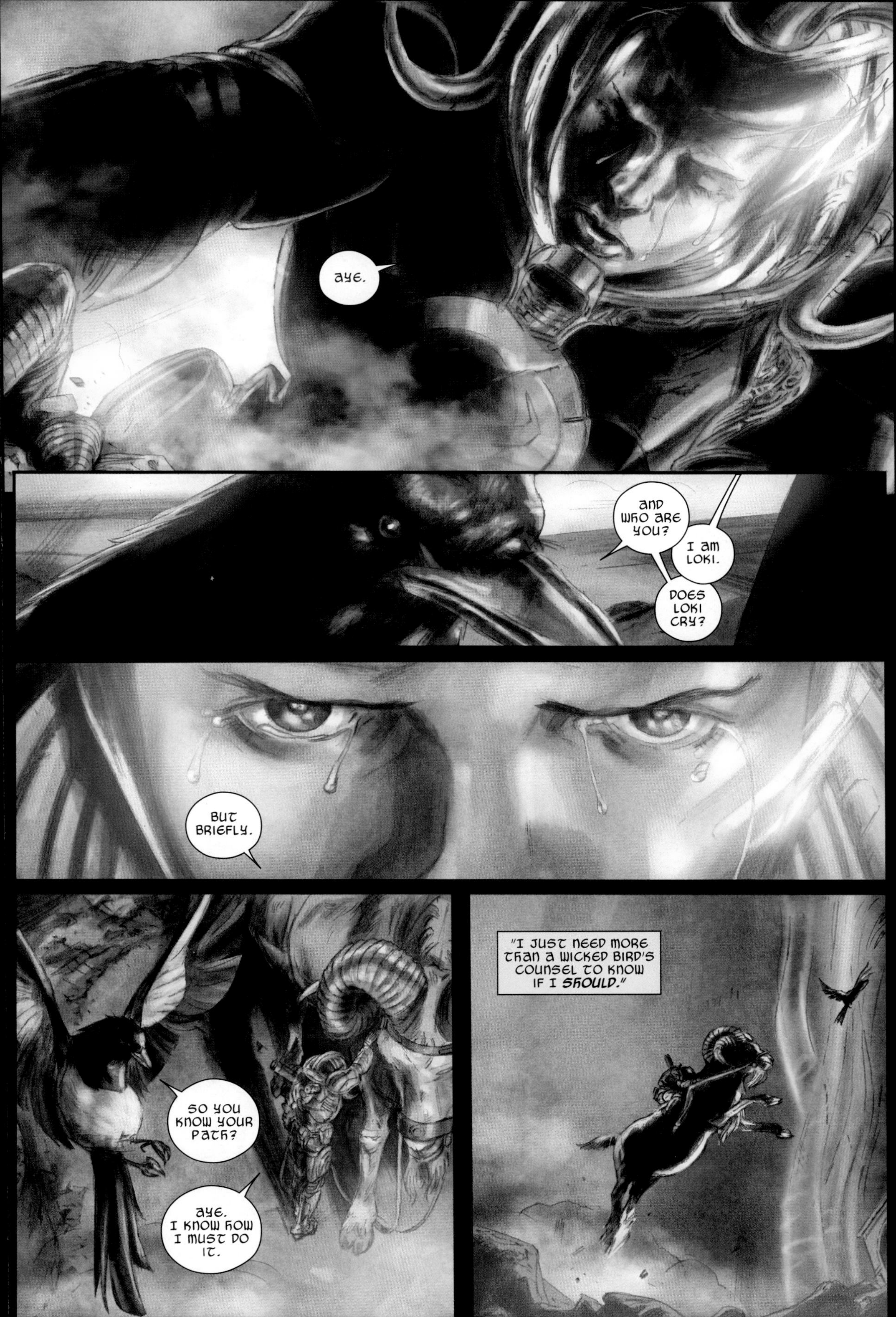
AYE.
AND WHO ARE YOU?
I AM LOKI.
DOES LOKI CRY?
BUT BRIEFLY.
SO YOU KNOW YOUR PATH?
AYE. I KNOW HOW I MUST DO IT.
"I JUST NEED MORE THAN A WICKED BIRD'S COUNSEL TO KNOW IF I *SHOULD*."

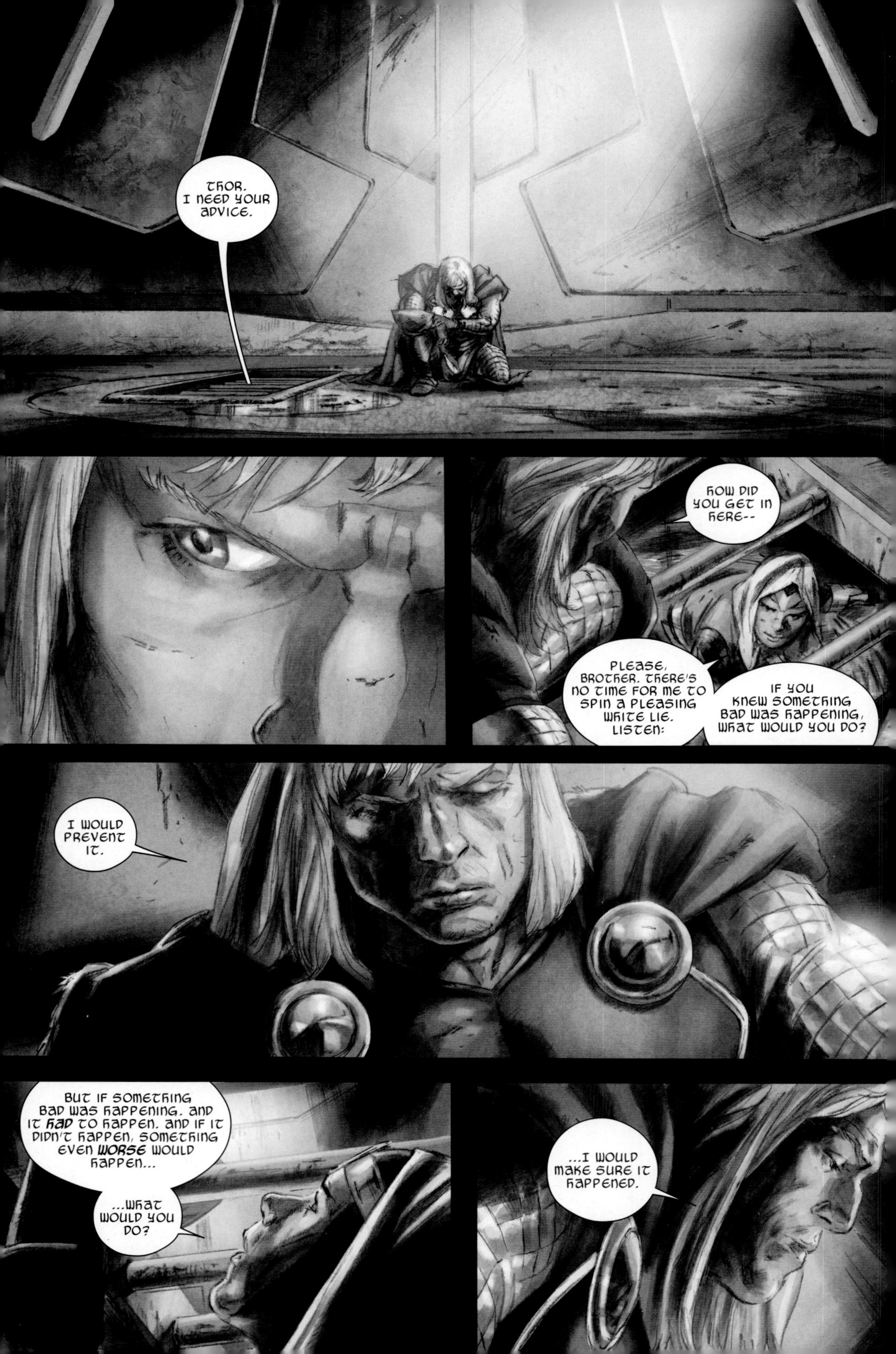
THOR. I NEED YOUR ADVICE.
HOW DID YOU GET IN HERE--
PLEASE, BROTHER. THERE'S NO TIME FOR ME TO SPIN A PLEASING WHITE LIE. LISTEN:
IF YOU KNEW SOMETHING BAD WAS HAPPENING, WHAT WOULD YOU DO?
I WOULD PREVENT IT.
BUT IF SOMETHING BAD WAS HAPPENING. AND IT HAD TO HAPPEN. AND IF IT DIDN'T HAPPEN, SOMETHING EVEN WORSE WOULD HAPPEN...
...WHAT WOULD YOU DO?
...I WOULD MAKE SURE IT HAPPENED.

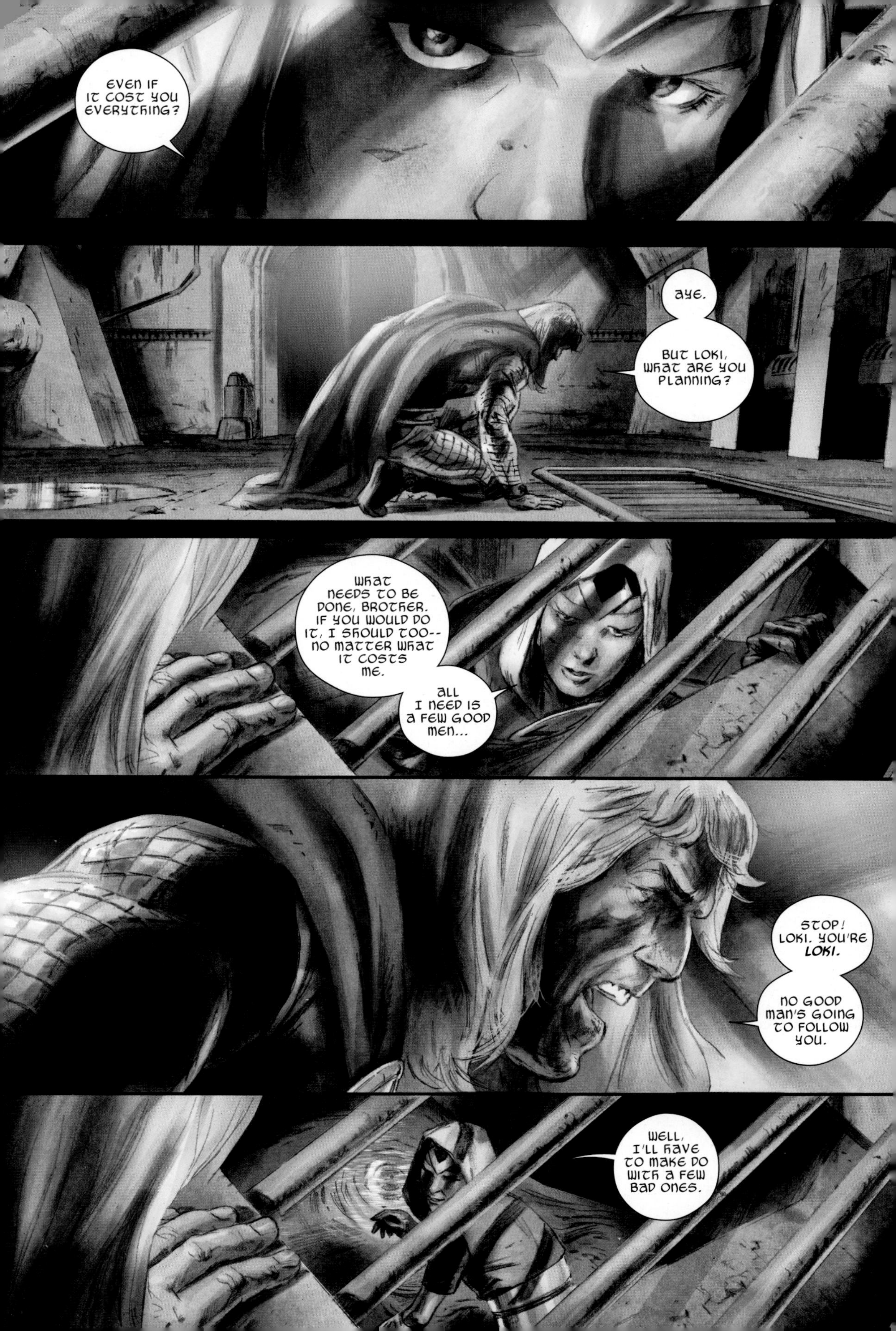
EVEN IF IT COST YOU EVERYTHING?
AYE.
BUT LOKI, WHAT ARE YOU PLANNING?
WHAT NEEDS TO BE DONE, BROTHER. IF YOU WOULD DO IT, I SHOULD TOO-- NO MATTER WHAT IT COSTS ME.
ALL I NEED IS A FEW GOOD MEN...
STOP! LOKI. YOU'RE **LOKI.**
NO GOOD MAN'S GOING TO FOLLOW YOU.
WELL, I'LL HAVE TO MAKE DO WITH A FEW BAD ONES.

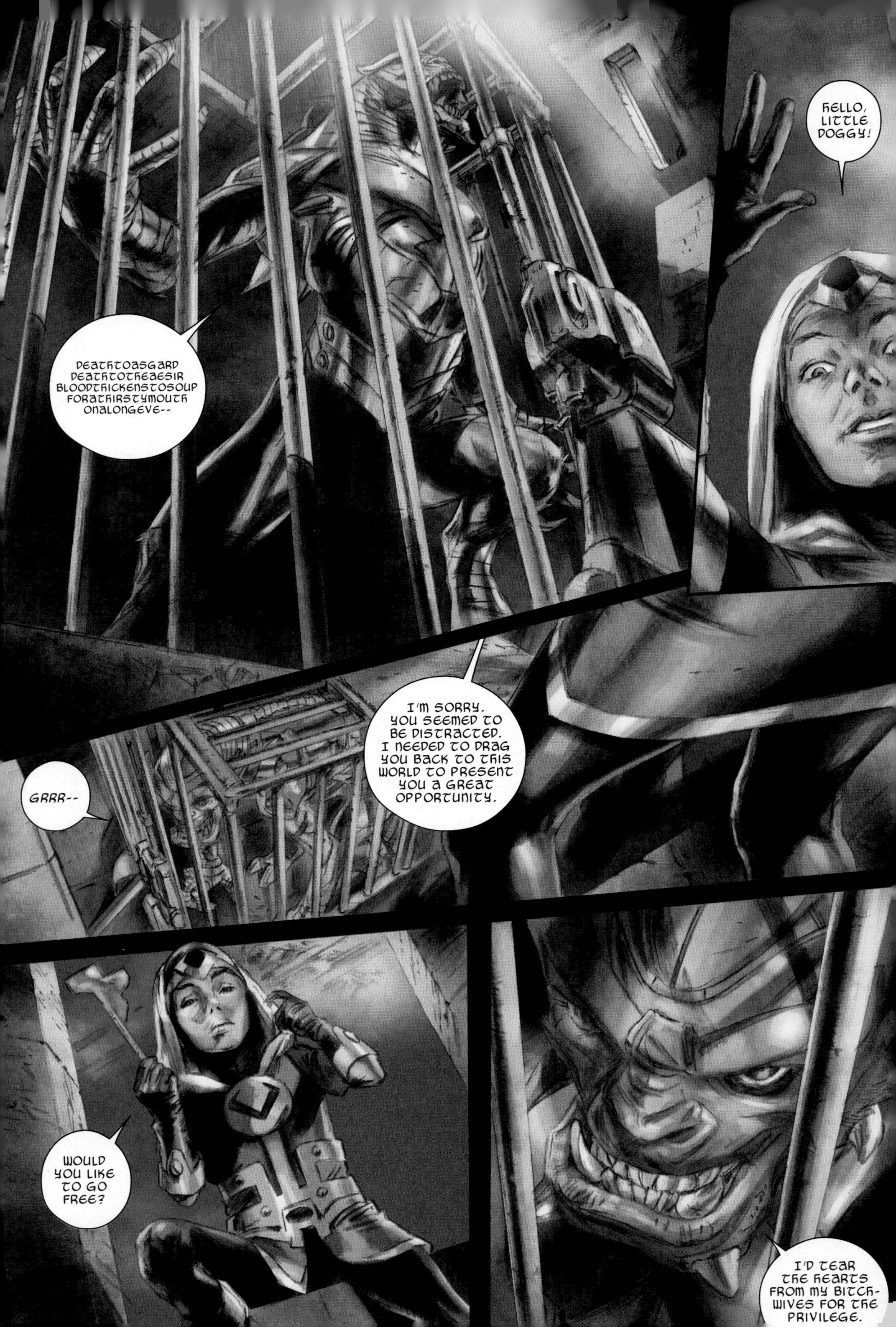
DEATHTOASGARD DEATHTOTHEAESIR BLOODTHICKENSTOSOUP FORATHIRSTYMOUTH ONALONGEVE--
HELLO, LITTLE DOGGY!
GRRR--
I'M SORRY. YOU SEEMED TO BE DISTRACTED. I NEEDED TO DRAG YOU BACK TO THIS WORLD TO PRESENT YOU A GREAT OPPORTUNITY.
WOULD YOU LIKE TO GO FREE?
I'D TEAR THE HEARTS FROM MY BITCH-WIVES FOR THE PRIVILEGE.

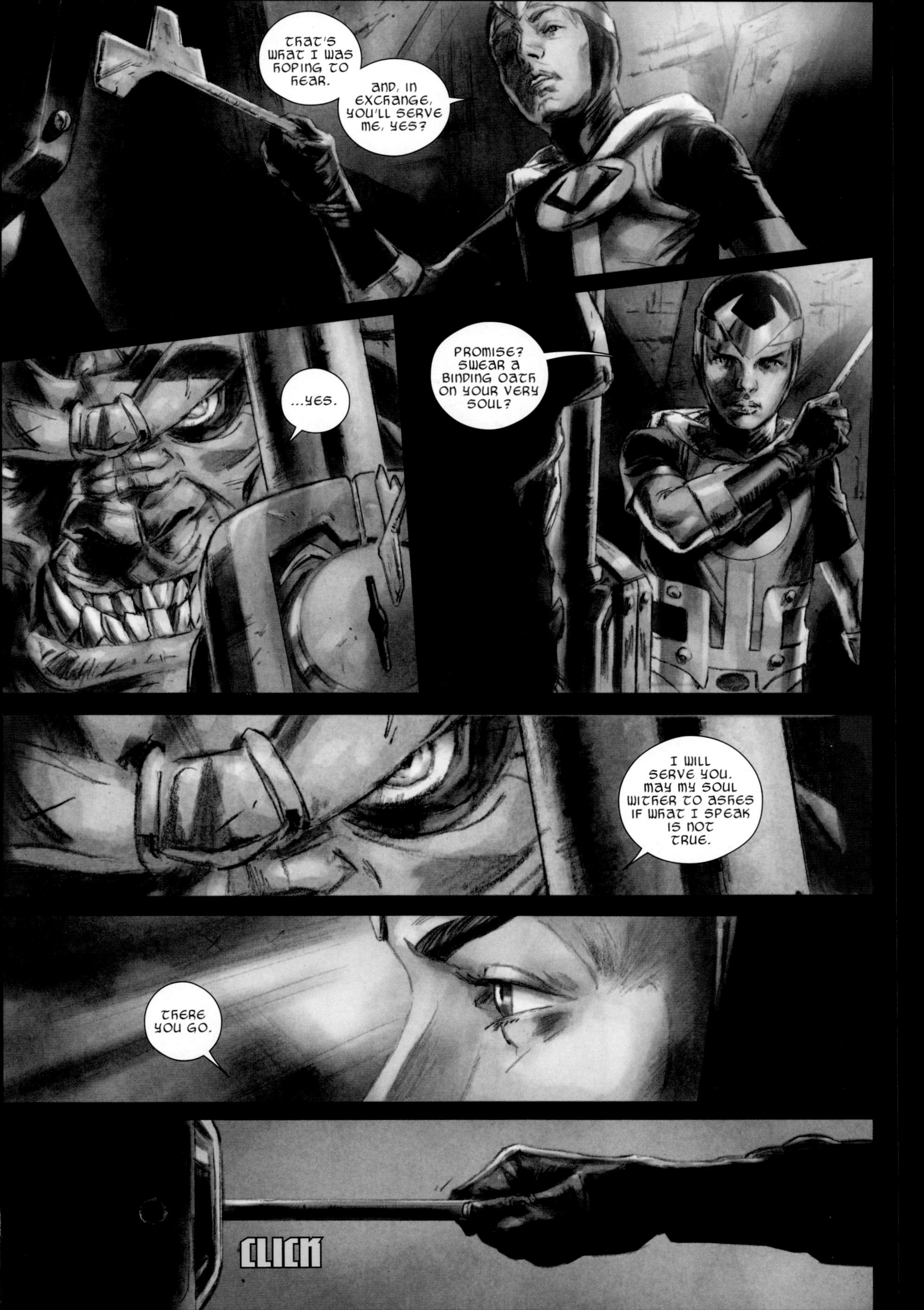
THAT'S WHAT I WAS HOPING TO HEAR.
AND, IN EXCHANGE, YOU'LL SERVE ME, YES?
...YES.
PROMISE? SWEAR A BINDING OATH ON YOUR VERY SOUL?
I WILL SERVE YOU. MAY MY SOUL WITHER TO ASHES IF WHAT I SPEAK IS NOT TRUE.
THERE YOU GO.
CLICK

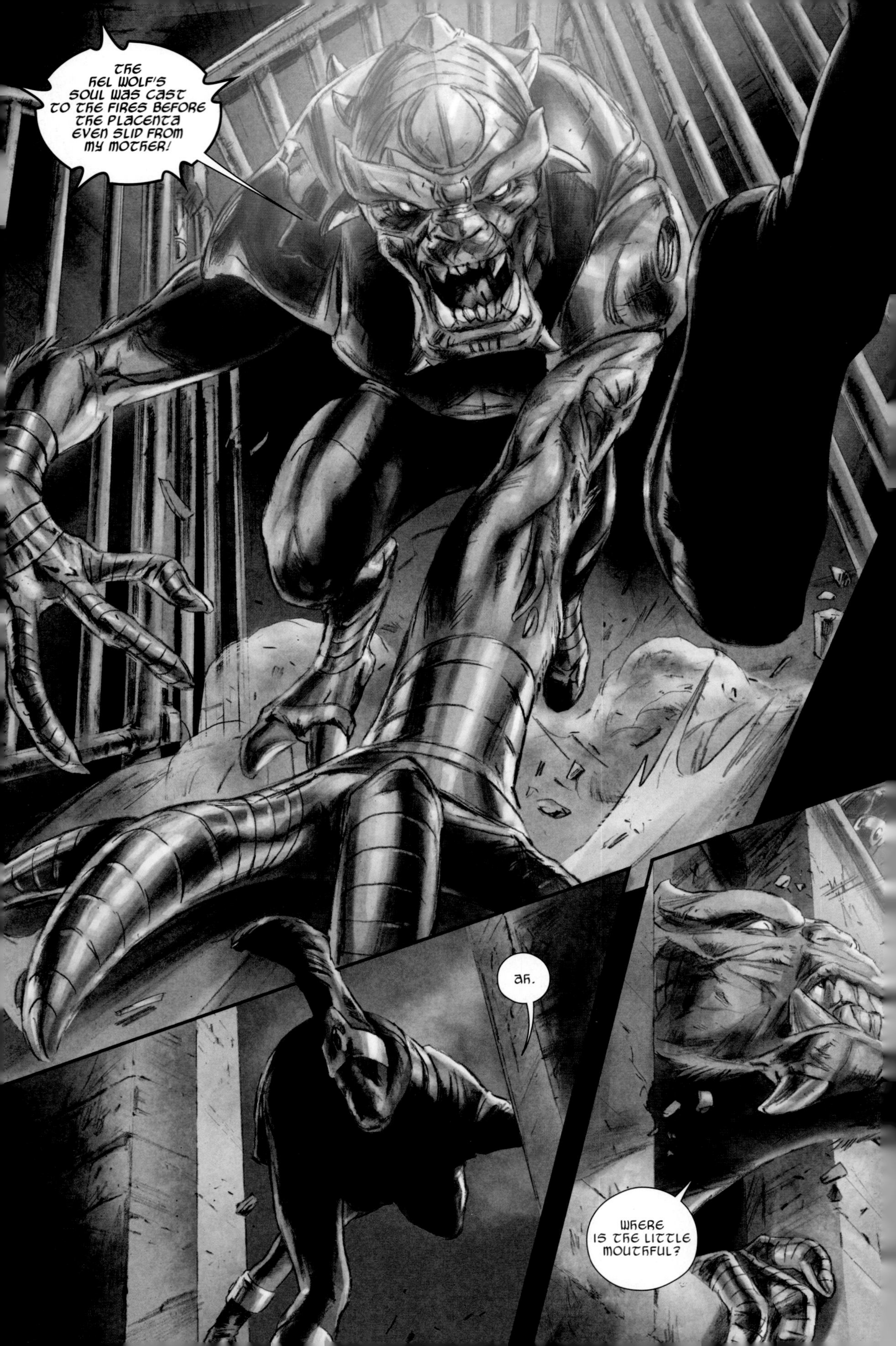
THE HEL WOLF'S SOUL WAS CAST TO THE FIRES BEFORE THE PLACENTA EVEN SLID FROM MY MOTHER!
AH.
WHERE IS THE LITTLE MOUTHFUL?

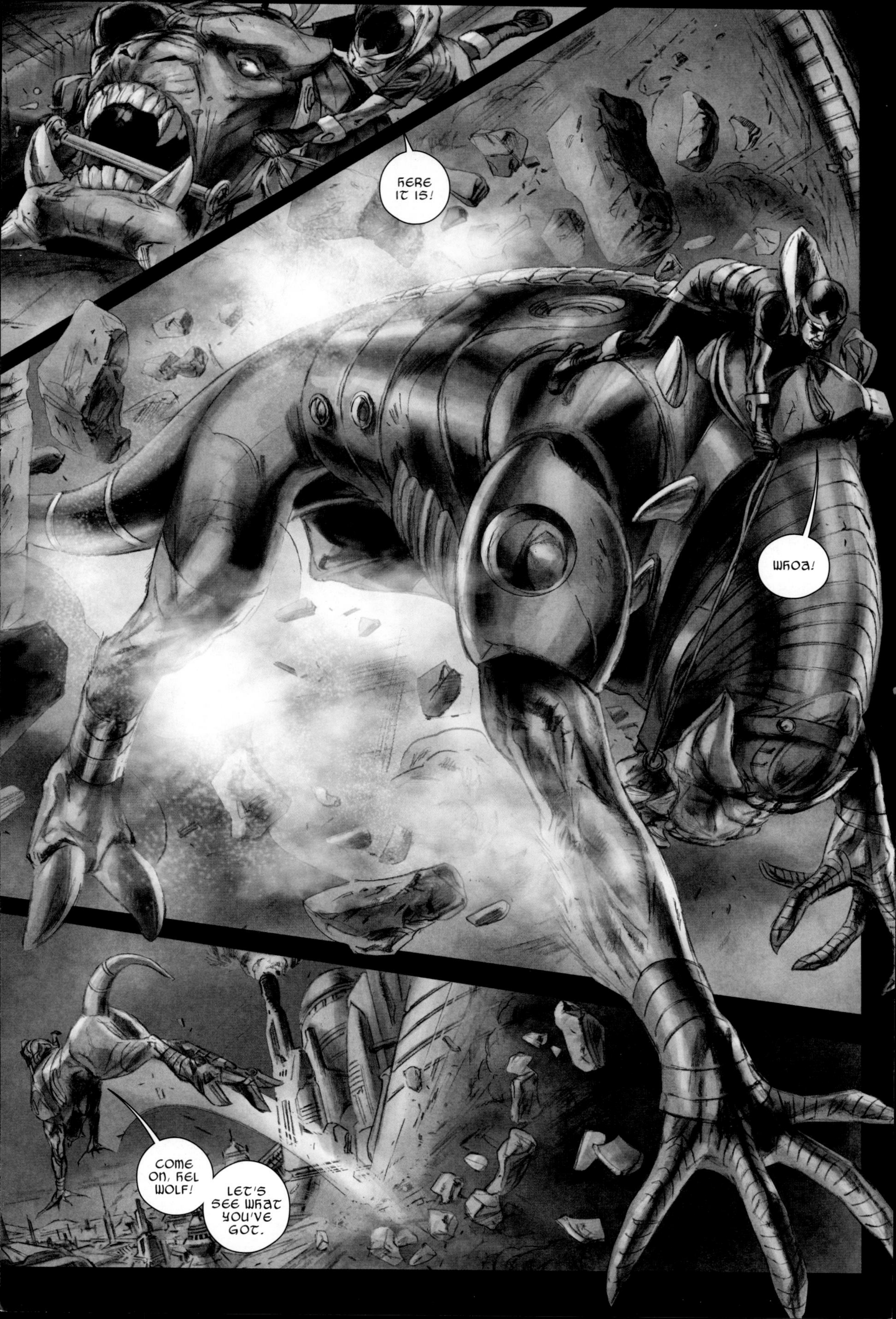
HERE IT IS!
WHOA!
COME ON, HEL WOLF!
LET'S SEE WHAT YOU'VE GOT.

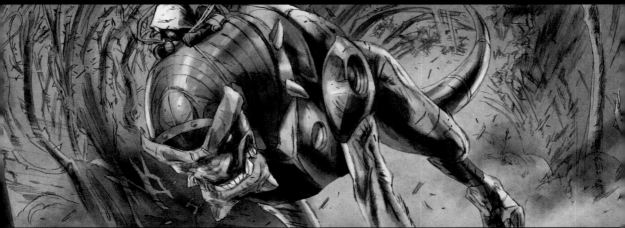

NO MORE. NO MORE.

YOU TRIED, BUT YOU MUST UNDERSTAND--THIS BRIDLE BROKE *GOATS.* ENORMOUS, DUNG-DEPOSITING BEASTS OF A MOST WILLFUL NATURE.

A MONSTER OF THE PITS ITSELF DOESN'T EXACTLY MEASURE UP.

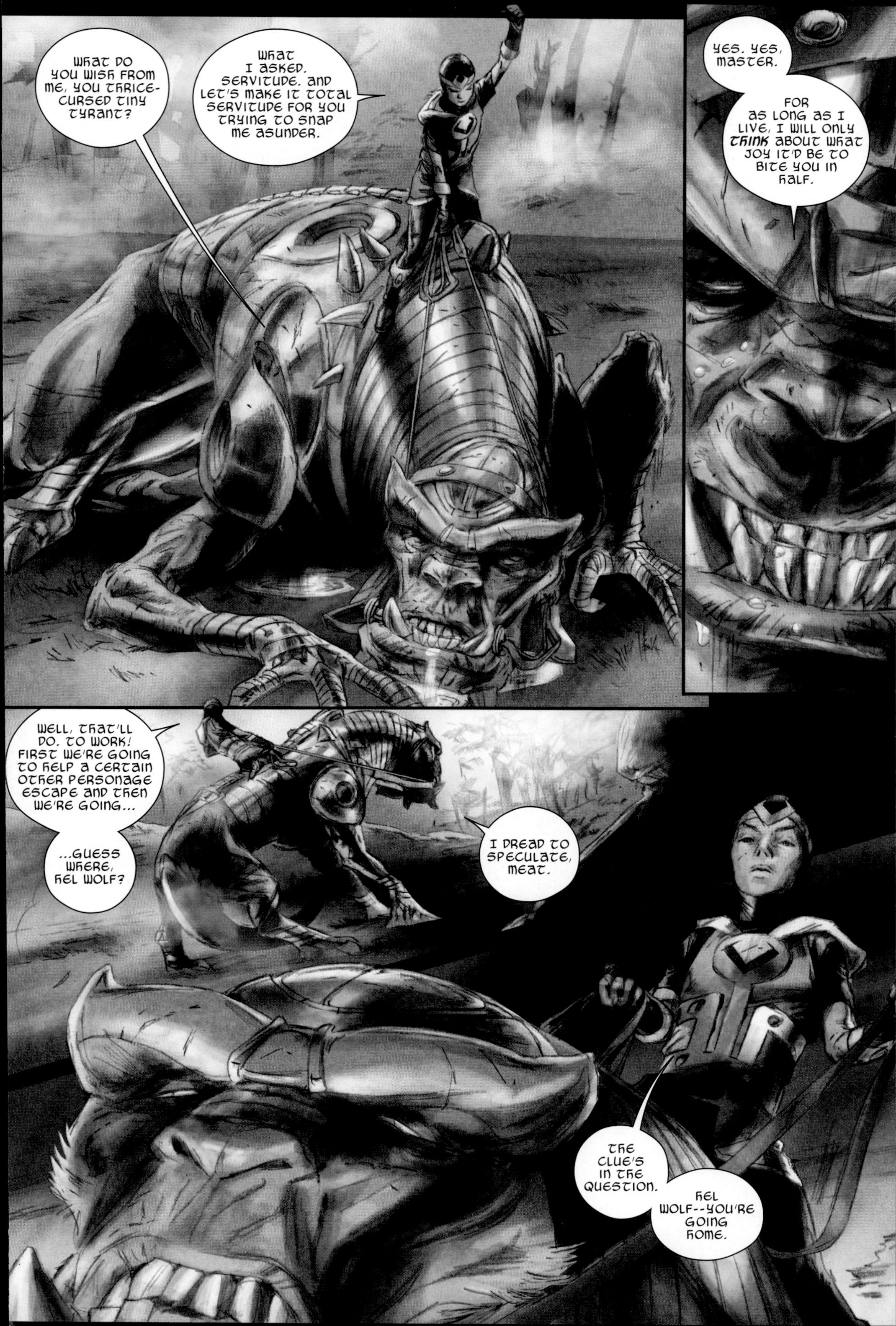
WHAT DO YOU WISH FROM ME, YOU THRICE-CURSED TINY TYRANT?
WHAT I ASKED. SERVITUDE. AND LET'S MAKE IT TOTAL SERVITUDE FOR YOU TRYING TO SNAP ME ASUNDER.
YES. YES, MASTER.
FOR AS LONG AS I LIVE, I WILL ONLY THINK ABOUT WHAT JOY IT'D BE TO BITE YOU IN HALF.
WELL, THAT'LL DO. TO WORK! FIRST WE'RE GOING TO HELP A CERTAIN OTHER PERSONAGE ESCAPE AND THEN WE'RE GOING...
...GUESS WHERE, HEL WOLF?
I DREAD TO SPECULATE, MEAT.
THE CLUE'S IN THE QUESTION.
HEL WOLF--YOU'RE GOING HOME.

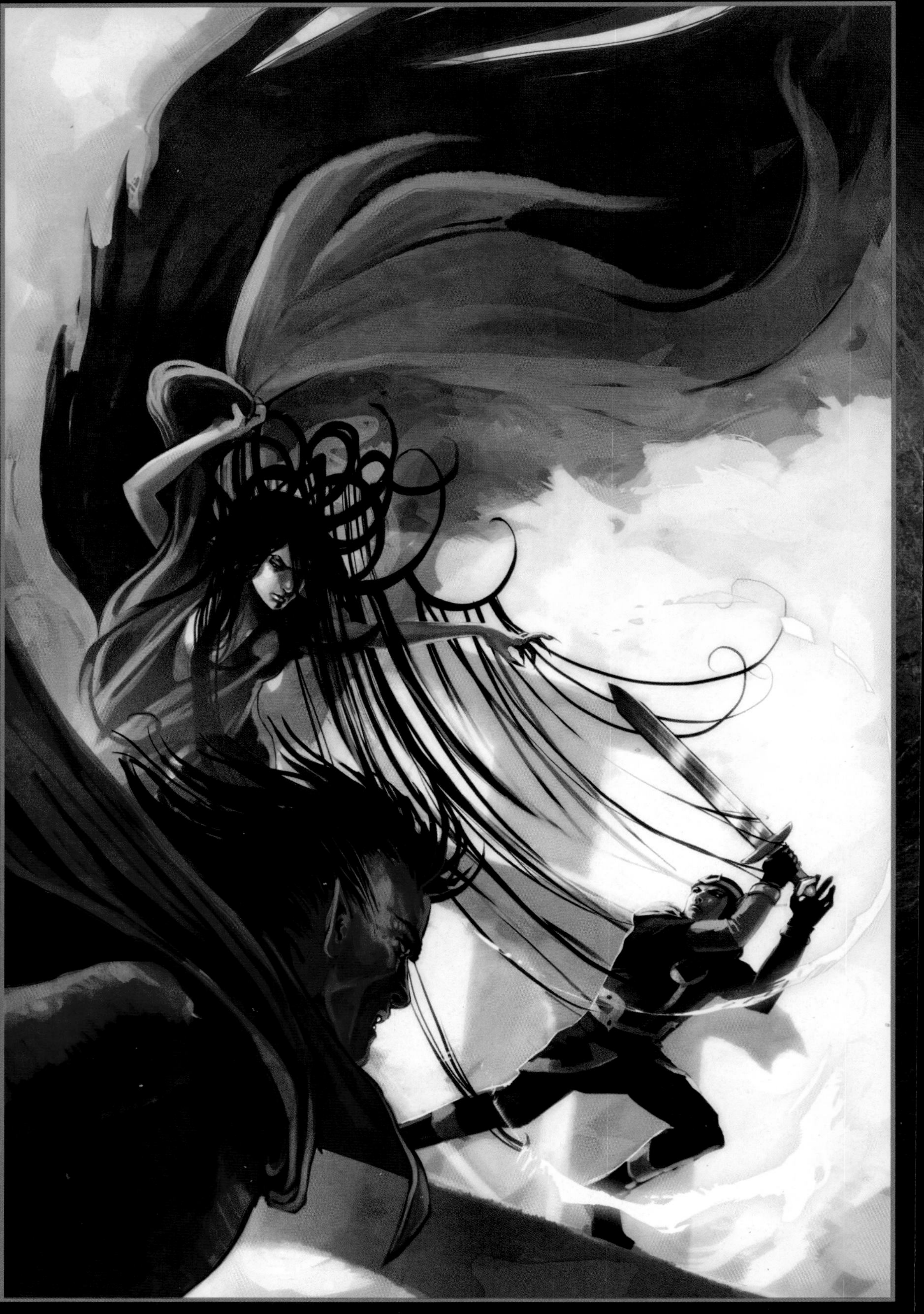

JOURNEY INTO MYSTERY #624

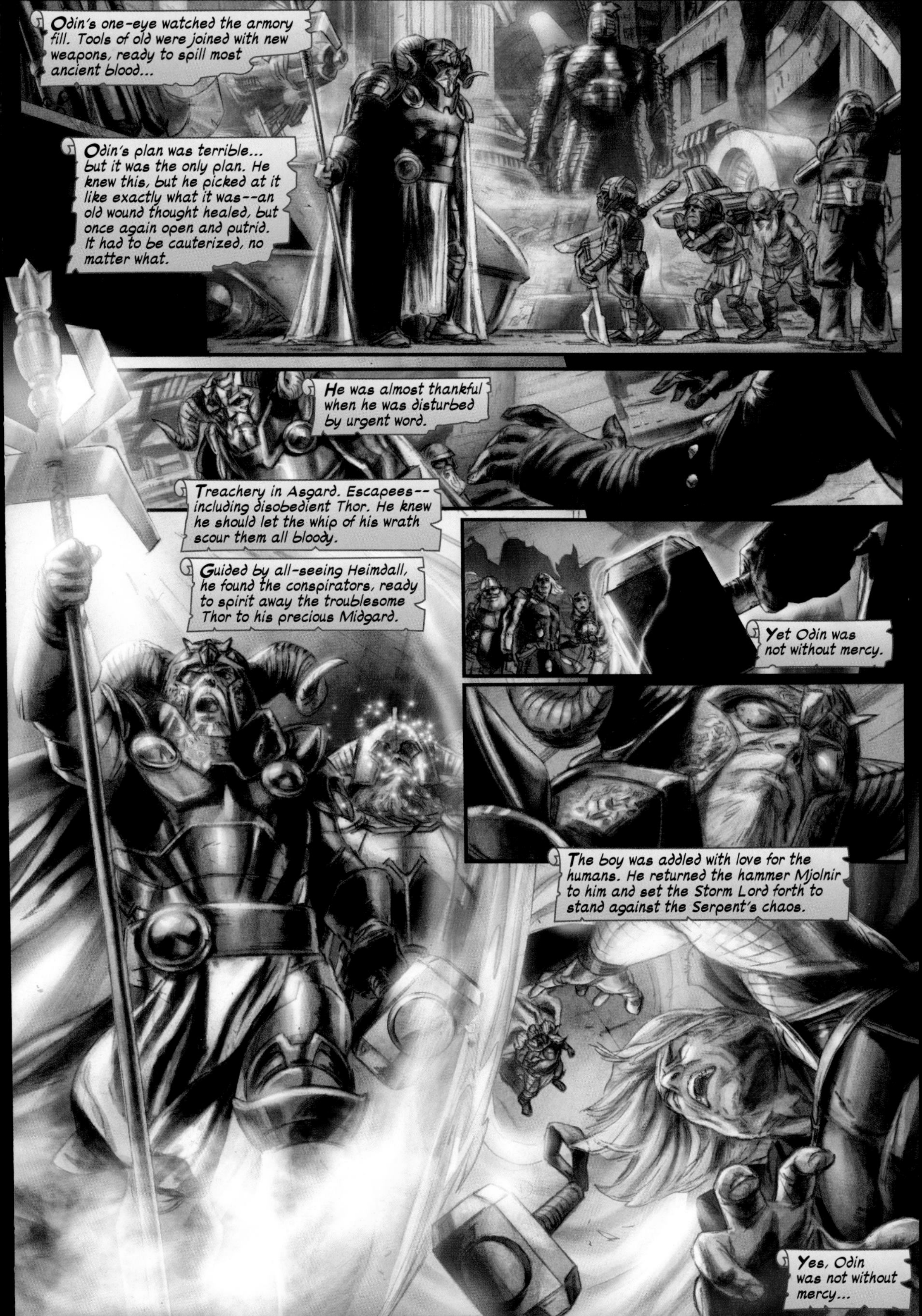
Odin's one-eye watched the armory fill. Tools of old were joined with new weapons, ready to spill most ancient blood...
Odin's plan was terrible... but it was the only plan. He knew this, but he picked at it like exactly what it was--an old wound thought healed, but once again open and putrid. It had to be cauterized, no matter what.
He was almost thankful when he was disturbed by urgent word.
Treachery in Asgard. Escapees--including disobedient Thor. He knew he should let the whip of his wrath scour them all bloody.
Guided by all-seeing Heimdall, he found the conspirators, ready to spirit away the troublesome Thor to his precious Midgard.
Yet Odin was not without mercy.
The boy was addled with love for the humans. He returned the hammer Mjolnir to him and set the Storm Lord forth to stand against the Serpent's chaos.
Yes, Odin was not without mercy...

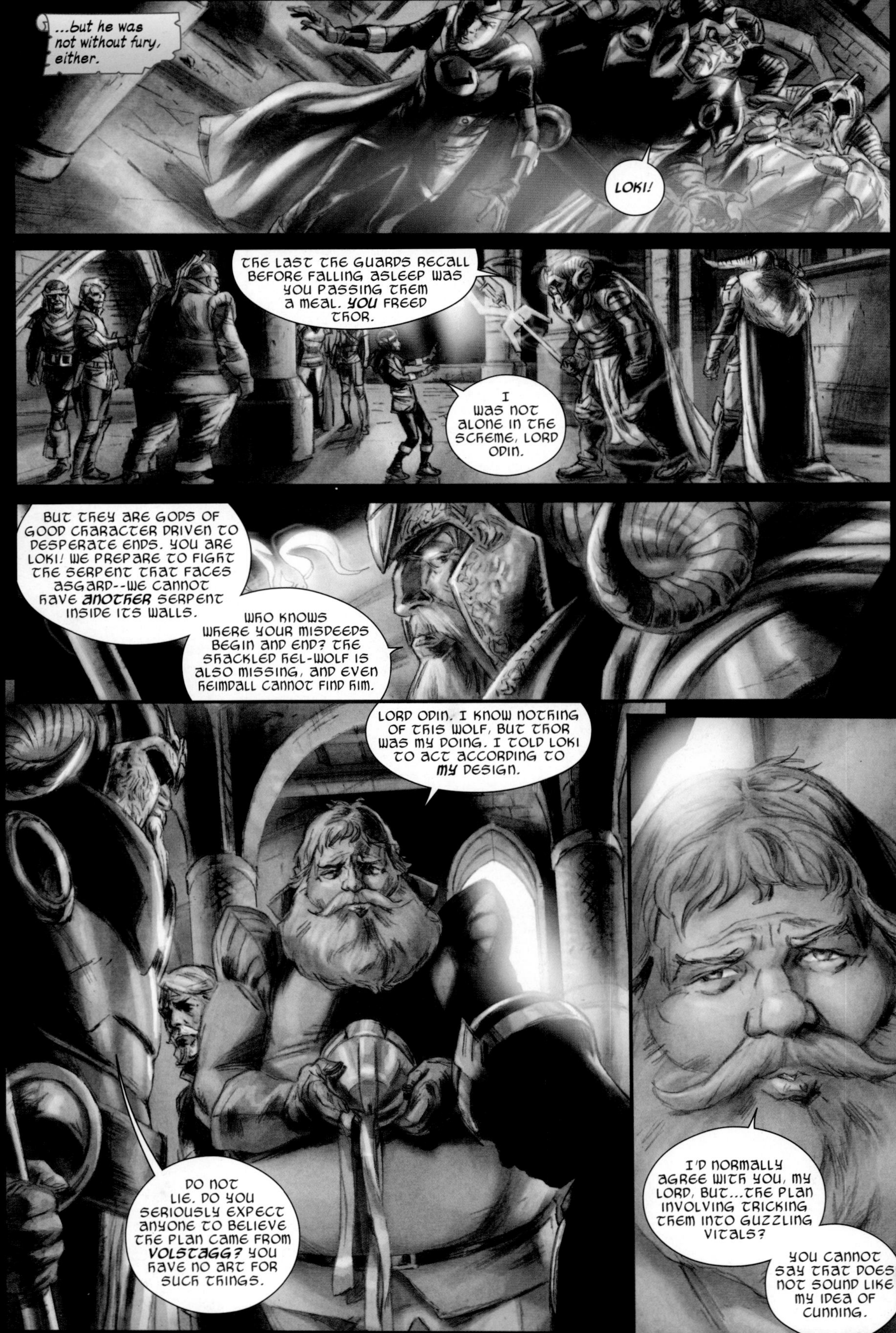
...but he was not without fury, either.
LOKI!
THE LAST THE GUARDS RECALL BEFORE FALLING ASLEEP WAS YOU PASSING THEM A MEAL. YOU FREED THOR.
I WAS NOT ALONE IN THE SCHEME, LORD ODIN.
BUT THEY ARE GODS OF GOOD CHARACTER DRIVEN TO DESPERATE ENDS. YOU ARE LOKI! WE PREPARE TO FIGHT THE SERPENT THAT FACES ASGARD--WE CANNOT HAVE ANOTHER SERPENT INSIDE ITS WALLS.
WHO KNOWS WHERE YOUR MISDEEDS BEGIN AND END? THE SHACKLED HEL-WOLF IS ALSO MISSING, AND EVEN HEIMDALL CANNOT FIND HIM.
LORD ODIN. I KNOW NOTHING OF THIS WOLF, BUT THOR WAS MY DOING. I TOLD LOKI TO ACT ACCORDING TO MY DESIGN.
DO NOT LIE. DO YOU SERIOUSLY EXPECT ANYONE TO BELIEVE THE PLAN CAME FROM VOLSTAGG? YOU HAVE NO ART FOR SUCH THINGS.
I'D NORMALLY AGREE WITH YOU, MY LORD, BUT...THE PLAN INVOLVING TRICKING THEM INTO GUZZLING VITALS?
YOU CANNOT SAY THAT DOES NOT SOUND LIKE MY IDEA OF CUNNING.

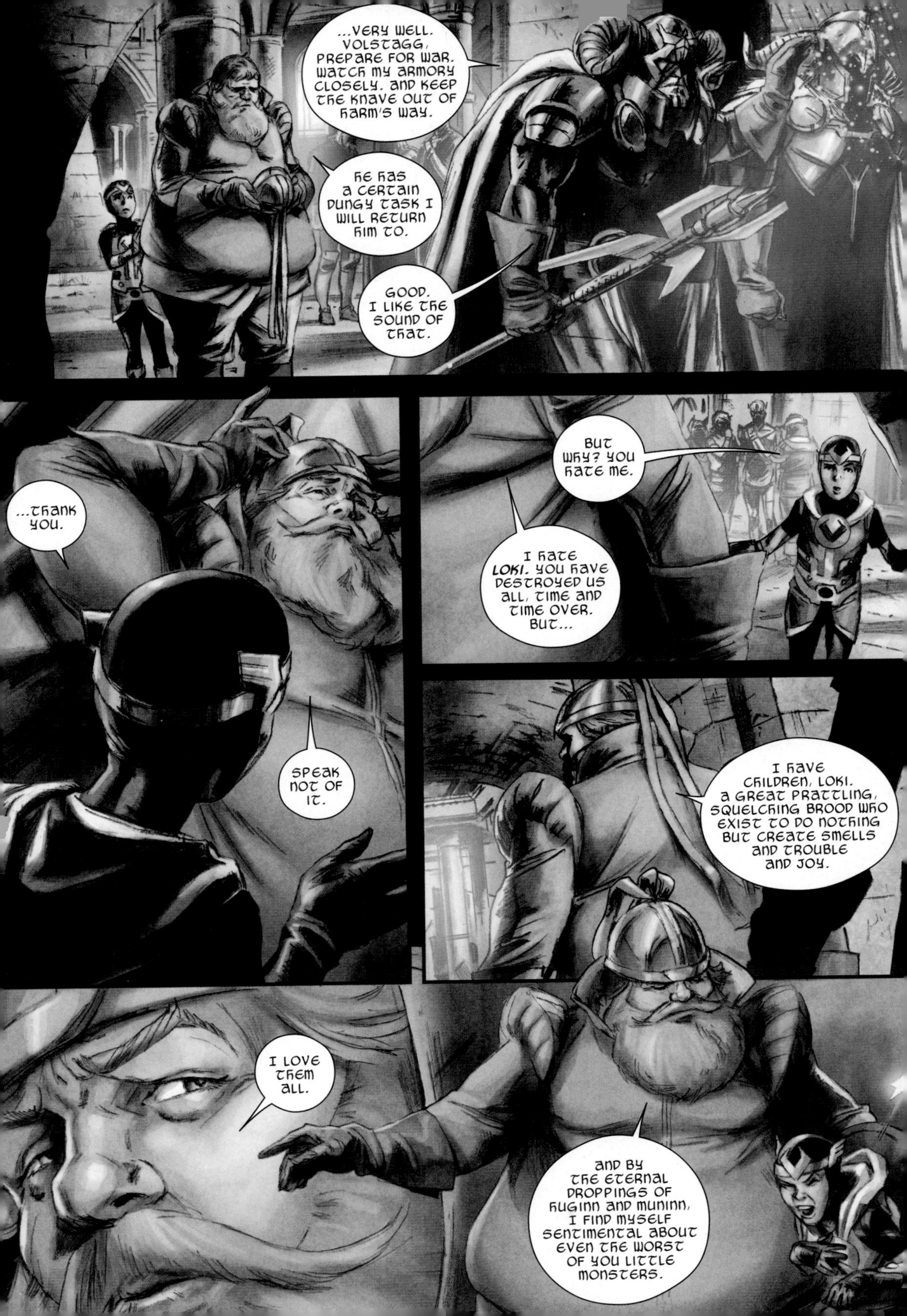
...VERY WELL. VOLSTAGG, PREPARE FOR WAR. WATCH MY ARMORY CLOSELY. AND KEEP THE KNAVE OUT OF HARM'S WAY.
HE HAS A CERTAIN DUNGY TASK I WILL RETURN HIM TO.
GOOD. I LIKE THE SOUND OF THAT.
...THANK YOU.
SPEAK NOT OF IT.
BUT WHY? YOU HATE ME.
I HATE **LOKI.** YOU HAVE DESTROYED US ALL, TIME AND TIME OVER. BUT...
I HAVE CHILDREN, LOKI. A GREAT PRATTLING, SQUELCHING BROOD WHO EXIST TO DO NOTHING BUT CREATE SMELLS AND TROUBLE AND JOY.
I LOVE THEM ALL.
AND BY THE ETERNAL DROPPINGS OF HUGINN AND MUNINN, I FIND MYSELF SENTIMENTAL ABOUT EVEN THE WORST OF YOU LITTLE MONSTERS.

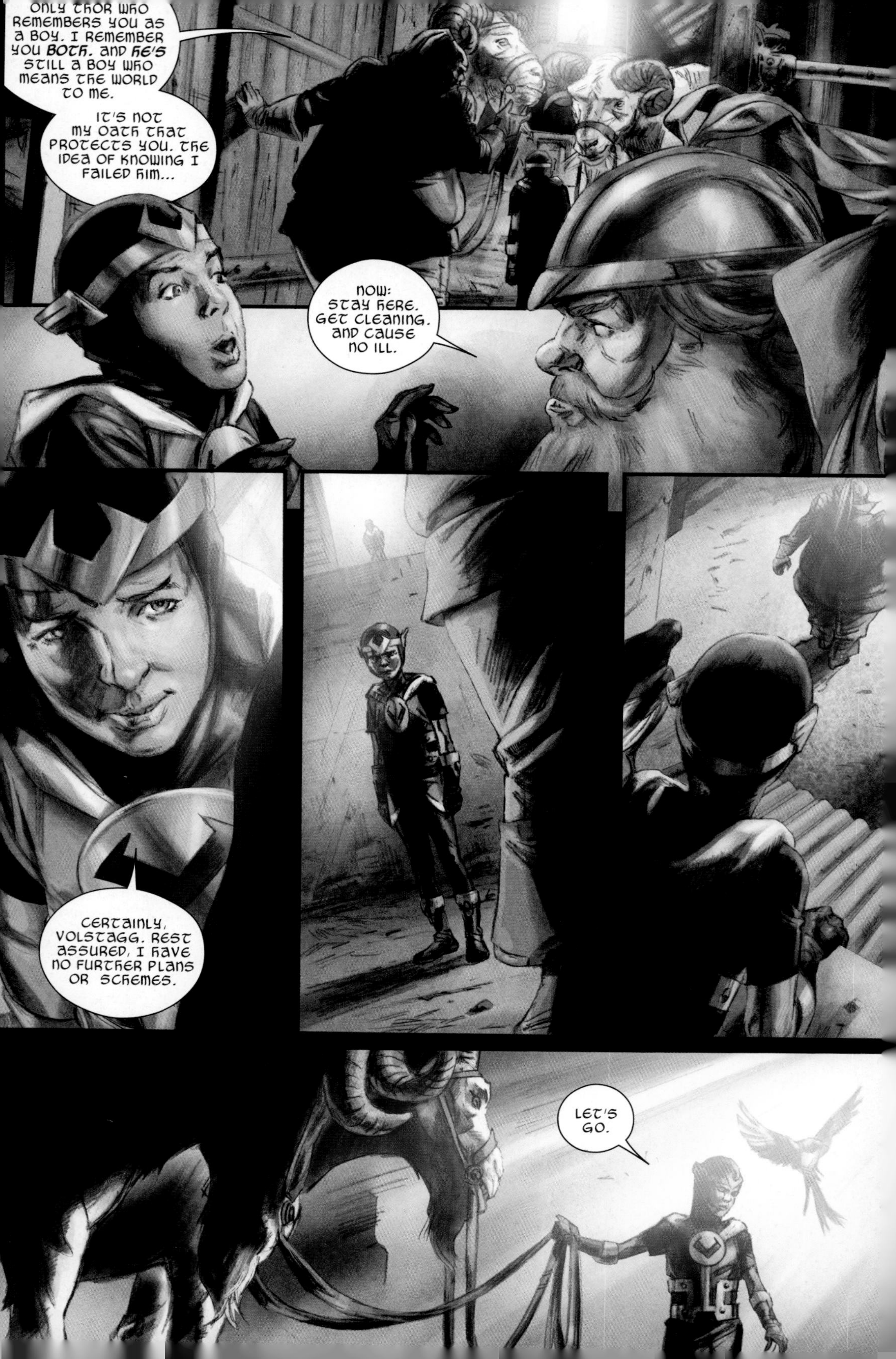
ONLY THOR WHO REMEMBERS YOU AS A BOY. I REMEMBER YOU *BOTH.* AND *HE'S* STILL A BOY WHO MEANS THE WORLD TO ME.
IT'S NOT MY OATH THAT PROTECTS YOU. THE IDEA OF KNOWING I FAILED HIM...
NOW: STAY HERE. GET CLEANING. AND CAUSE NO ILL.
CERTAINLY, VOLSTAGG. REST ASSURED, I HAVE NO FURTHER PLANS OR SCHEMES.
LET'S GO.

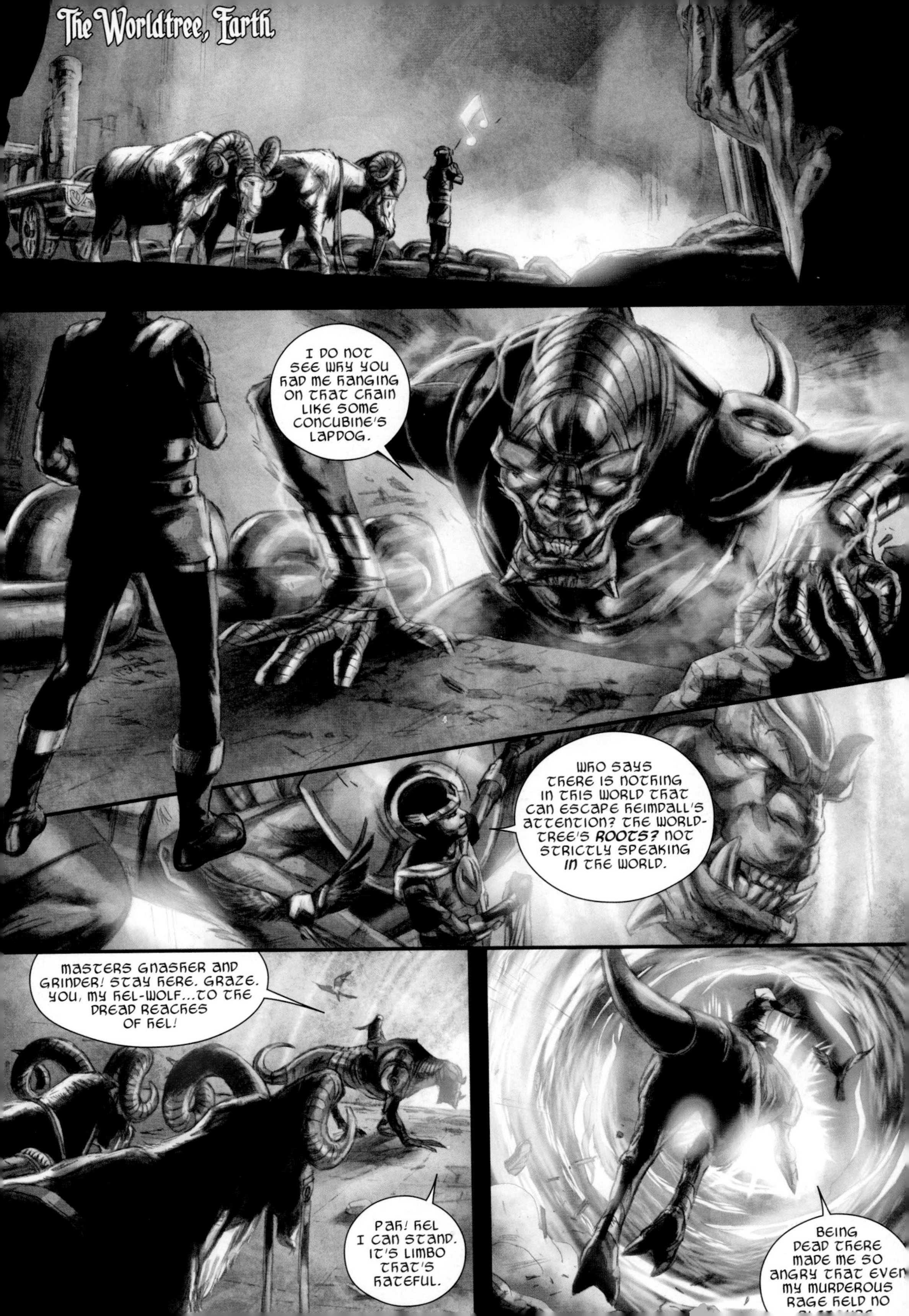
The Worldtree, Earth.
I DO NOT SEE WHY YOU HAD ME HANGING ON THAT CHAIN LIKE SOME CONCUBINE'S LAPDOG.
WHO SAYS THERE IS NOTHING IN THIS WORLD THAT CAN ESCAPE HEIMDALL'S ATTENTION? THE WORLD-TREE'S **ROOTS?** NOT STRICTLY SPEAKING **IN** THE WORLD.
MASTERS GNASHER AND GRINDER! STAY HERE. GRAZE. YOU, MY HEL-WOLF...TO THE DREAD REACHES OF HEL!
PAH! HEL I CAN STAND. IT'S LIMBO THAT'S HATEFUL.
BEING DEAD THERE MADE ME SO ANGRY THAT EVEN MY MURDEROUS RAGE HELD NO

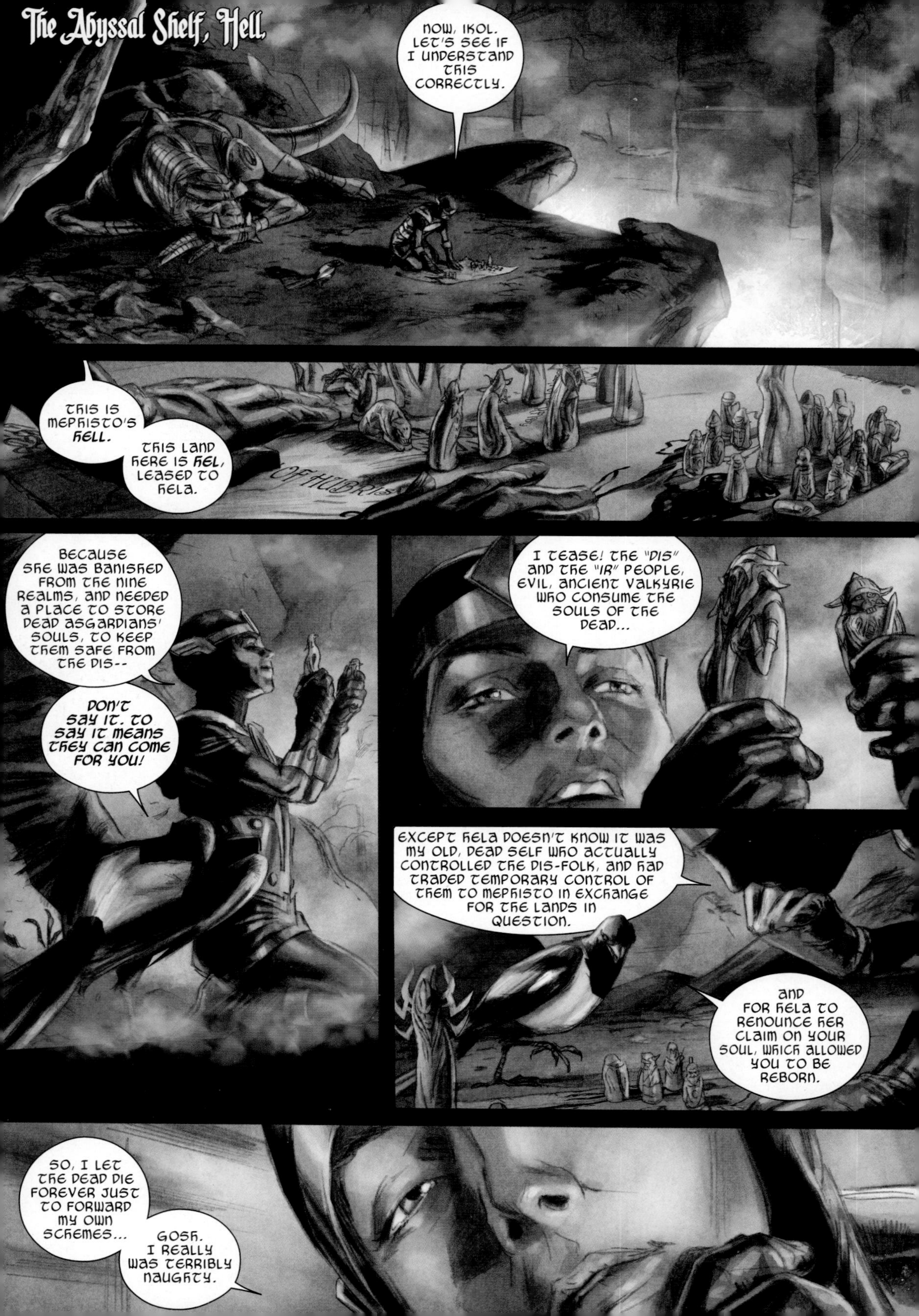
The Abyssal Shelf, Hell.
NOW, IKOL. LET'S SEE IF I UNDERSTAND THIS CORRECTLY.
THIS IS MEPHISTO'S **HELL.**
THIS LAND HERE IS **HEL**, LEASED TO HELA.
OF HUBRIS
BECAUSE SHE WAS BANISHED FROM THE NINE REALMS, AND NEEDED A PLACE TO STORE DEAD ASGARDIANS' SOULS, TO KEEP THEM SAFE FROM THE DIS--
DON'T SAY IT. TO SAY IT MEANS THEY CAN COME FOR YOU!
I TEASE! THE "*DIS*" AND THE "*IR*" PEOPLE, EVIL, ANCIENT VALKYRIE WHO CONSUME THE SOULS OF THE DEAD...
EXCEPT HELA DOESN'T KNOW IT WAS MY OLD, DEAD SELF WHO ACTUALLY CONTROLLED THE DIS-FOLK, AND HAD TRADED TEMPORARY CONTROL OF THEM TO MEPHISTO IN EXCHANGE FOR THE LANDS IN QUESTION.
AND FOR HELA TO RENOUNCE HER CLAIM ON YOUR SOUL, WHICH ALLOWED YOU TO BE REBORN.
SO, I LET THE DEAD DIE FOREVER JUST TO FORWARD MY OWN SCHEMES...
GOSH. I REALLY WAS TERRIBLY NAUGHTY.

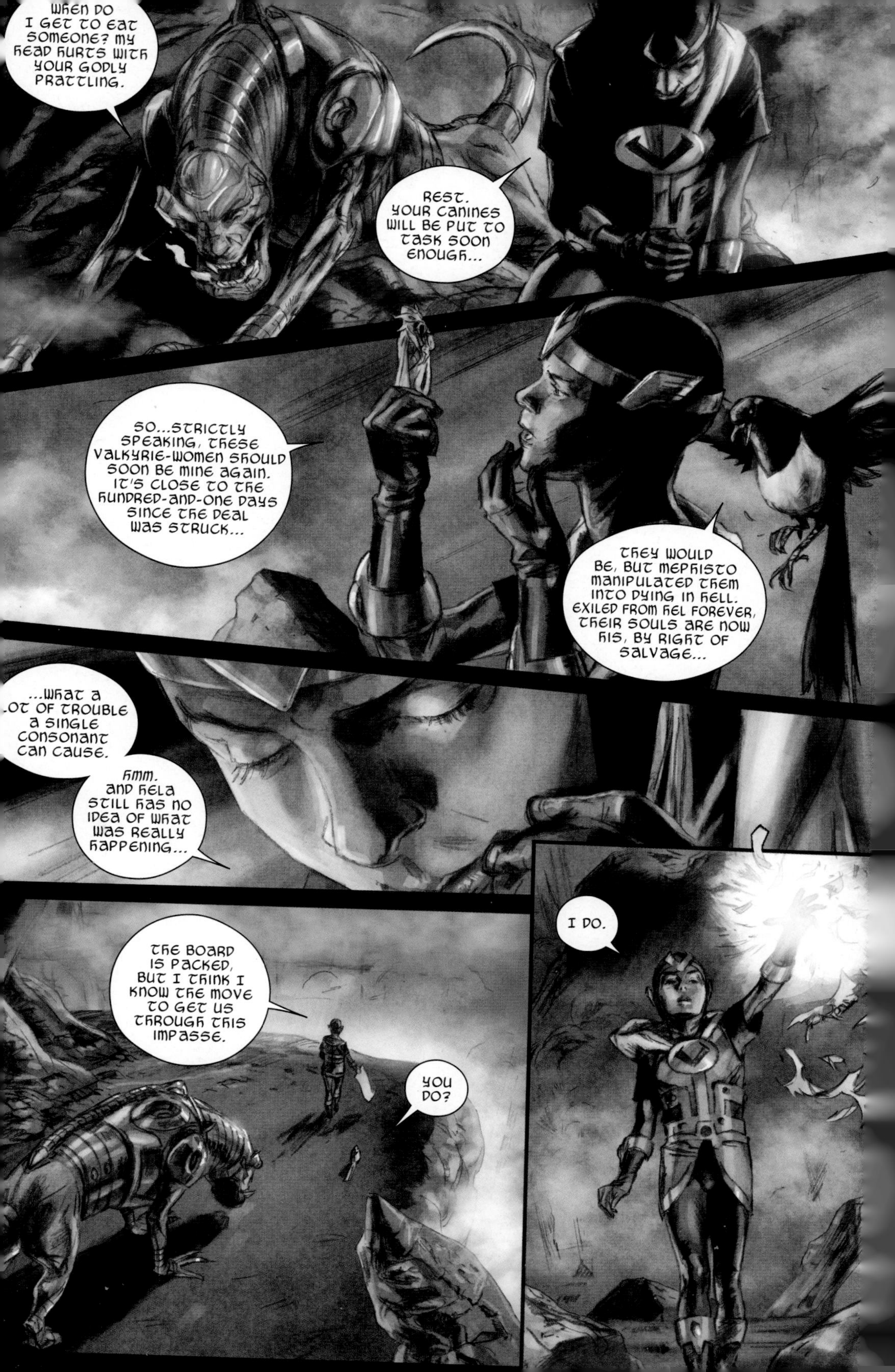
WHEN DO I GET TO EAT SOMEONE? MY HEAD HURTS WITH YOUR GODLY PRATTLING.
REST. YOUR CANINES WILL BE PUT TO TASK SOON ENOUGH...
SO...STRICTLY SPEAKING, THESE VALKYRIE-WOMEN SHOULD SOON BE MINE AGAIN. IT'S CLOSE TO THE HUNDRED-AND-ONE DAYS SINCE THE DEAL WAS STRUCK...
THEY WOULD BE, BUT MEPHISTO MANIPULATED THEM INTO DYING IN HELL. EXILED FROM HEL FOREVER, THEIR SOULS ARE NOW HIS, BY RIGHT OF SALVAGE...
...WHAT A LOT OF TROUBLE A SINGLE CONSONANT CAN CAUSE.
HMM. AND HELA STILL HAS NO IDEA OF WHAT WAS REALLY HAPPENING...
THE BOARD IS PACKED, BUT I THINK I KNOW THE MOVE TO GET US THROUGH THIS IMPASSE.
YOU DO?
I DO.

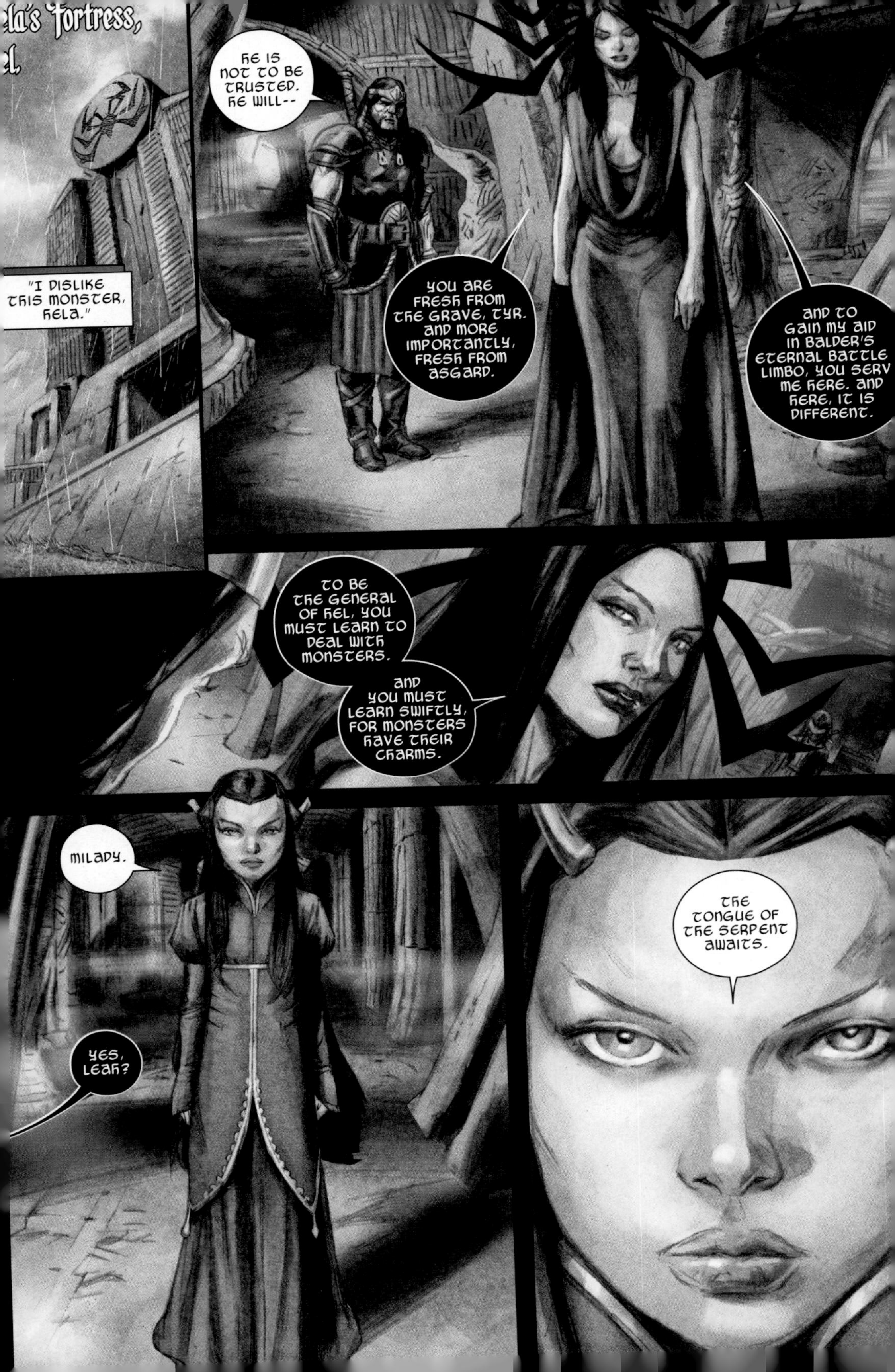
la's Fortress,
l,
"I DISLIKE THIS MONSTER, HELA."
HE IS NOT TO BE TRUSTED. HE WILL--
YOU ARE FRESH FROM THE GRAVE, TYR. AND MORE IMPORTANTLY, FRESH FROM ASGARD.
AND TO GAIN MY AID IN BALDER'S ETERNAL BATTLE LIMBO, YOU SERV ME HERE. AND HERE, IT IS DIFFERENT.
TO BE THE GENERAL OF HEL, YOU MUST LEARN TO DEAL WITH MONSTERS.
AND YOU MUST LEARN SWIFTLY, FOR MONSTERS HAVE THEIR CHARMS.
MILADY.
YES, LEAH?
THE TONGUE OF THE SERPENT AWAITS.

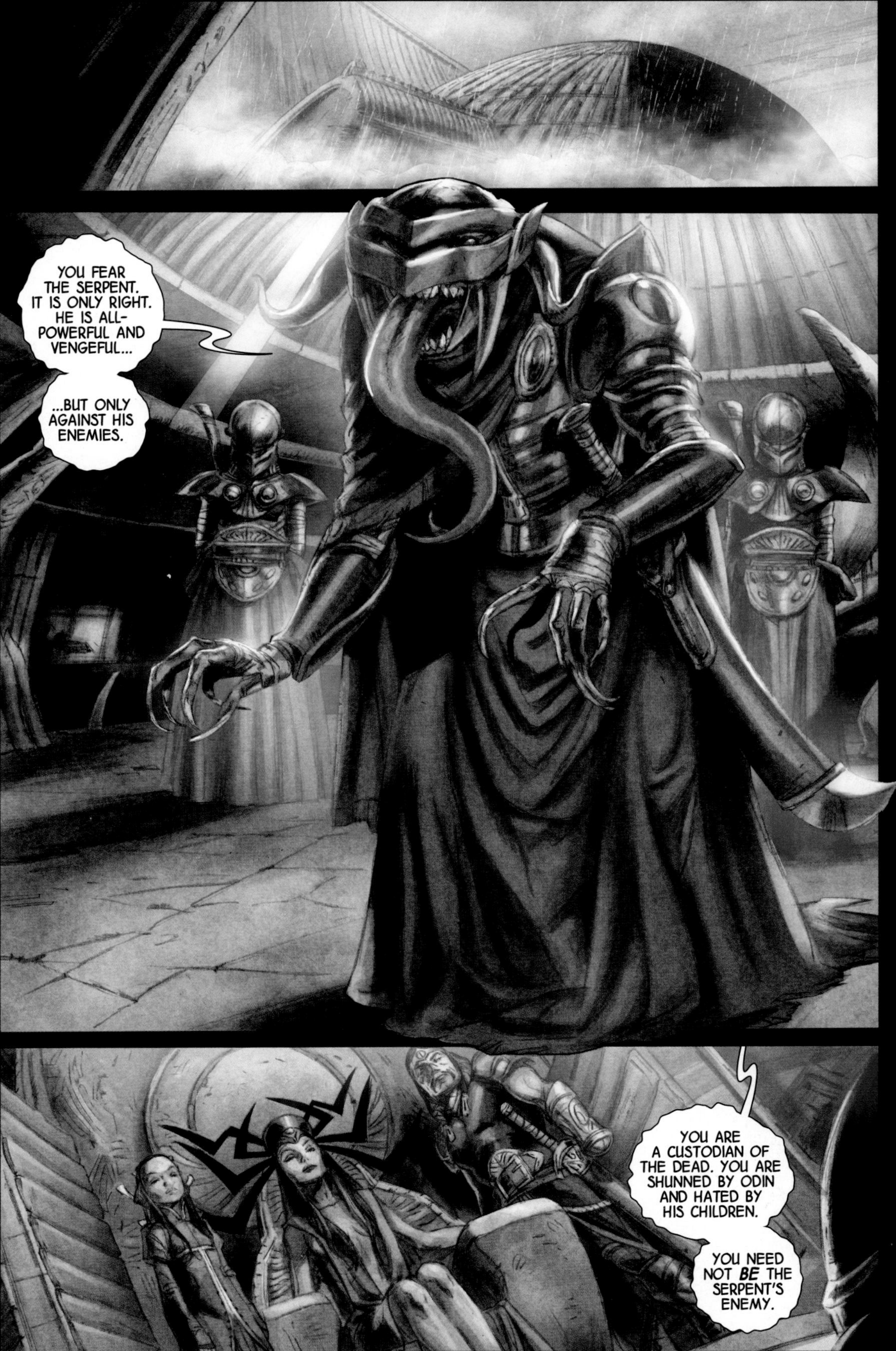
YOU FEAR THE SERPENT. IT IS ONLY RIGHT. HE IS ALL-POWERFUL AND VENGEFUL...
...BUT ONLY AGAINST HIS ENEMIES.
YOU ARE A CUSTODIAN OF THE DEAD. YOU ARE SHUNNED BY ODIN AND HATED BY HIS CHILDREN.
YOU NEED NOT BE THE SERPENT'S ENEMY.

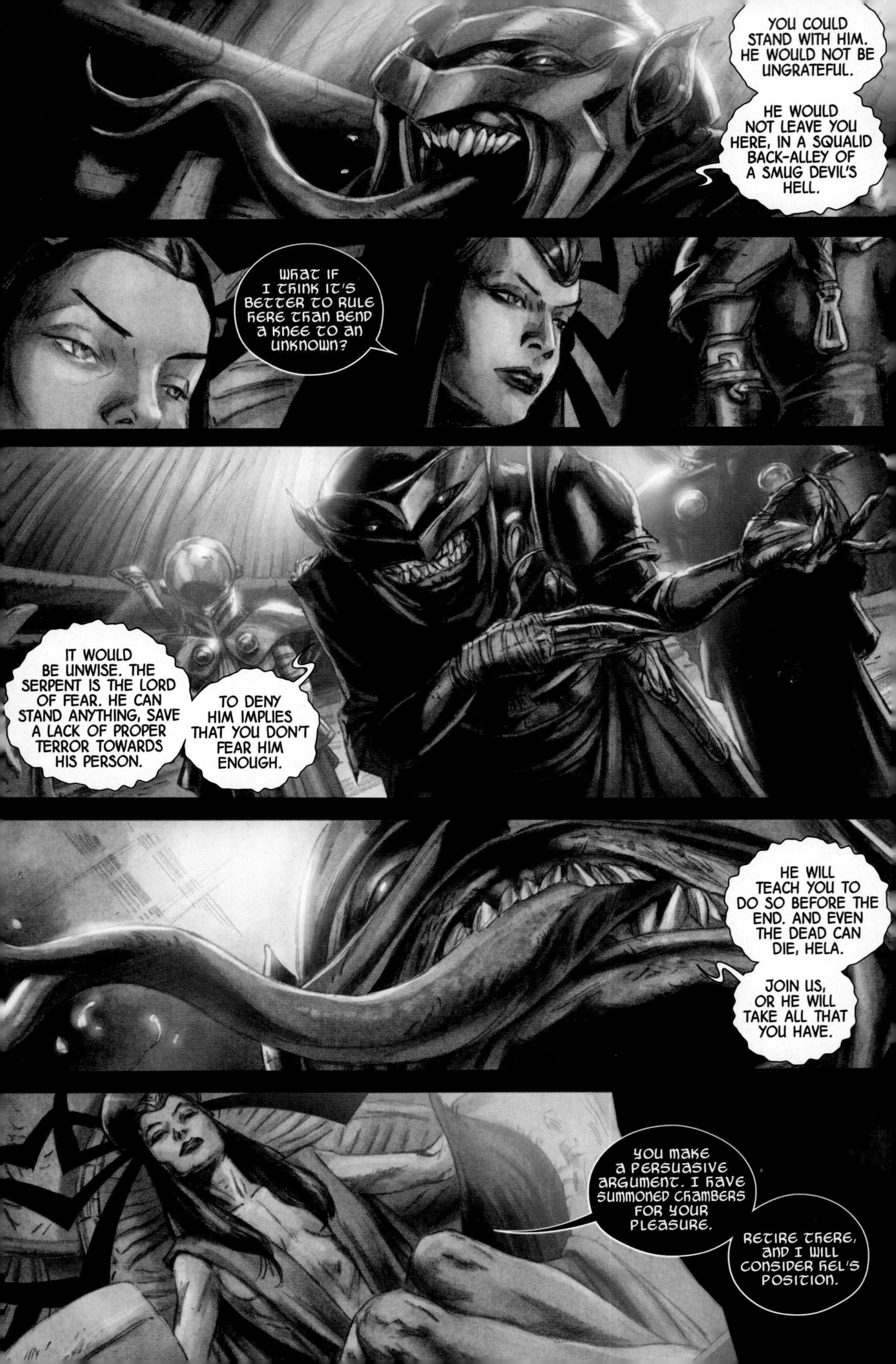

YOU COULD STAND WITH HIM. HE WOULD NOT BE UNGRATEFUL.
HE WOULD NOT LEAVE YOU HERE, IN A SQUALID BACK-ALLEY OF A SMUG DEVIL'S HELL.
WHAT IF I THINK IT'S BETTER TO RULE HERE THAN BEND A KNEE TO AN UNKNOWN?
IT WOULD BE UNWISE. THE SERPENT IS THE LORD OF FEAR. HE CAN STAND ANYTHING, SAVE A LACK OF PROPER TERROR TOWARDS HIS PERSON.
TO DENY HIM IMPLIES THAT YOU DON'T FEAR HIM ENOUGH.
HE WILL TEACH YOU TO DO SO BEFORE THE END. AND EVEN THE DEAD CAN DIE, HELA.
JOIN US, OR HE WILL TAKE ALL THAT YOU HAVE.
YOU MAKE A PERSUASIVE ARGUMENT. I HAVE SUMMONED CHAMBERS FOR YOUR PLEASURE.
RETIRE THERE, AND I WILL CONSIDER HEL'S POSITION.

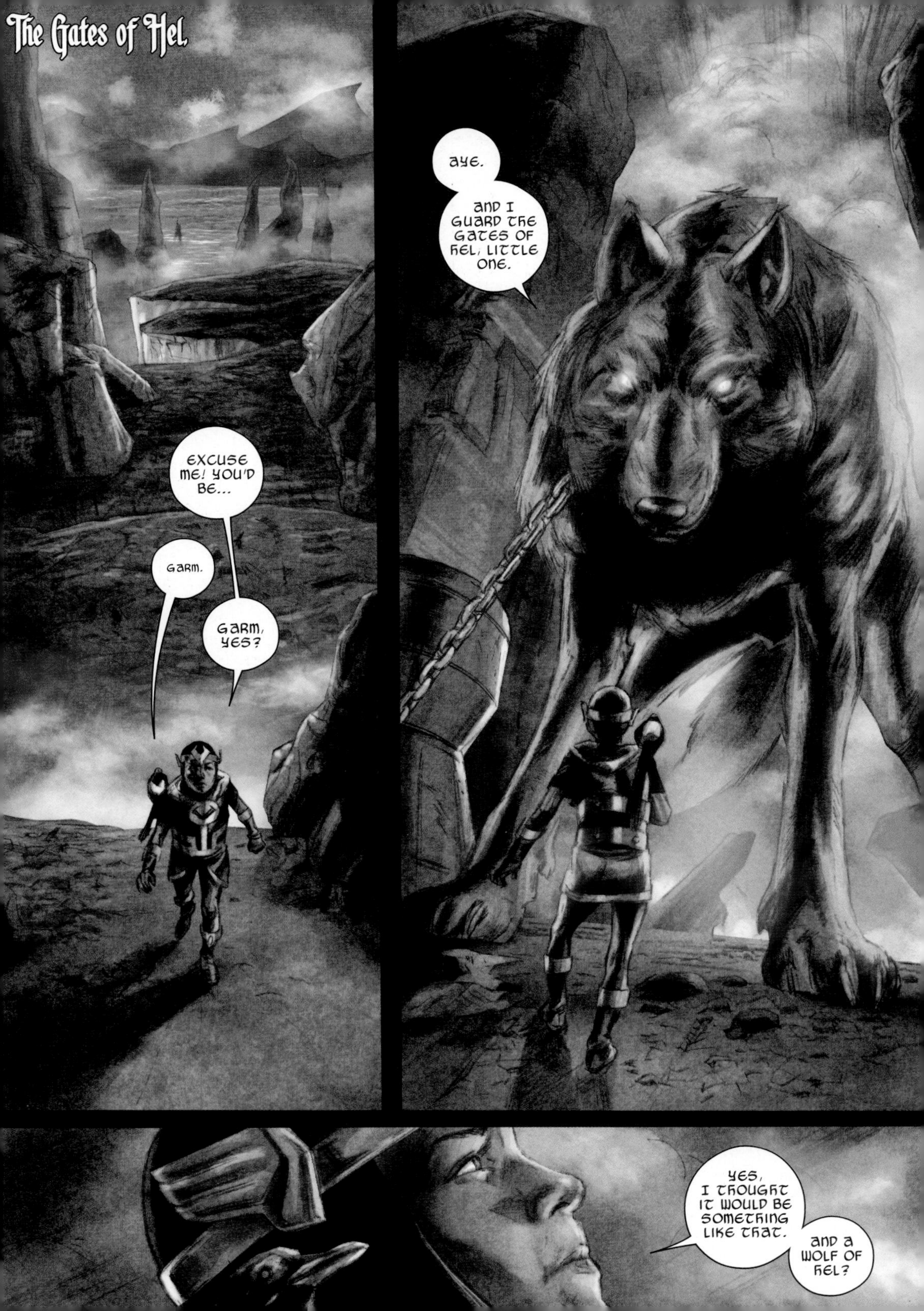
The Gates of Hel.
EXCUSE ME! YOU'D BE...
GARM.
GARM, YES?
AYE.
AND I GUARD THE GATES OF HEL, LITTLE ONE.
YES, I THOUGHT IT WOULD BE SOMETHING LIKE THAT.
AND A WOLF OF HEL?

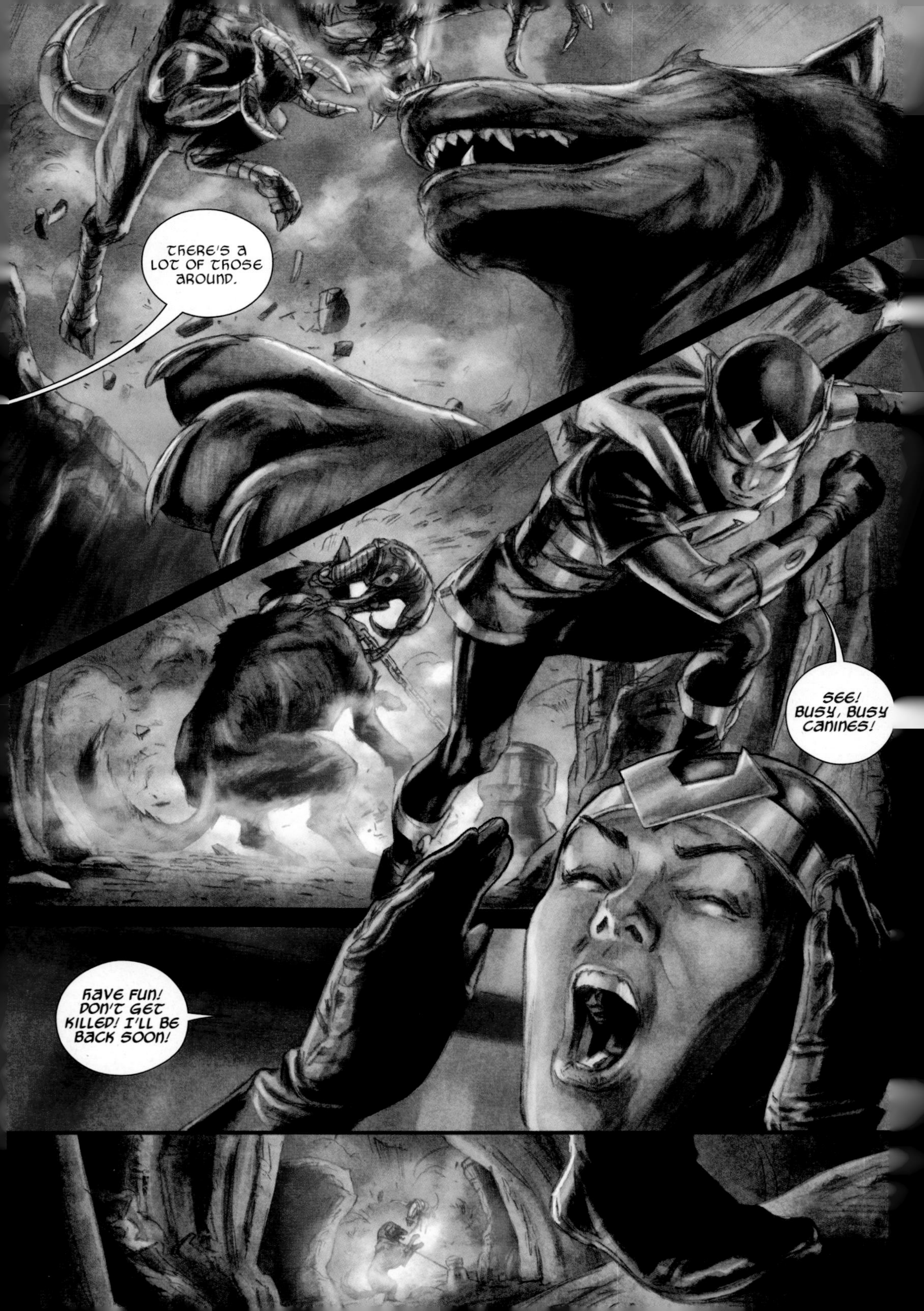
THERE'S A LOT OF THOSE AROUND.
SEE! BUSY, BUSY CANINES!
HAVE FUN! DON'T GET KILLED! I'LL BE BACK SOON!

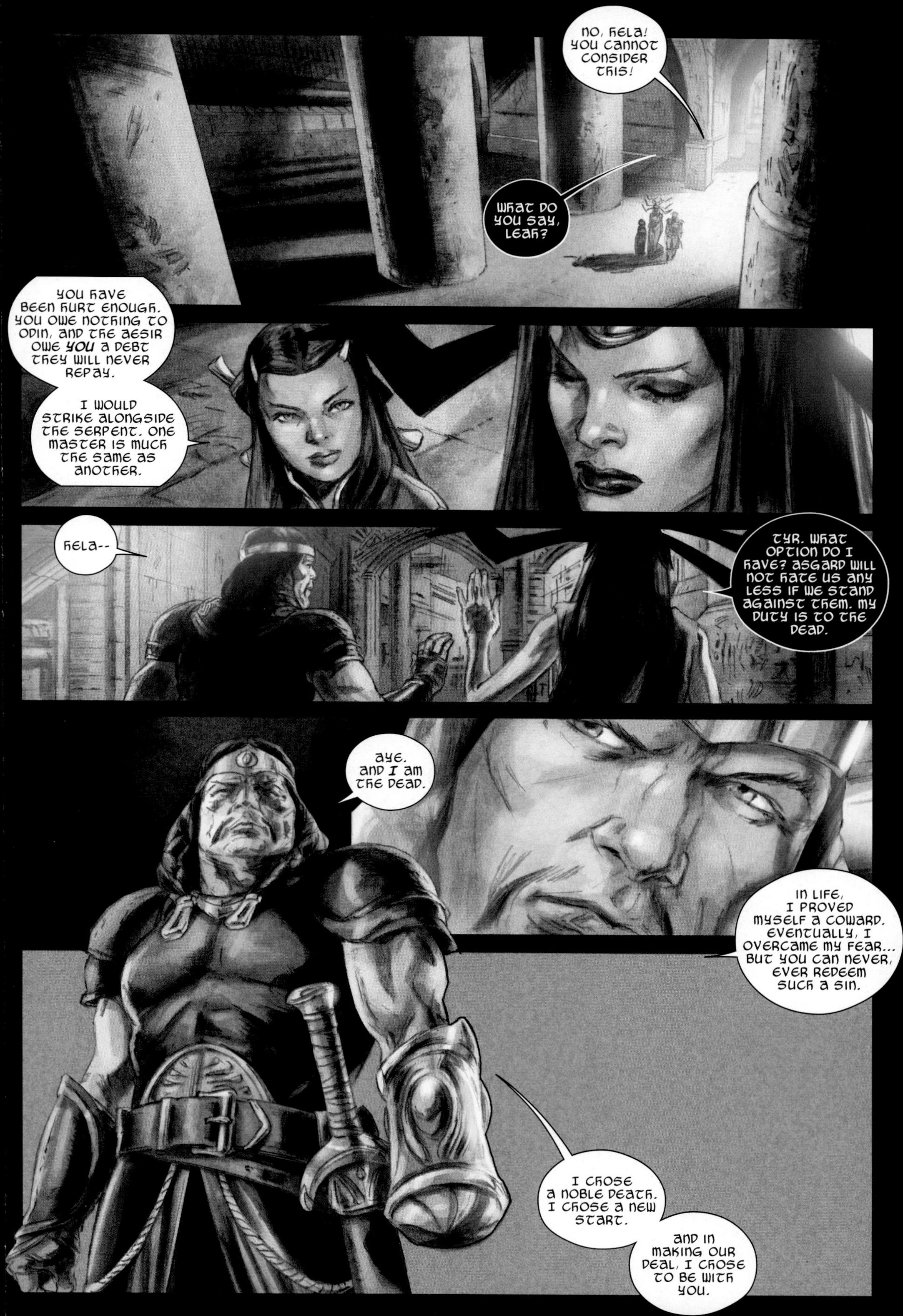
NO, HELA! YOU CANNOT CONSIDER THIS!
WHAT DO YOU SAY, LEAH?
YOU HAVE BEEN HURT ENOUGH. YOU OWE NOTHING TO ODIN, AND THE AESIR OWE *YOU* A DEBT THEY WILL NEVER REPAY.
I WOULD STRIKE ALONGSIDE THE SERPENT. ONE MASTER IS MUCH THE SAME AS ANOTHER.
HELA--
TYR. WHAT OPTION DO I HAVE? ASGARD WILL NOT HATE US ANY LESS IF WE STAND AGAINST THEM. MY DUTY IS TO THE DEAD.
AYE. AND *I* AM THE DEAD.
IN LIFE, I PROVED MYSELF A COWARD. EVENTUALLY, I OVERCAME MY FEAR... BUT YOU CAN NEVER, EVER REDEEM SUCH A SIN.
I CHOSE A NOBLE DEATH. I CHOSE A NEW START.
AND IN MAKING OUR DEAL, I CHOSE TO BE WITH YOU.

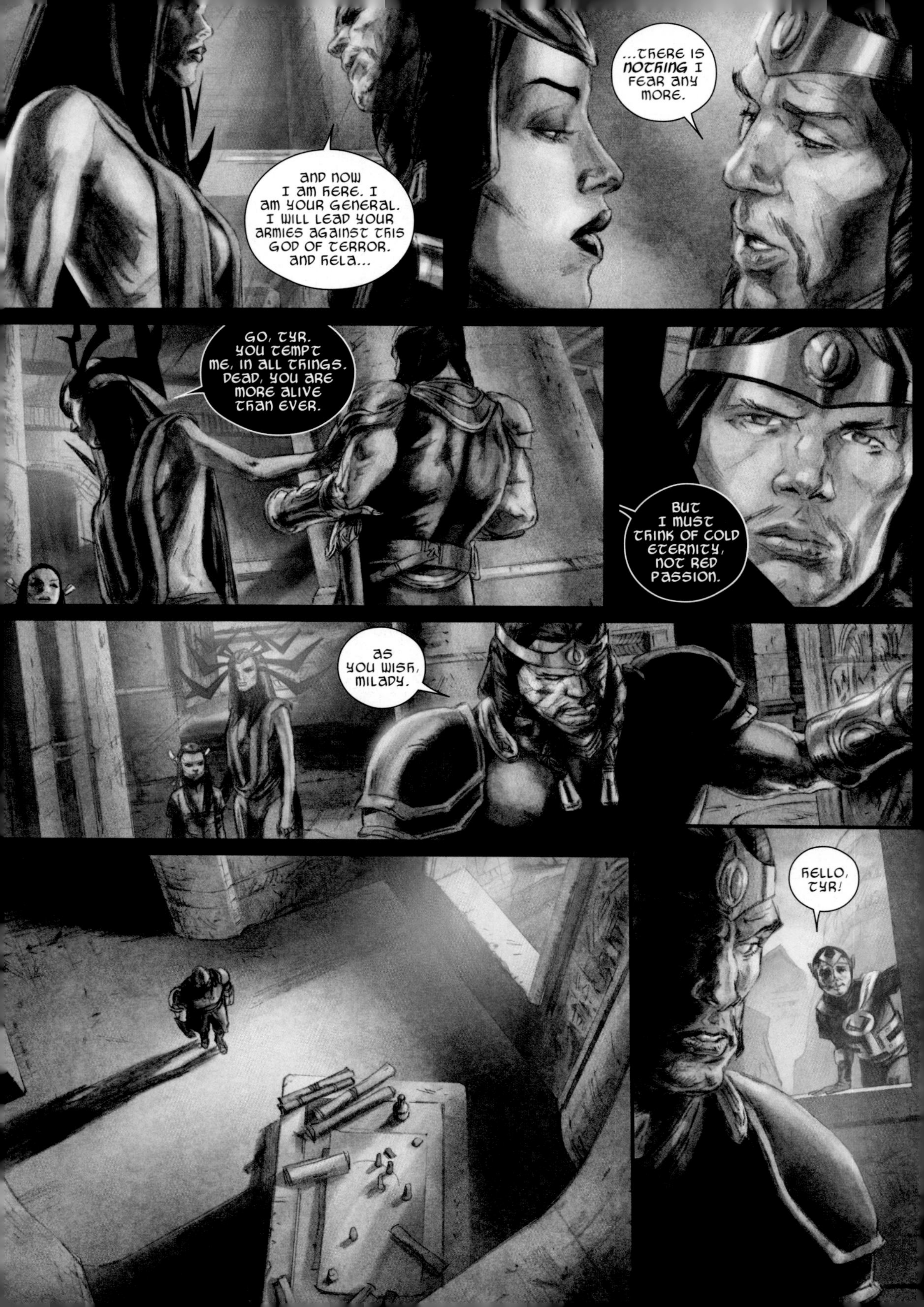
AND NOW I AM HERE. I AM YOUR GENERAL. I WILL LEAD YOUR ARMIES AGAINST THIS GOD OF TERROR. AND HELA...
...THERE IS NOTHING I FEAR ANY MORE.
GO, TYR. YOU TEMPT ME, IN ALL THINGS. DEAD, YOU ARE MORE ALIVE THAN EVER.
BUT I MUST THINK OF COLD ETERNITY, NOT RED PASSION.
AS YOU WISH, MILADY.
HELLO, TYR!

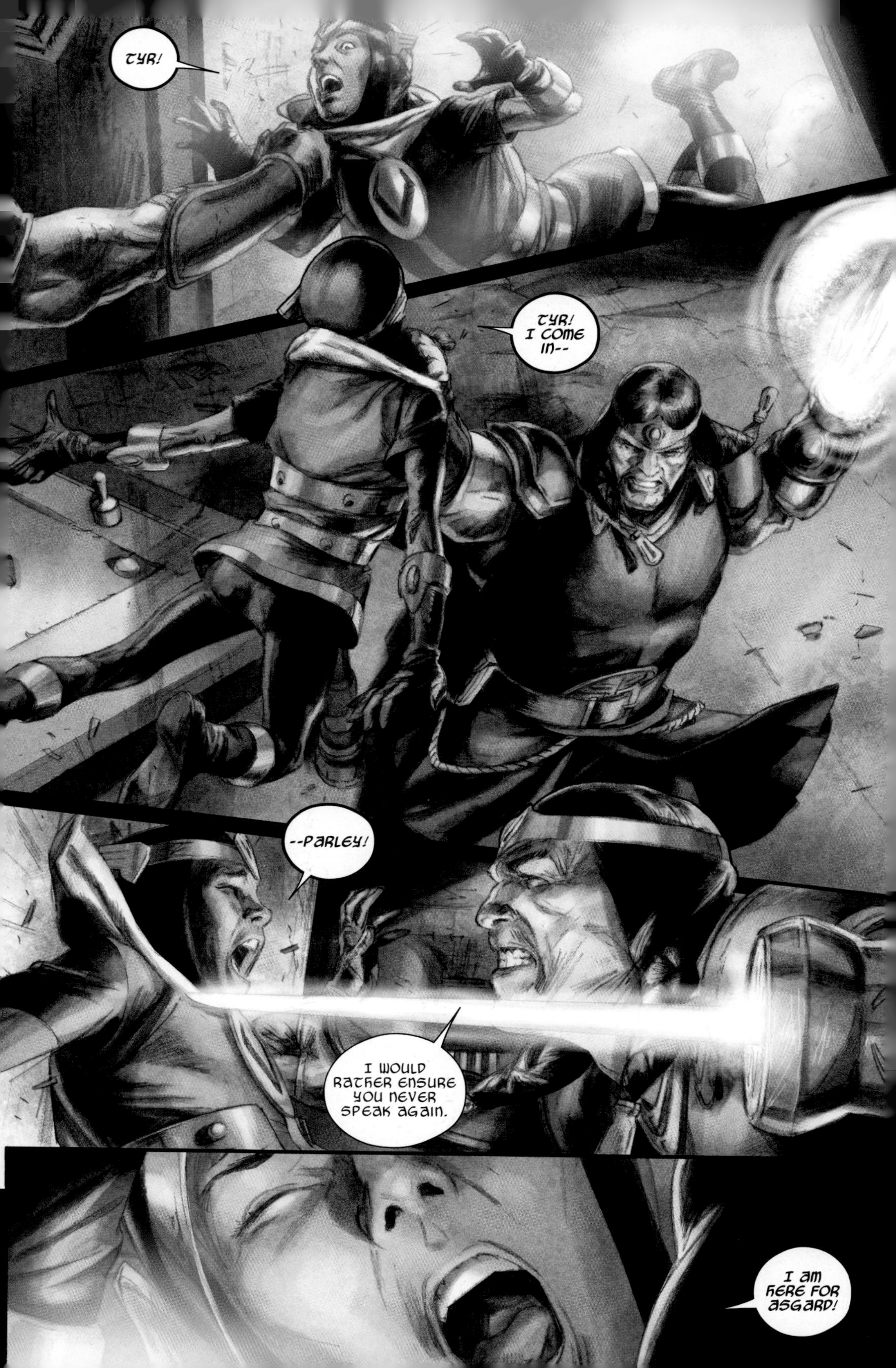
TYR!
TYR! I COME IN--
--PARLEY!
I WOULD RATHER ENSURE YOU NEVER SPEAK AGAIN.
I AM HERE FOR ASGARD!

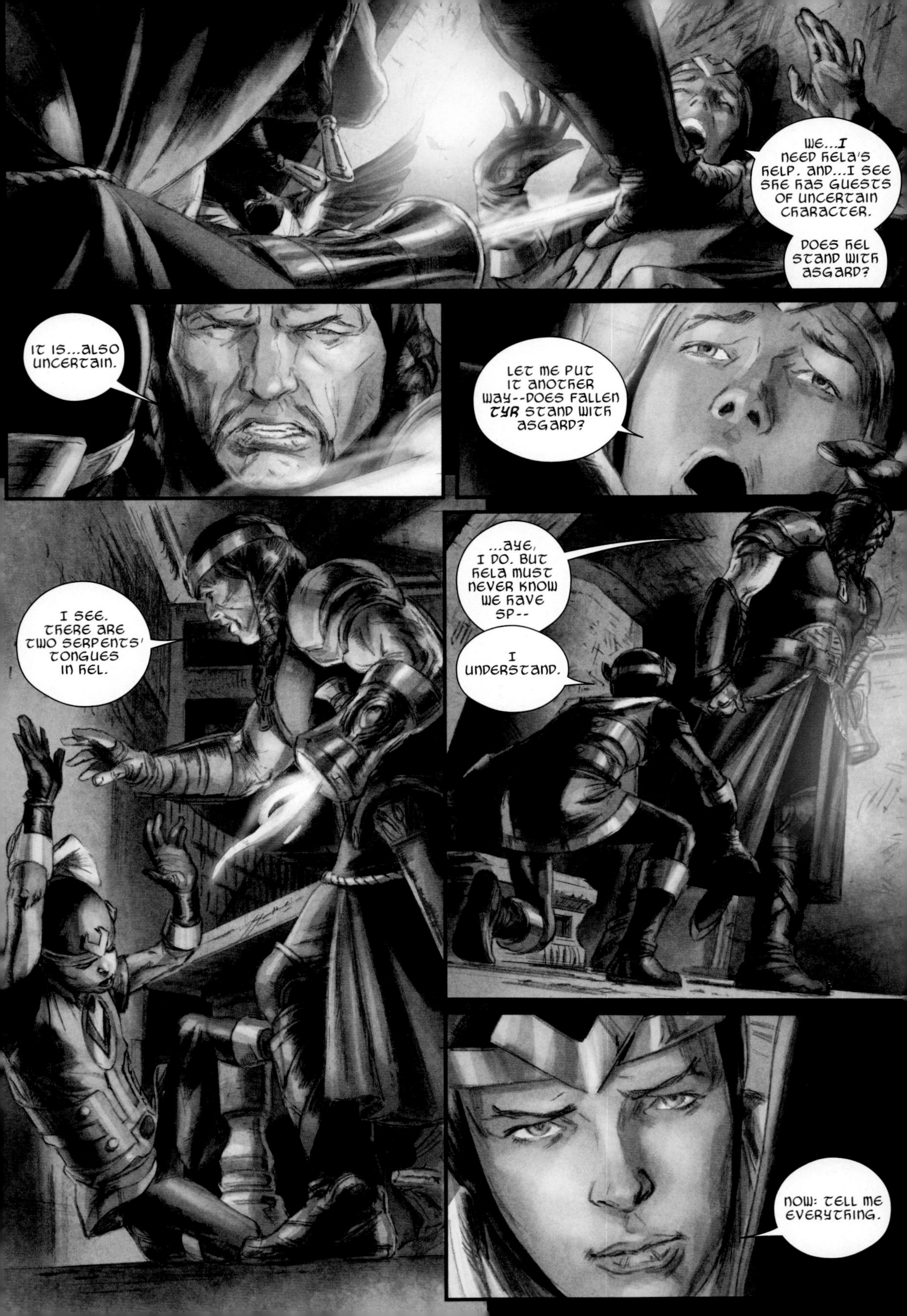
WE...I NEED HELA'S HELP. AND...I SEE SHE HAS GUESTS OF UNCERTAIN CHARACTER.
DOES HEL STAND WITH ASGARD?
IT IS...ALSO UNCERTAIN.
LET ME PUT IT ANOTHER WAY--DOES FALLEN TYR STAND WITH ASGARD?
I SEE. THERE ARE TWO SERPENTS' TONGUES IN HEL.
...AYE, I DO. BUT HELA MUST NEVER KNOW WE HAVE SP--
I UNDERSTAND.
NOW: TELL ME EVERYTHING.

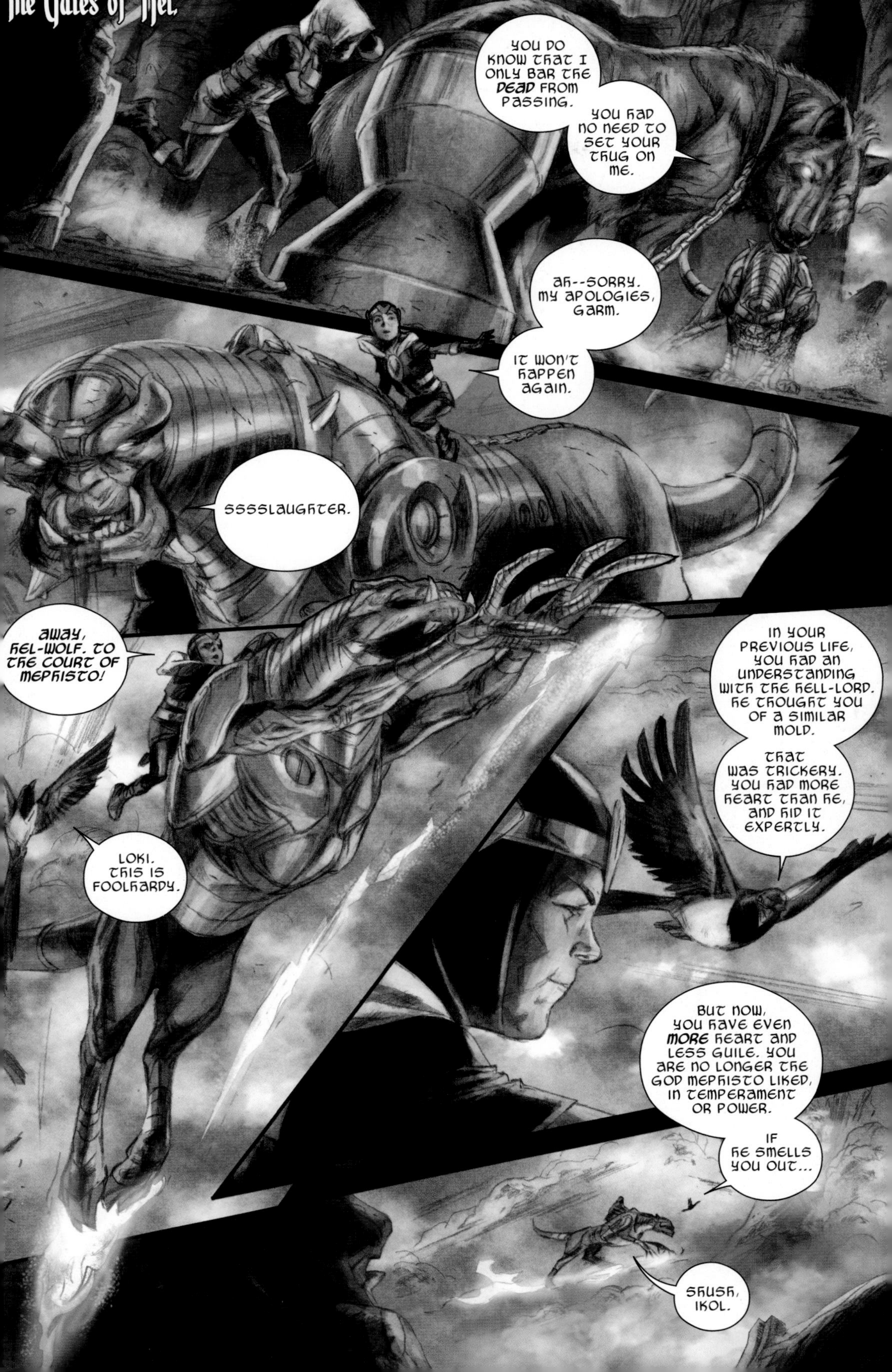
YOU DO KNOW THAT I ONLY BAR THE DEAD FROM PASSING.
YOU HAD NO NEED TO SET YOUR THUG ON ME.
AH--SORRY. MY APOLOGIES, GARM.
IT WON'T HAPPEN AGAIN.
SSSSLAUGHTER.
AWAY, HEL-WOLF. TO THE COURT OF MEPHISTO!
LOKI. THIS IS FOOLHARDY.
IN YOUR PREVIOUS LIFE, YOU HAD AN UNDERSTANDING WITH THE HELL-LORD. HE THOUGHT YOU OF A SIMILAR MOLD.
THAT WAS TRICKERY. YOU HAD MORE HEART THAN HE, AND HID IT EXPERTLY.
BUT NOW, YOU HAVE EVEN MORE HEART AND LESS GUILE. YOU ARE NO LONGER THE GOD MEPHISTO LIKED, IN TEMPERAMENT OR POWER.
IF HE SMELLS YOU OUT...
SHUSH, IKOL.

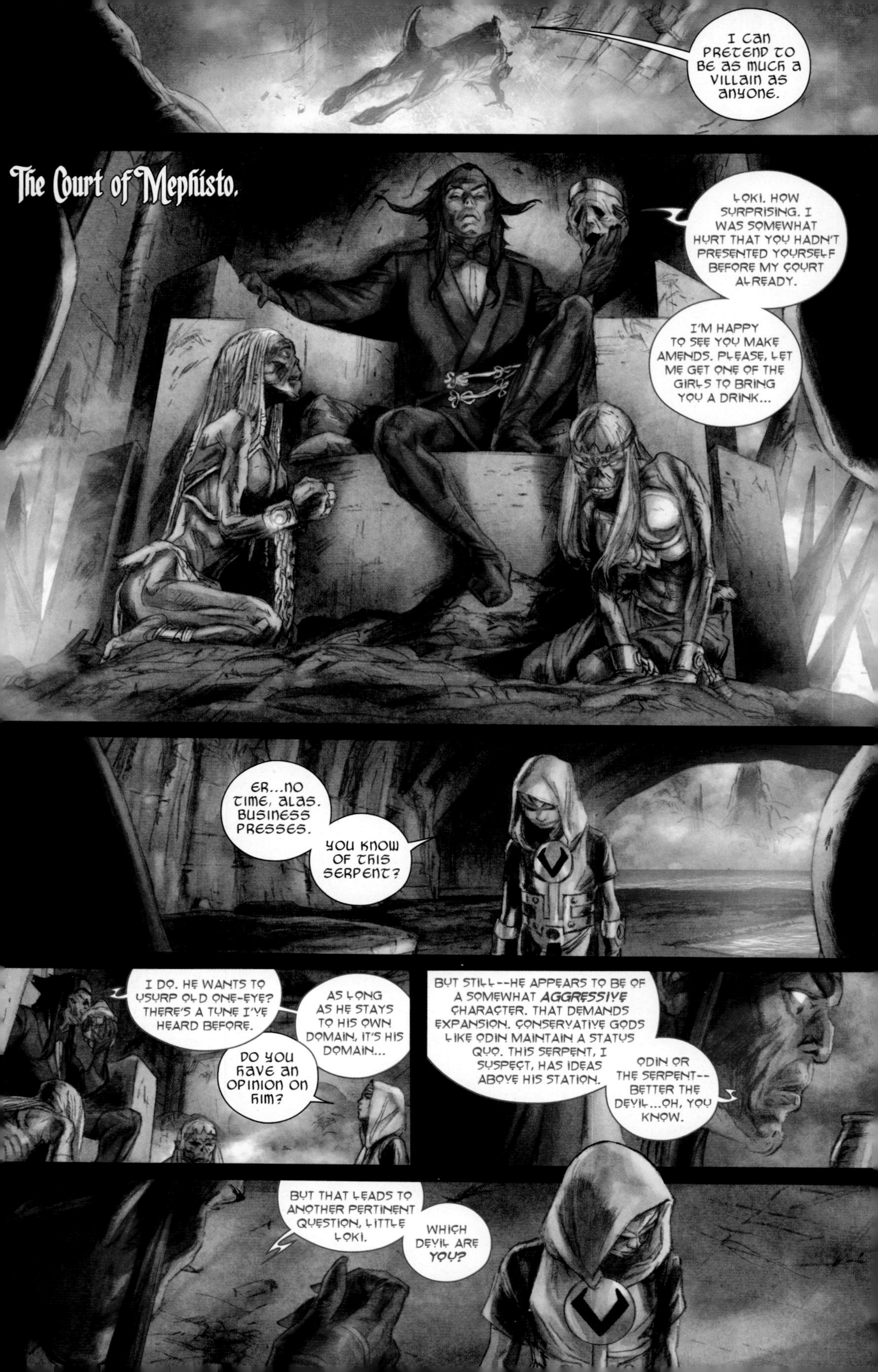
I CAN PRETEND TO BE AS MUCH A VILLAIN AS ANYONE.
The Court of Mephisto.
LOKI. HOW SURPRISING. I WAS SOMEWHAT HURT THAT YOU HADN'T PRESENTED YOURSELF BEFORE MY COURT ALREADY.
I'M HAPPY TO SEE YOU MAKE AMENDS. PLEASE, LET ME GET ONE OF THE GIRLS TO BRING YOU A DRINK...
ER...NO TIME, ALAS. BUSINESS PRESSES.
YOU KNOW OF THIS SERPENT?
I DO. HE WANTS TO USURP OLD ONE-EYE? THERE'S A TUNE I'VE HEARD BEFORE.
AS LONG AS HE STAYS TO HIS OWN DOMAIN, IT'S HIS DOMAIN...
DO YOU HAVE AN OPINION ON HIM?
BUT STILL--HE APPEARS TO BE OF A SOMEWHAT AGGRESSIVE CHARACTER. THAT DEMANDS EXPANSION. CONSERVATIVE GODS LIKE ODIN MAINTAIN A STATUS QUO. THIS SERPENT, I SUSPECT, HAS IDEAS ABOVE HIS STATION.
ODIN OR THE SERPENT--BETTER THE DEVIL...OH, YOU KNOW.
BUT THAT LEADS TO ANOTHER PERTINENT QUESTION, LITTLE LOKI.
WHICH DEVIL ARE YOU?

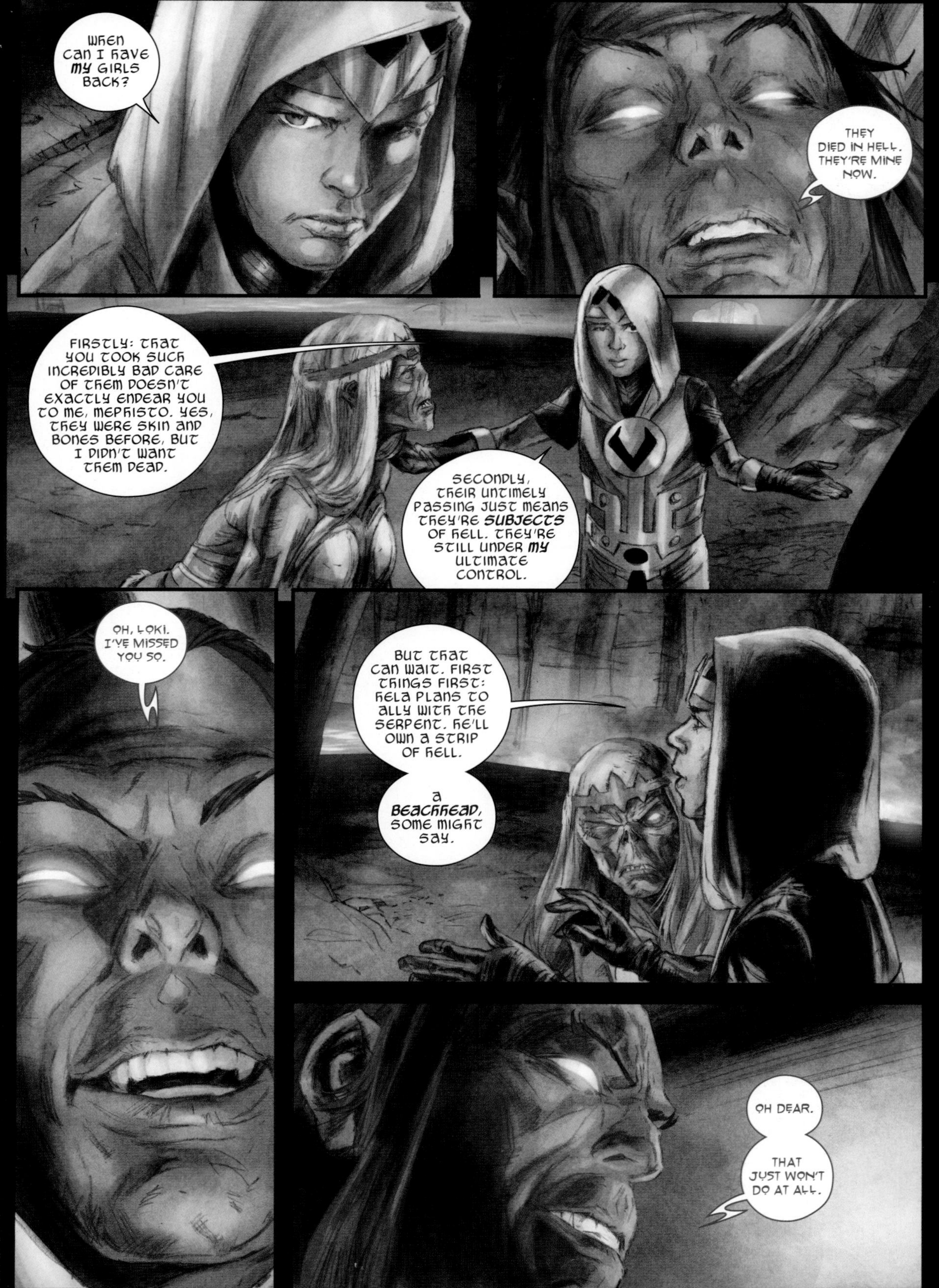
WHEN CAN I HAVE MY GIRLS BACK?
THEY DIED IN HELL. THEY'RE MINE NOW.
FIRSTLY: THAT YOU TOOK SUCH INCREDIBLY BAD CARE OF THEM DOESN'T EXACTLY ENDEAR YOU TO ME, MEPHISTO. YES, THEY WERE SKIN AND BONES BEFORE, BUT I DIDN'T WANT THEM DEAD.
SECONDLY, THEIR UNTIMELY PASSING JUST MEANS THEY'RE SUBJECTS OF HELL. THEY'RE STILL UNDER MY ULTIMATE CONTROL.
OH, LOKI. I'VE MISSED YOU SO.
BUT THAT CAN WAIT. FIRST THINGS FIRST: HELA PLANS TO ALLY WITH THE SERPENT. HE'LL OWN A STRIP OF HELL.
A BEACHHEAD, SOME MIGHT SAY.
OH DEAR.
THAT JUST WON'T DO AT ALL.

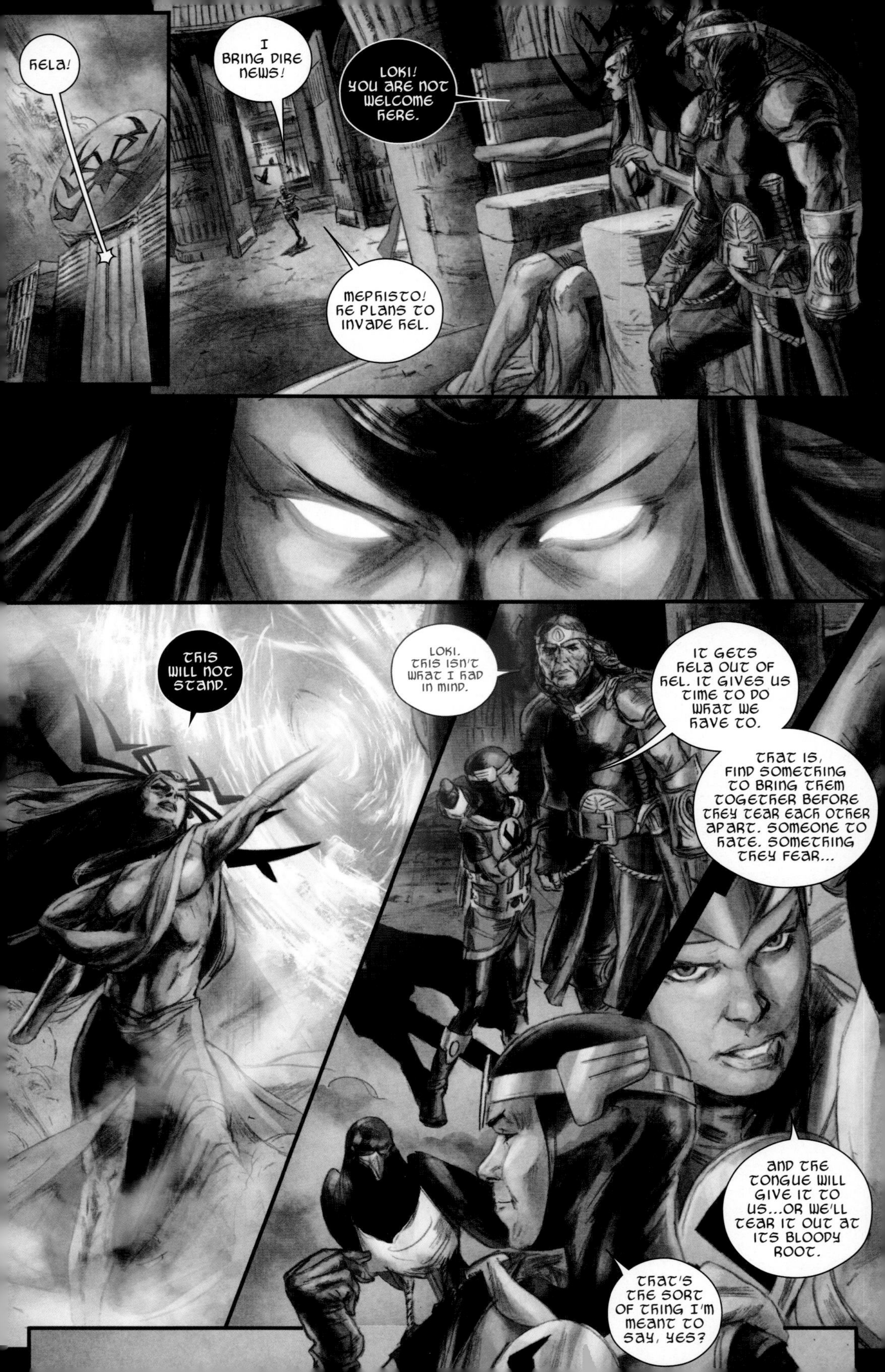
HELA!
I BRING DIRE NEWS!
LOKI! YOU ARE NOT WELCOME HERE.
MEPHISTO! HE PLANS TO INVADE HEL.
THIS WILL NOT STAND.
LOKI. THIS ISN'T WHAT I HAD IN MIND.
IT GETS HELA OUT OF HEL. IT GIVES US TIME TO DO WHAT WE HAVE TO.
THAT IS, FIND SOMETHING TO BRING THEM TOGETHER BEFORE THEY TEAR EACH OTHER APART. SOMEONE TO HATE. SOMETHING THEY FEAR...
AND THE TONGUE WILL GIVE IT TO US...OR WE'LL TEAR IT OUT AT ITS BLOODY ROOT.
THAT'S THE SORT OF THING I'M MEANT TO SAY, YES?

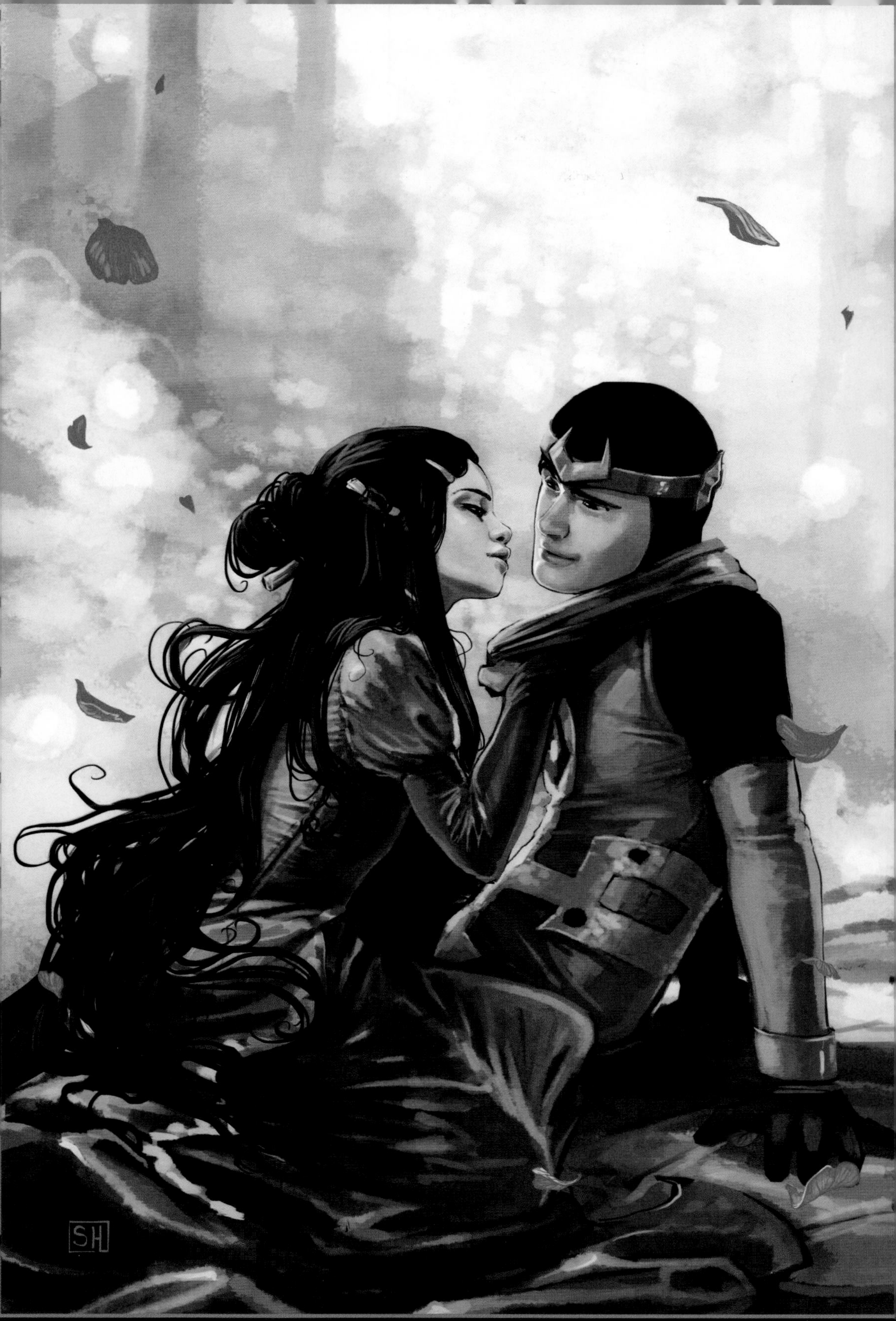
SH

JOURNEY INTO MYSTERY #625

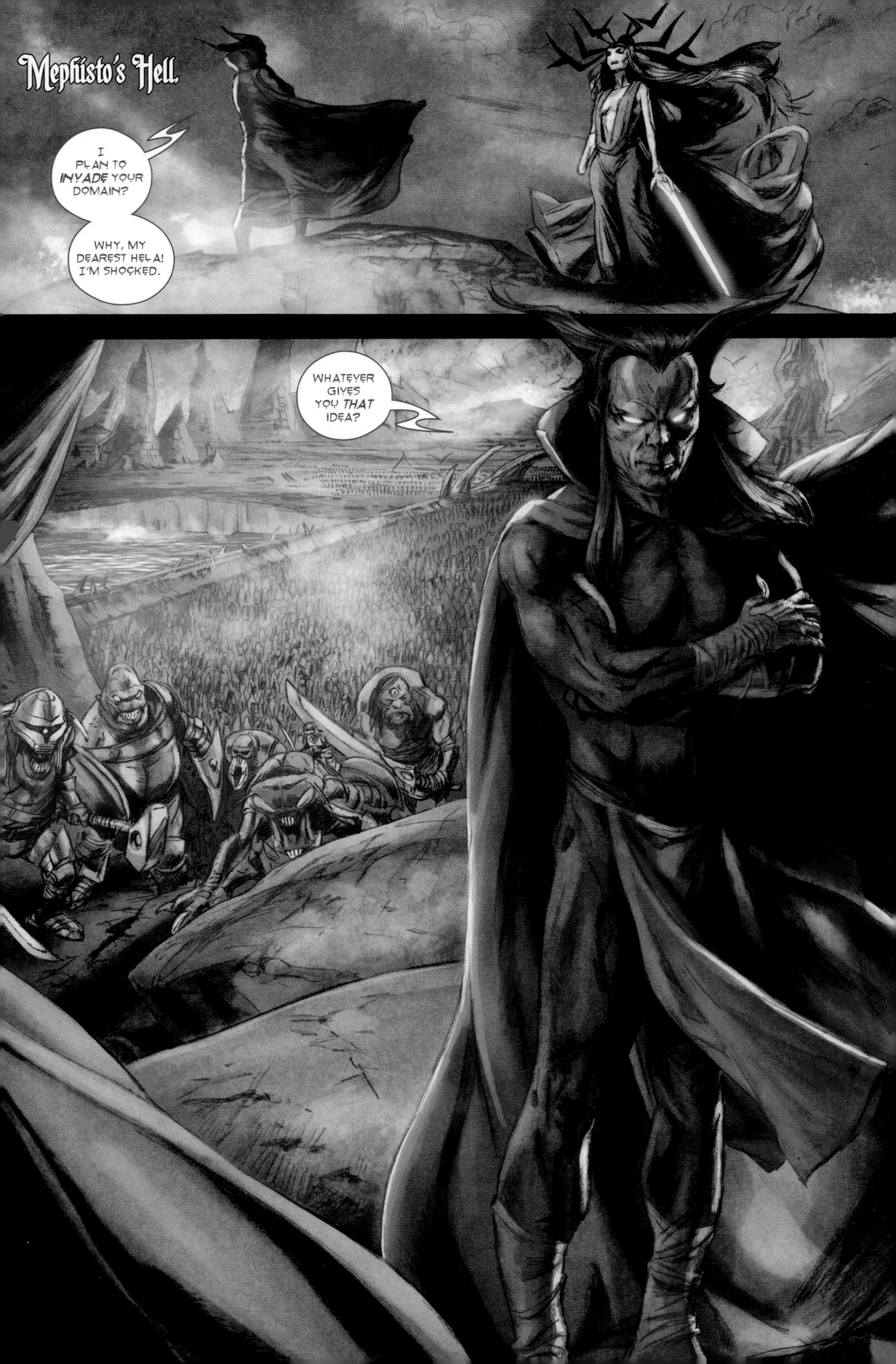
Mephisto's Hell.
I PLAN TO INVADE YOUR DOMAIN?
WHY, MY DEAREST HELA! I'M SHOCKED.
WHATEVER GIVES YOU THAT IDEA?

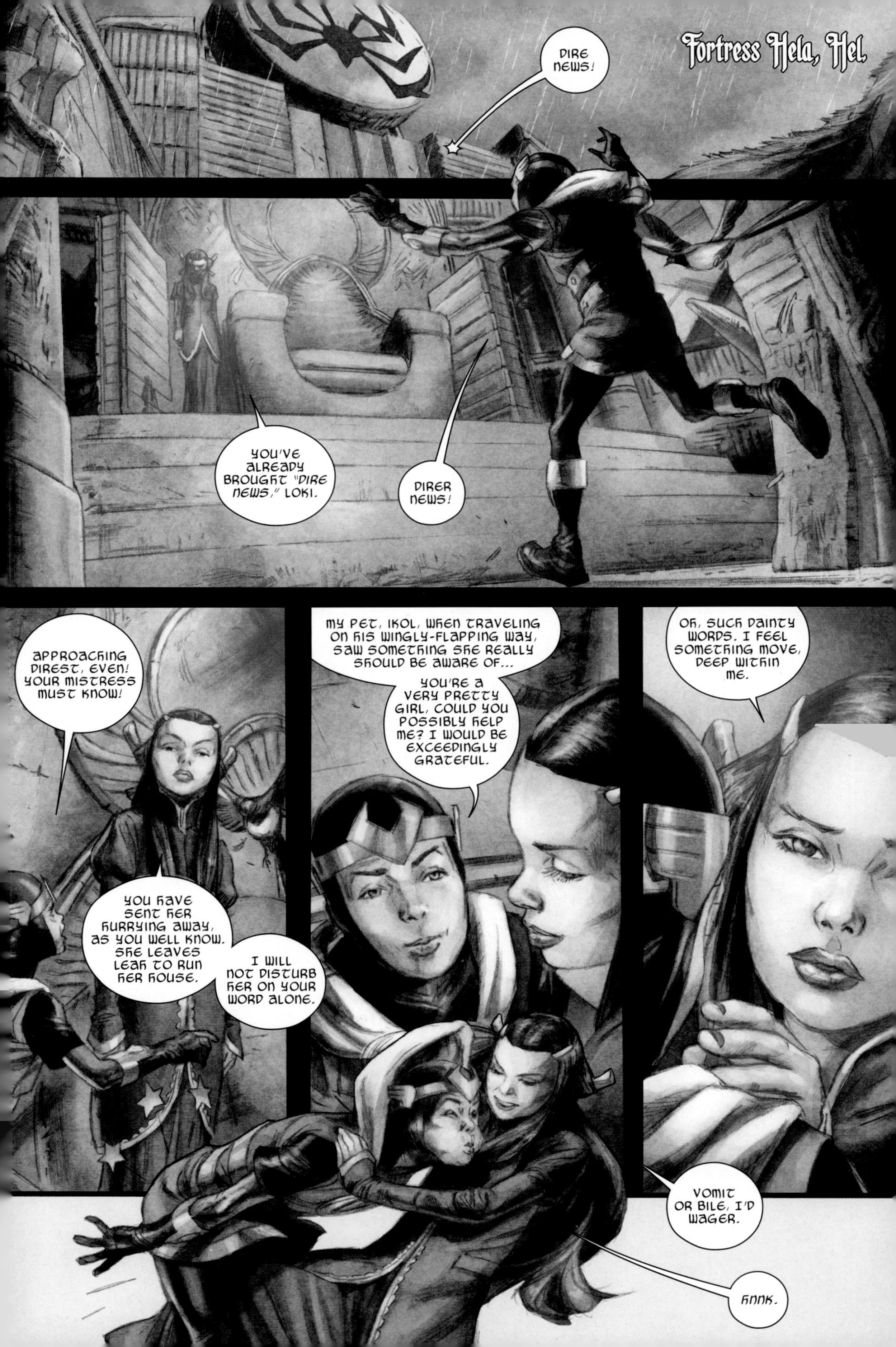
Fortress Hela, Hel.
DIRE NEWS!
YOU'VE ALREADY BROUGHT "DIRE NEWS," LOKI.
DIRER NEWS!
APPROACHING DIREST, EVEN! YOUR MISTRESS MUST KNOW!
YOU HAVE SENT HER HURRYING AWAY, AS YOU WELL KNOW. SHE LEAVES LEAH TO RUN HER HOUSE.
I WILL NOT DISTURB HER ON YOUR WORD ALONE.
MY PET, IKOL, WHEN TRAVELING ON HIS WINGLY-FLAPPING WAY, SAW SOMETHING SHE REALLY SHOULD BE AWARE OF...
YOU'RE A VERY PRETTY GIRL, COULD YOU POSSIBLY HELP ME? I WOULD BE EXCEEDINGLY GRATEFUL.
OH, SUCH DAINTY WORDS. I FEEL SOMETHING MOVE, DEEP WITHIN ME.
VOMIT OR BILE, I'D WAGER.
HNNK.

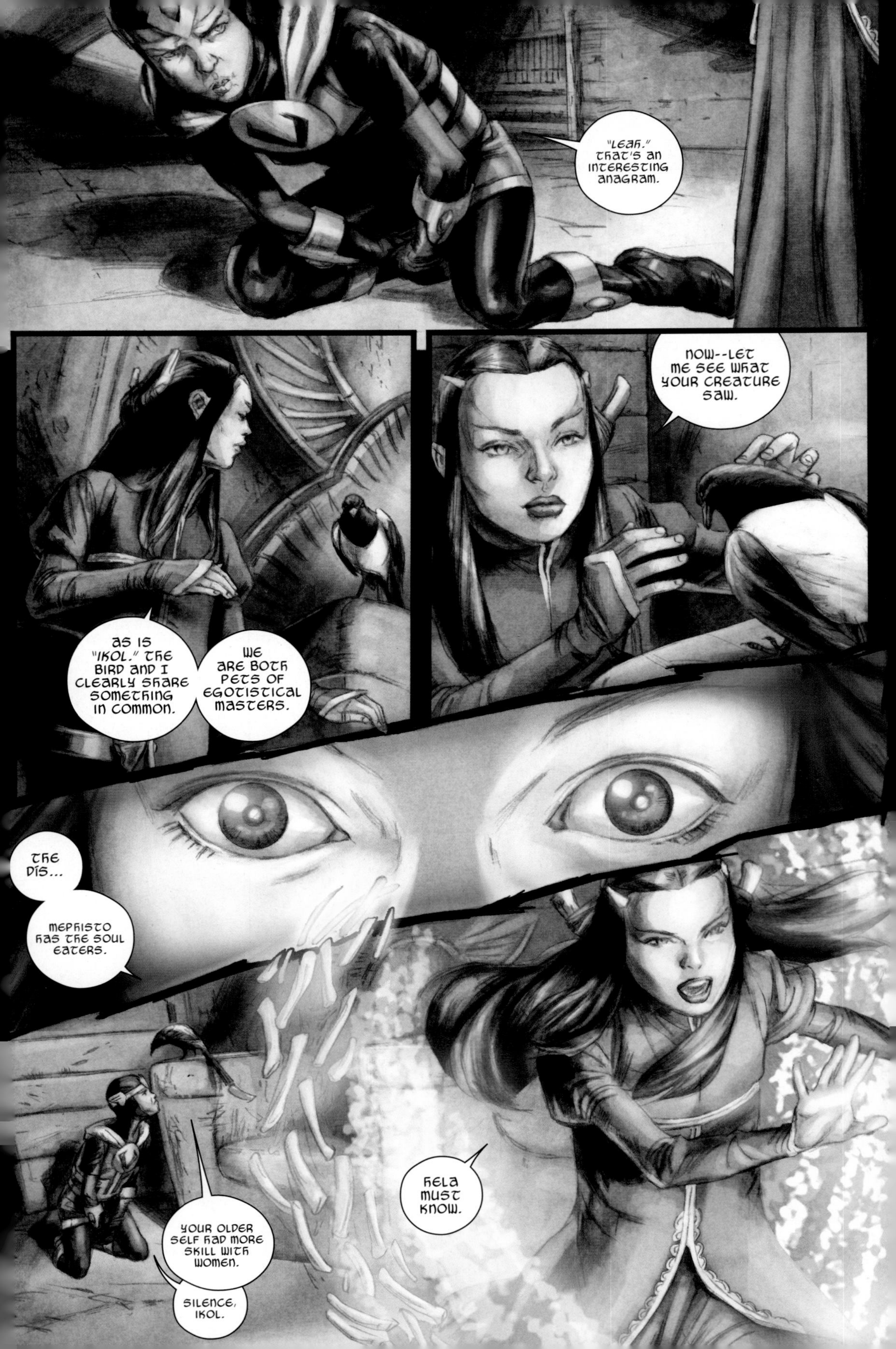
"LEAH." THAT'S AN INTERESTING ANAGRAM.
AS IS "IKOL." THE BIRD AND I CLEARLY SHARE SOMETHING IN COMMON.
WE ARE BOTH PETS OF EGOTISTICAL MASTERS.
NOW--LET ME SEE WHAT YOUR CREATURE SAW.
THE DÍS...
MEPHISTO HAS THE SOUL EATERS.
HELA MUST KNOW.
YOUR OLDER SELF HAD MORE SKILL WITH WOMEN.
SILENCE, IKOL.

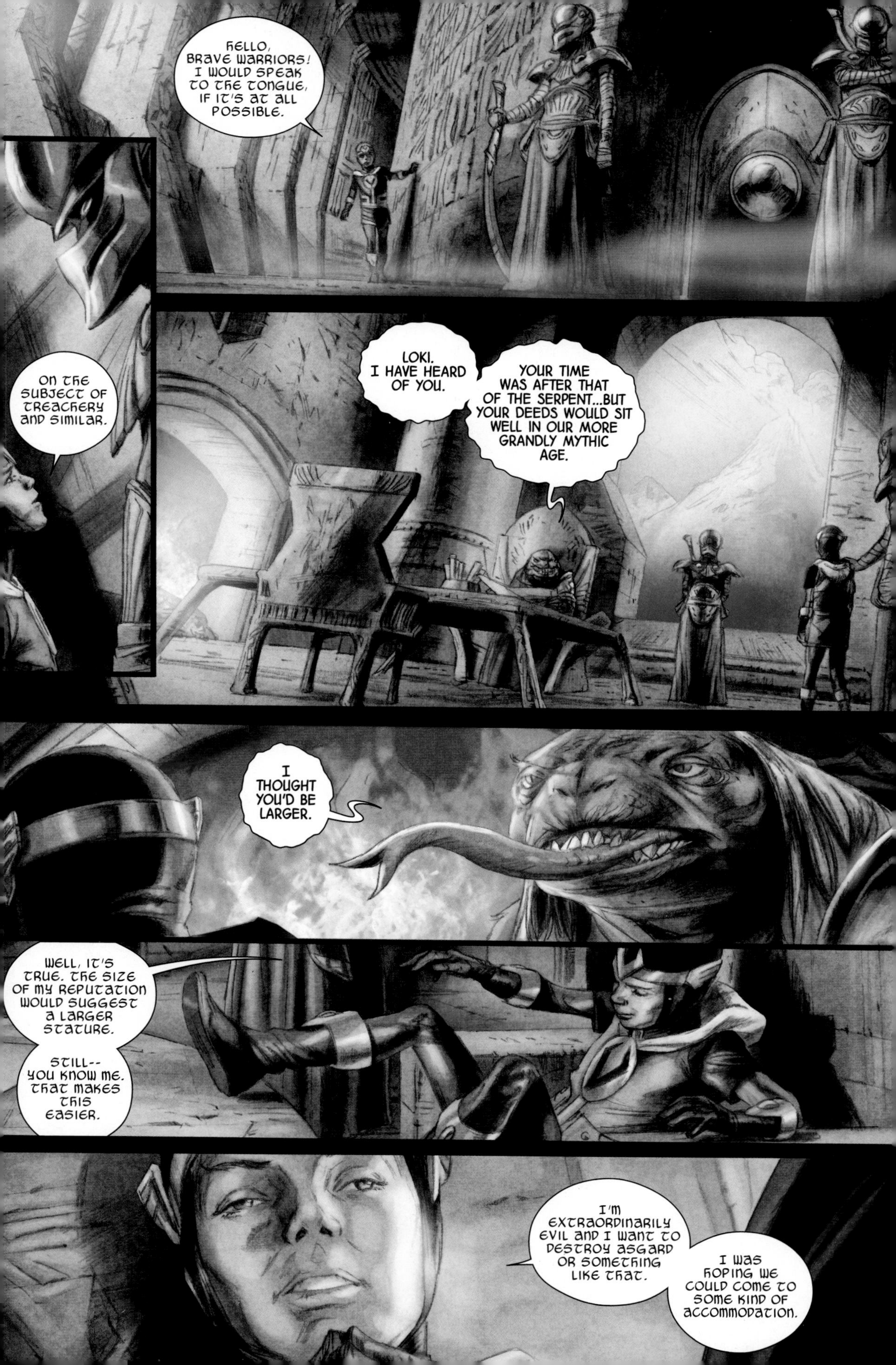
HELLO, BRAVE WARRIORS! I WOULD SPEAK TO THE TONGUE, IF IT'S AT ALL POSSIBLE.
ON THE SUBJECT OF TREACHERY AND SIMILAR.
LOKI. I HAVE HEARD OF YOU.
YOUR TIME WAS AFTER THAT OF THE SERPENT...BUT YOUR DEEDS WOULD SIT WELL IN OUR MORE GRANDLY MYTHIC AGE.
I THOUGHT YOU'D BE LARGER.
WELL, IT'S TRUE. THE SIZE OF MY REPUTATION WOULD SUGGEST A LARGER STATURE.
STILL-- YOU KNOW ME. THAT MAKES THIS EASIER.
I'M EXTRAORDINARILY EVIL AND I WANT TO DESTROY ASGARD OR SOMETHING LIKE THAT.
I WAS HOPING WE COULD COME TO SOME KIND OF ACCOMMODATION.

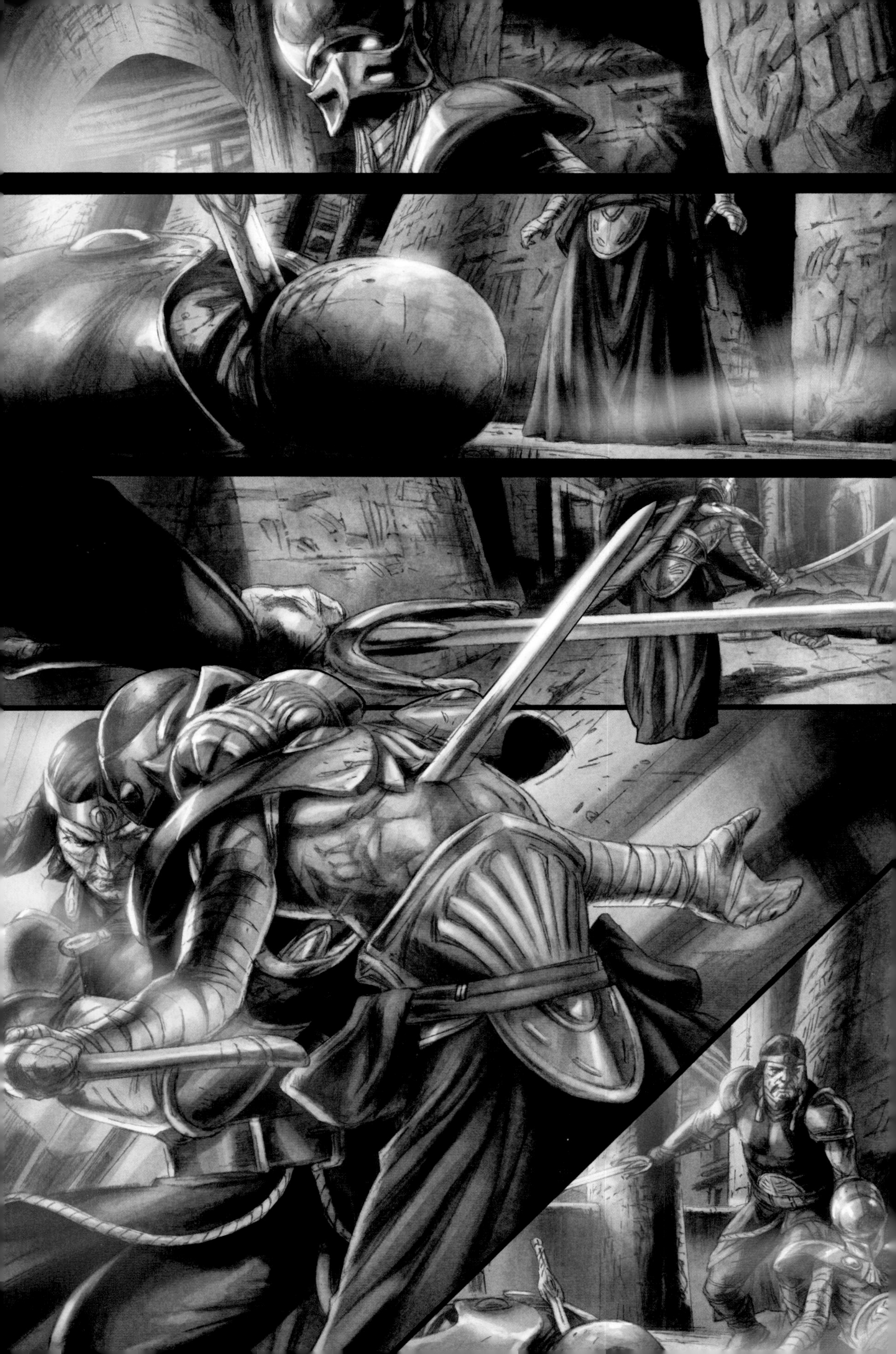

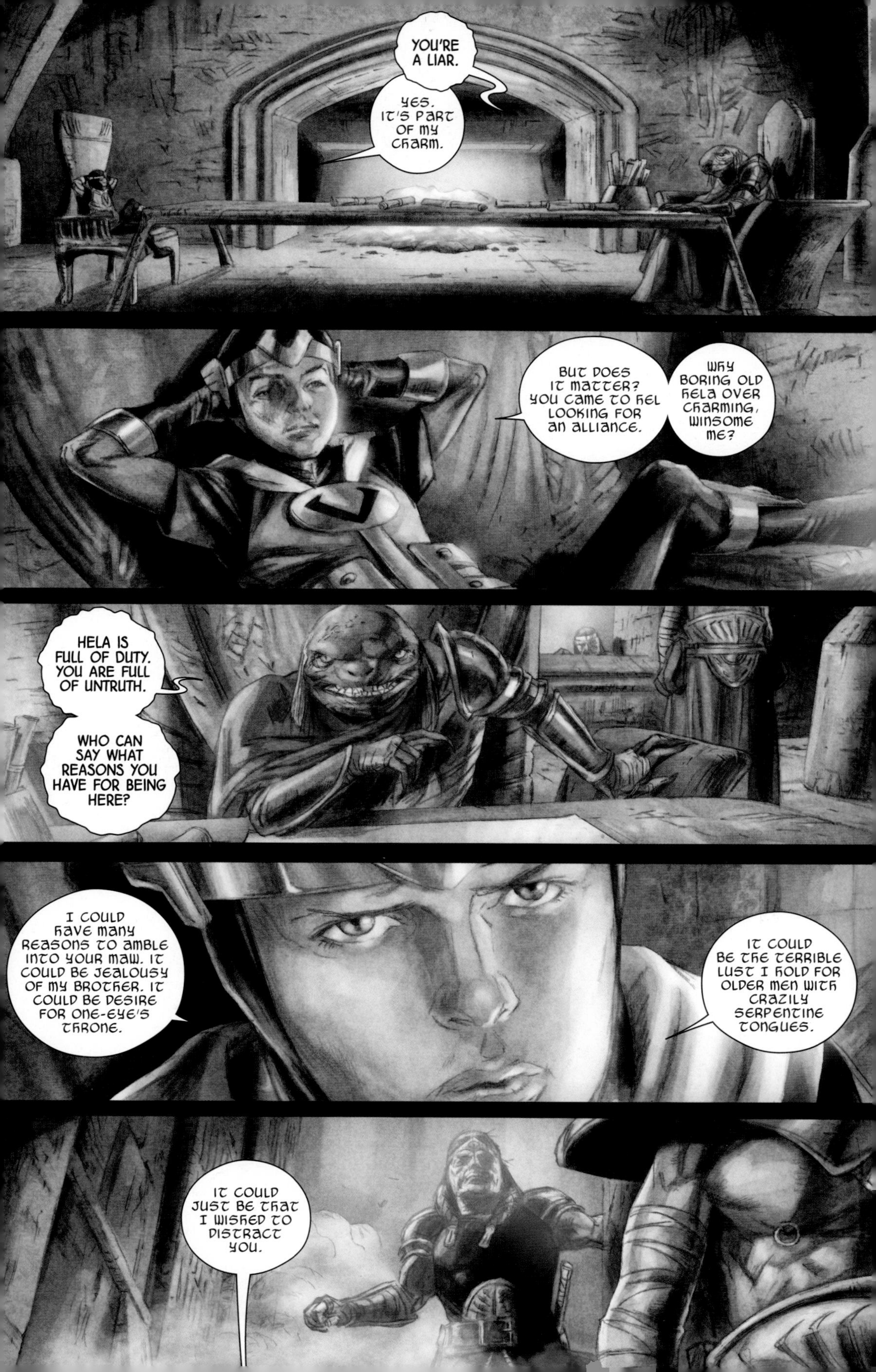
YOU'RE A LIAR.
YES. IT'S PART OF MY CHARM.
BUT DOES IT MATTER? YOU CAME TO HEL LOOKING FOR AN ALLIANCE.
WHY BORING OLD HELA OVER CHARMING, WINSOME ME?
HELA IS FULL OF DUTY. YOU ARE FULL OF UNTRUTH.
WHO CAN SAY WHAT REASONS YOU HAVE FOR BEING HERE?
I COULD HAVE MANY REASONS TO AMBLE INTO YOUR MAW. IT COULD BE JEALOUSY OF MY BROTHER. IT COULD BE DESIRE FOR ONE-EYE'S THRONE.
IT COULD BE THE TERRIBLE LUST I HOLD FOR OLDER MEN WITH CRAZILY SERPENTINE TONGUES.
IT COULD JUST BE THAT I WISHED TO DISTRACT YOU.

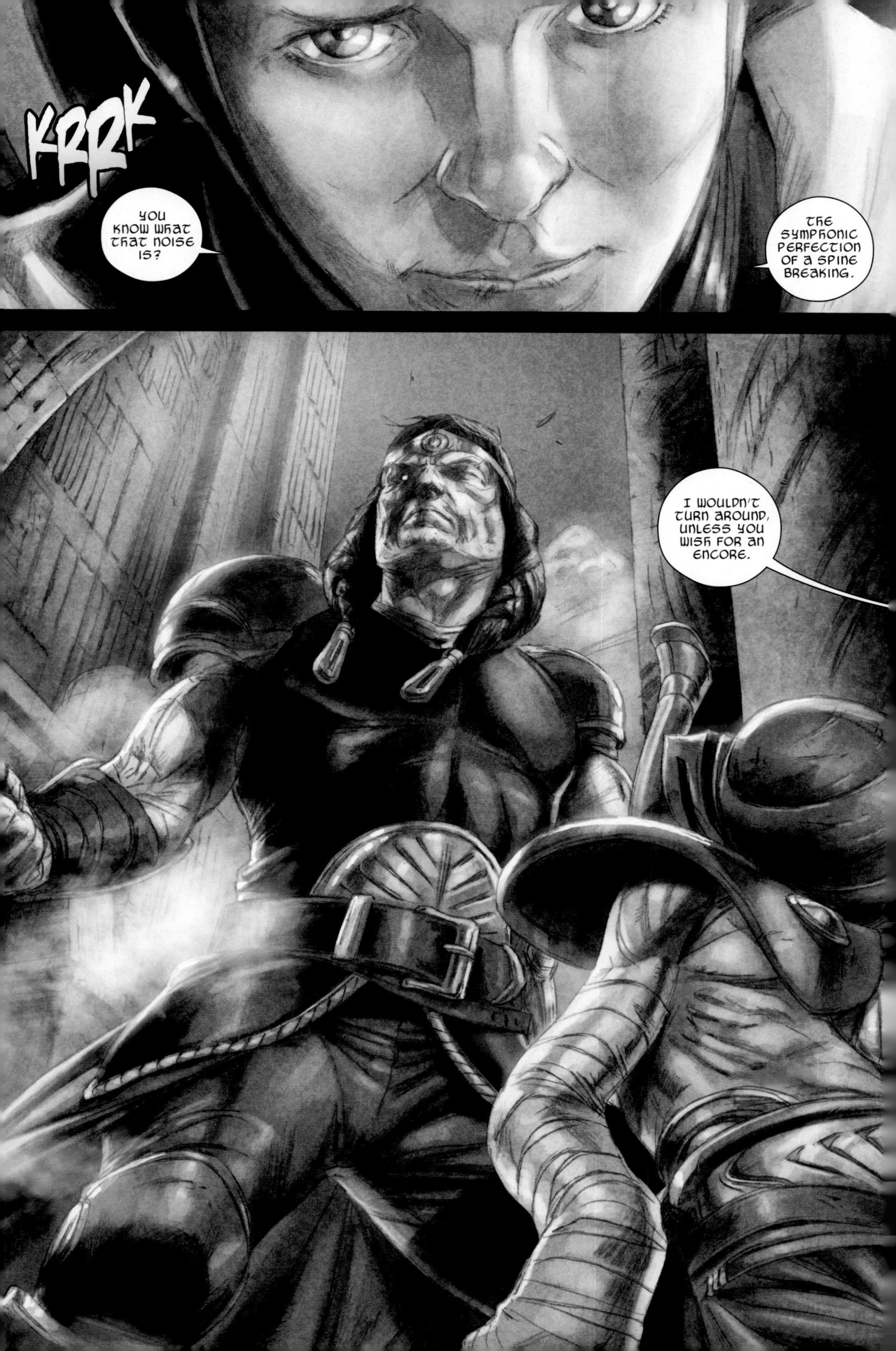
KRRK
YOU KNOW WHAT THAT NOISE IS?
THE SYMPHONIC PERFECTION OF A SPINE BREAKING.
I WOULDN'T TURN AROUND, UNLESS YOU WISH FOR AN ENCORE.

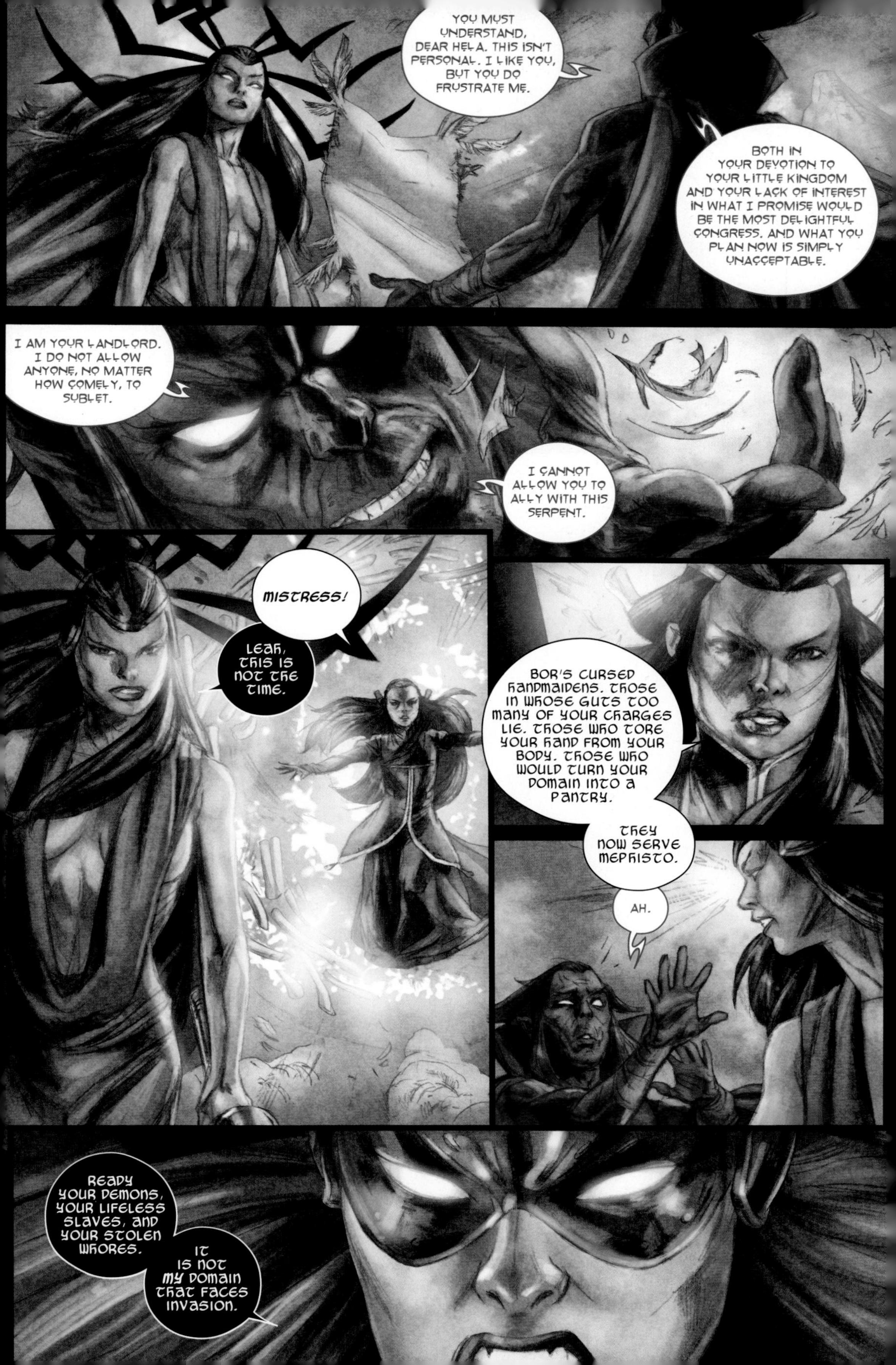
YOU MUST UNDERSTAND, DEAR HELA. THIS ISN'T PERSONAL. I LIKE YOU, BUT YOU DO FRUSTRATE ME.
BOTH IN YOUR DEVOTION TO YOUR LITTLE KINGDOM AND YOUR LACK OF INTEREST IN WHAT I PROMISE WOULD BE THE MOST DELIGHTFUL CONGRESS. AND WHAT YOU PLAN NOW IS SIMPLY UNACCEPTABLE.
I AM YOUR LANDLORD. I DO NOT ALLOW ANYONE, NO MATTER HOW COMELY, TO SUBLET.
I CANNOT ALLOW YOU TO ALLY WITH THIS SERPENT.
MISTRESS!
LEAH, THIS IS NOT THE TIME.
BOR'S CURSED HANDMAIDENS. THOSE IN WHOSE GUTS TOO MANY OF YOUR CHARGES LIE. THOSE WHO TORE YOUR HAND FROM YOUR BODY. THOSE WHO WOULD TURN YOUR DOMAIN INTO A PANTRY.
THEY NOW SERVE MEPHISTO.
AH.
READY YOUR DEMONS, YOUR LIFELESS SLAVES, AND YOUR STOLEN WHORES.
IT IS NOT MY DOMAIN THAT FACES INVASION.

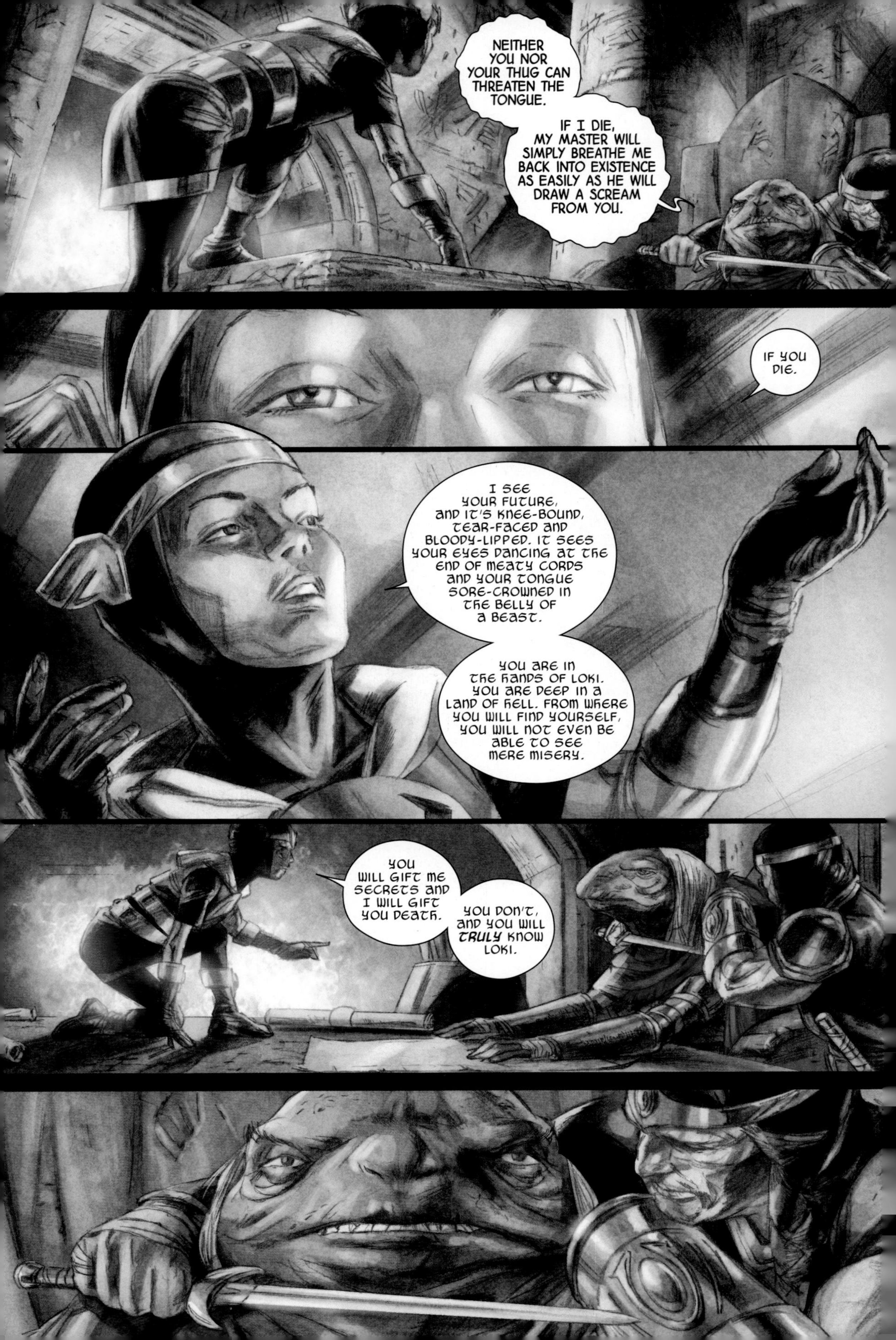
NEITHER YOU NOR YOUR THUG CAN THREATEN THE TONGUE.
IF I DIE, MY MASTER WILL SIMPLY BREATHE ME BACK INTO EXISTENCE AS EASILY AS HE WILL DRAW A SCREAM FROM YOU.
IF YOU DIE.
I SEE YOUR FUTURE, AND IT'S KNEE-BOUND, TEAR-FACED AND BLOODY-LIPPED. IT SEES YOUR EYES DANCING AT THE END OF MEATY CORDS AND YOUR TONGUE SORE-CROWNED IN THE BELLY OF A BEAST.
YOU ARE IN THE HANDS OF LOKI. YOU ARE DEEP IN A LAND OF HELL. FROM WHERE YOU WILL FIND YOURSELF, YOU WILL NOT EVEN BE ABLE TO SEE MERE MISERY.
YOU WILL GIFT ME SECRETS AND I WILL GIFT YOU DEATH.
YOU DON'T, AND YOU WILL *TRULY* KNOW LOKI.

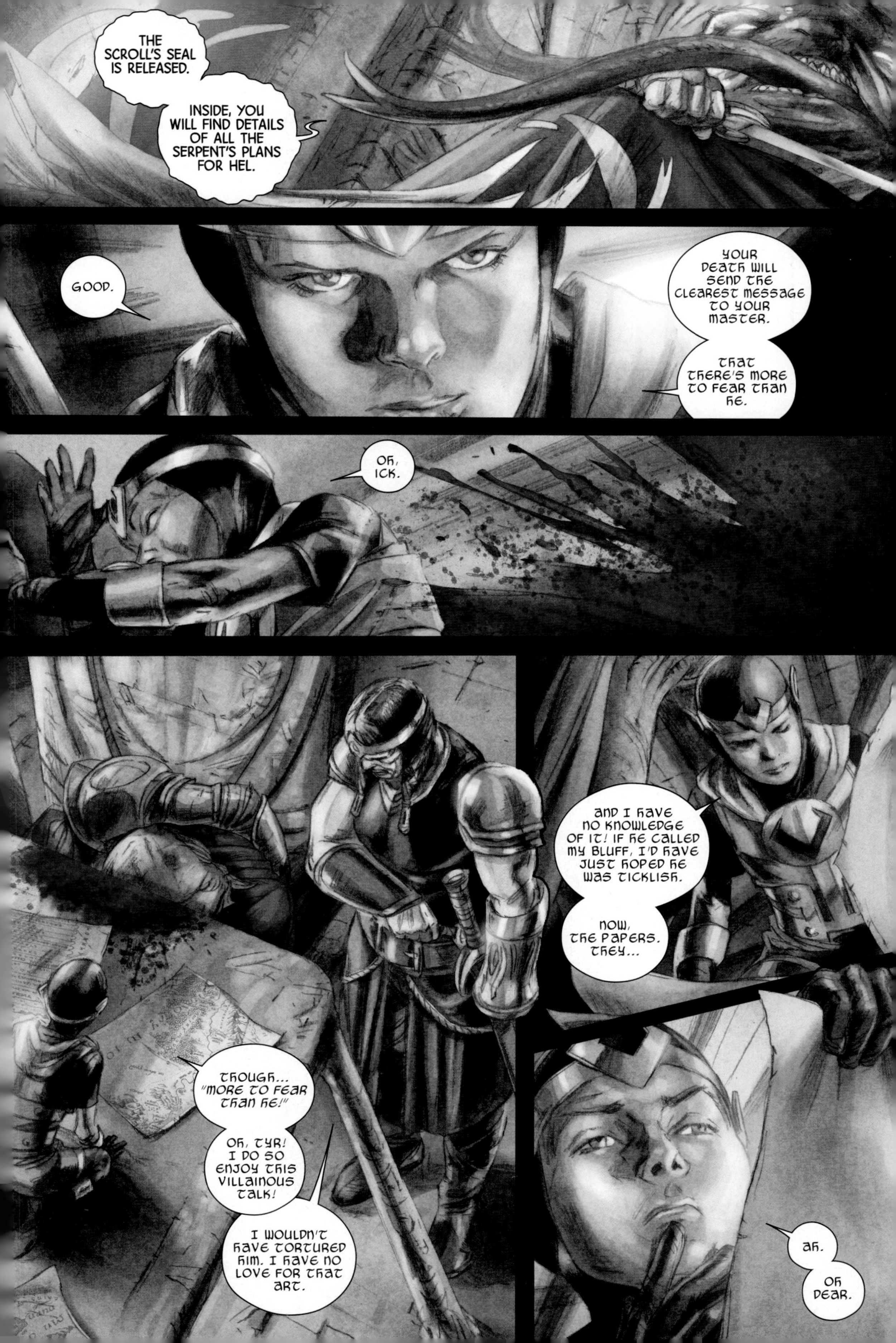
THE SCROLL'S SEAL IS RELEASED.
INSIDE, YOU WILL FIND DETAILS OF ALL THE SERPENT'S PLANS FOR HEL.
GOOD.
YOUR DEATH WILL SEND THE CLEAREST MESSAGE TO YOUR MASTER.
THAT THERE'S MORE TO FEAR THAN HE.
OH, ICK.
AND I HAVE NO KNOWLEDGE OF IT! IF HE CALLED MY BLUFF, I'D HAVE JUST HOPED HE WAS TICKLISH.
NOW, THE PAPERS. THEY...
THOUGH... "MORE TO FEAR THAN HE!"
OH, TYR! I DO SO ENJOY THIS VILLAINOUS TALK!
I WOULDN'T HAVE TORTURED HIM. I HAVE NO LOVE FOR THAT ART.
AH.
OH DEAR.

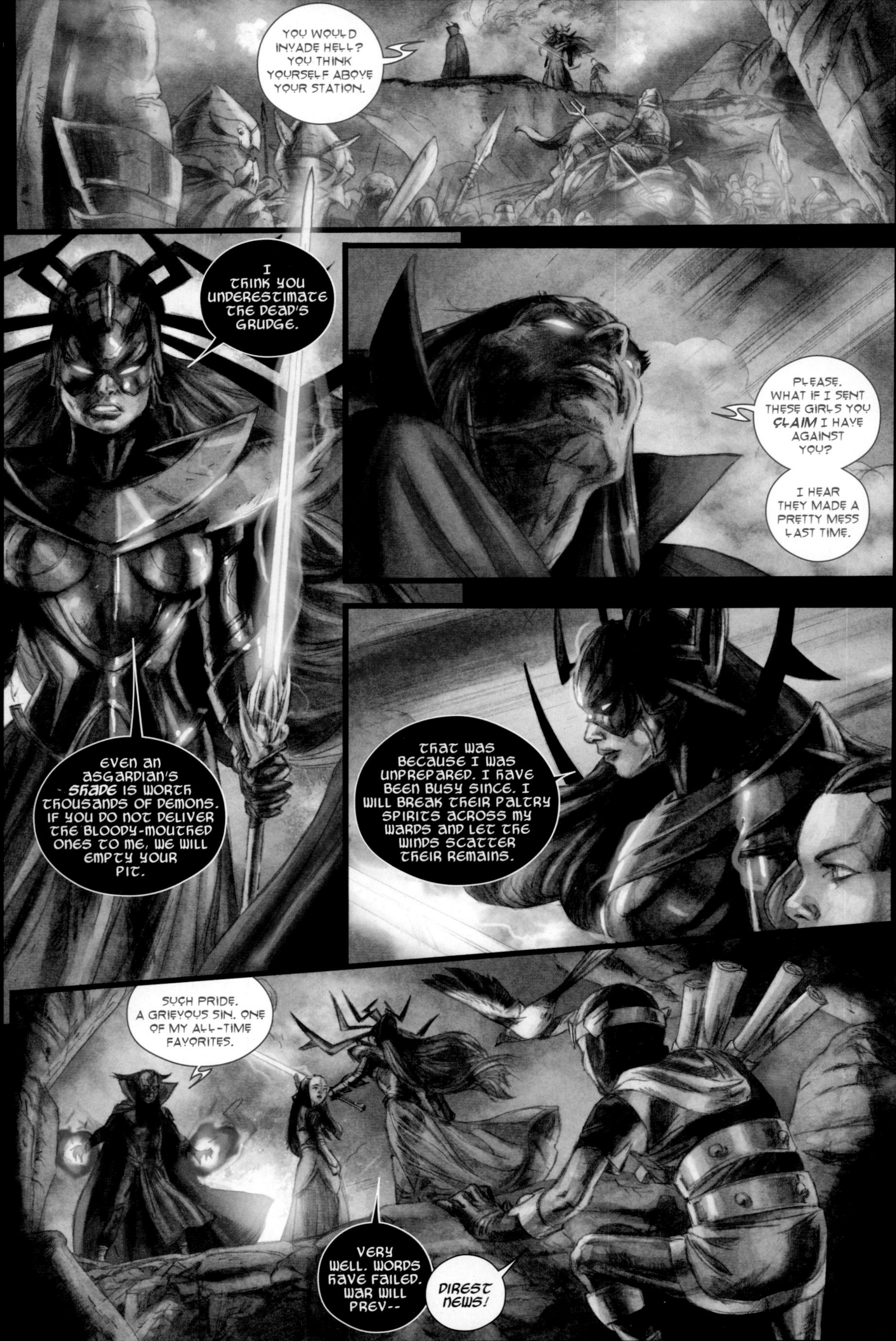

YOU WOULD INVADE HELL? YOU THINK YOURSELF ABOVE YOUR STATION.
I THINK YOU UNDERESTIMATE THE DEAD'S GRUDGE.
PLEASE. WHAT IF I SENT THESE GIRLS YOU CLAIM I HAVE AGAINST YOU?
I HEAR THEY MADE A PRETTY MESS LAST TIME.
EVEN AN ASGARDIAN'S SHADE IS WORTH THOUSANDS OF DEMONS. IF YOU DO NOT DELIVER THE BLOODY-MOUTHED ONES TO ME, WE WILL EMPTY YOUR PIT.
THAT WAS BECAUSE I WAS UNPREPARED. I HAVE BEEN BUSY SINCE. I WILL BREAK THEIR PALTRY SPIRITS ACROSS MY WARDS AND LET THE WINDS SCATTER THEIR REMAINS.
SUCH PRIDE. A GRIEVOUS SIN. ONE OF MY ALL-TIME FAVORITES.
VERY WELL. WORDS HAVE FAILED. WAR WILL PREV--
DIREST NEWS!

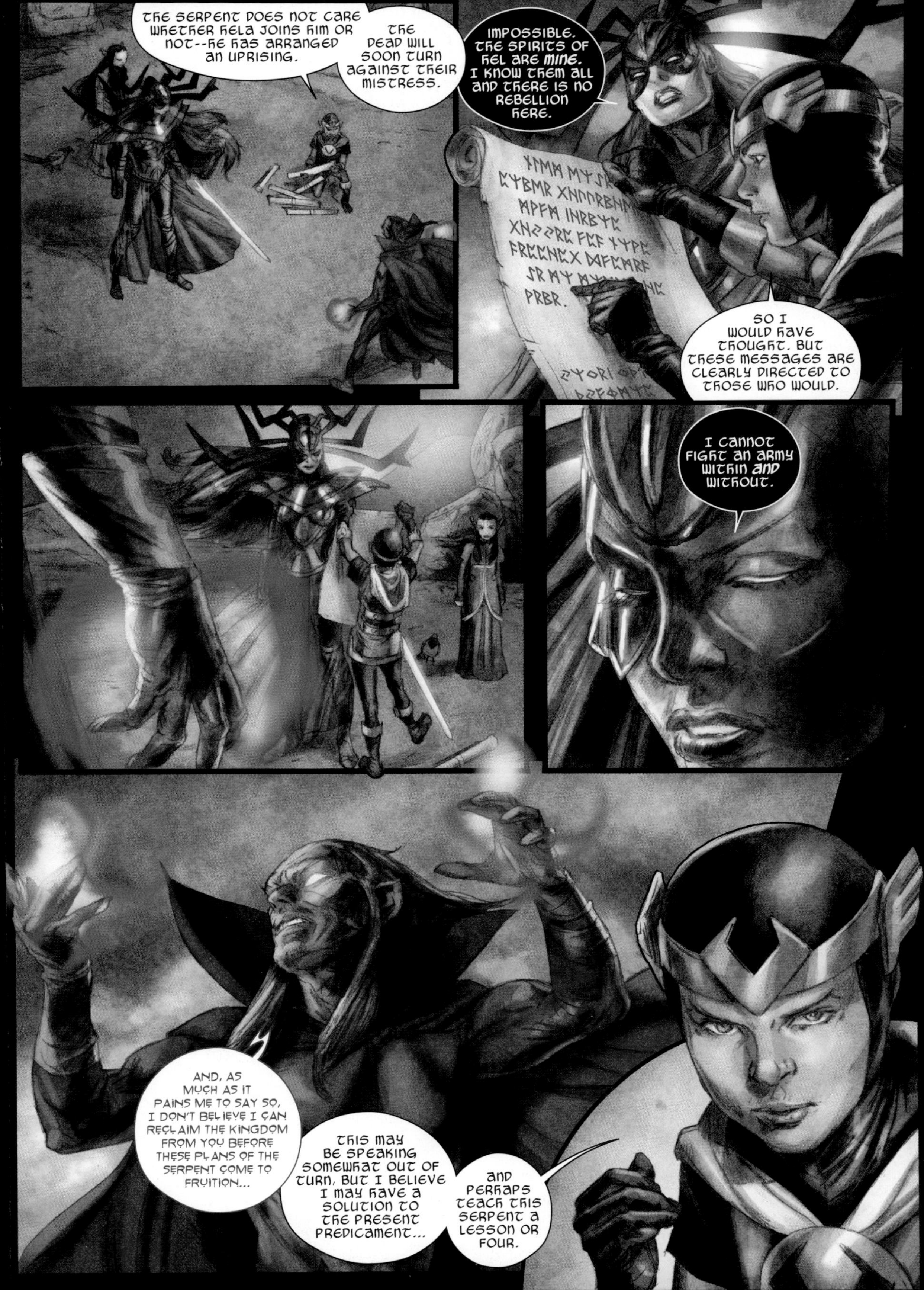
THE SERPENT DOES NOT CARE WHETHER HELA JOINS HIM OR NOT--HE HAS ARRANGED AN UPRISING.
THE DEAD WILL SOON TURN AGAINST THEIR MISTRESS.
IMPOSSIBLE. THE SPIRITS OF HEL ARE MINE. I KNOW THEM ALL AND THERE IS NO REBELLION HERE.
SO I WOULD HAVE THOUGHT. BUT THESE MESSAGES ARE CLEARLY DIRECTED TO THOSE WHO WOULD.
I CANNOT FIGHT AN ARMY WITHIN AND WITHOUT.
AND, AS MUCH AS IT PAINS ME TO SAY SO, I DON'T BELIEVE I CAN RECLAIM THE KINGDOM FROM YOU BEFORE THESE PLANS OF THE SERPENT COME TO FRUITION...
THIS MAY BE SPEAKING SOMEWHAT OUT OF TURN, BUT I BELIEVE I MAY HAVE A SOLUTION TO THE PRESENT PREDICAMENT...
AND PERHAPS TEACH THIS SERPENT A LESSON OR FOUR.

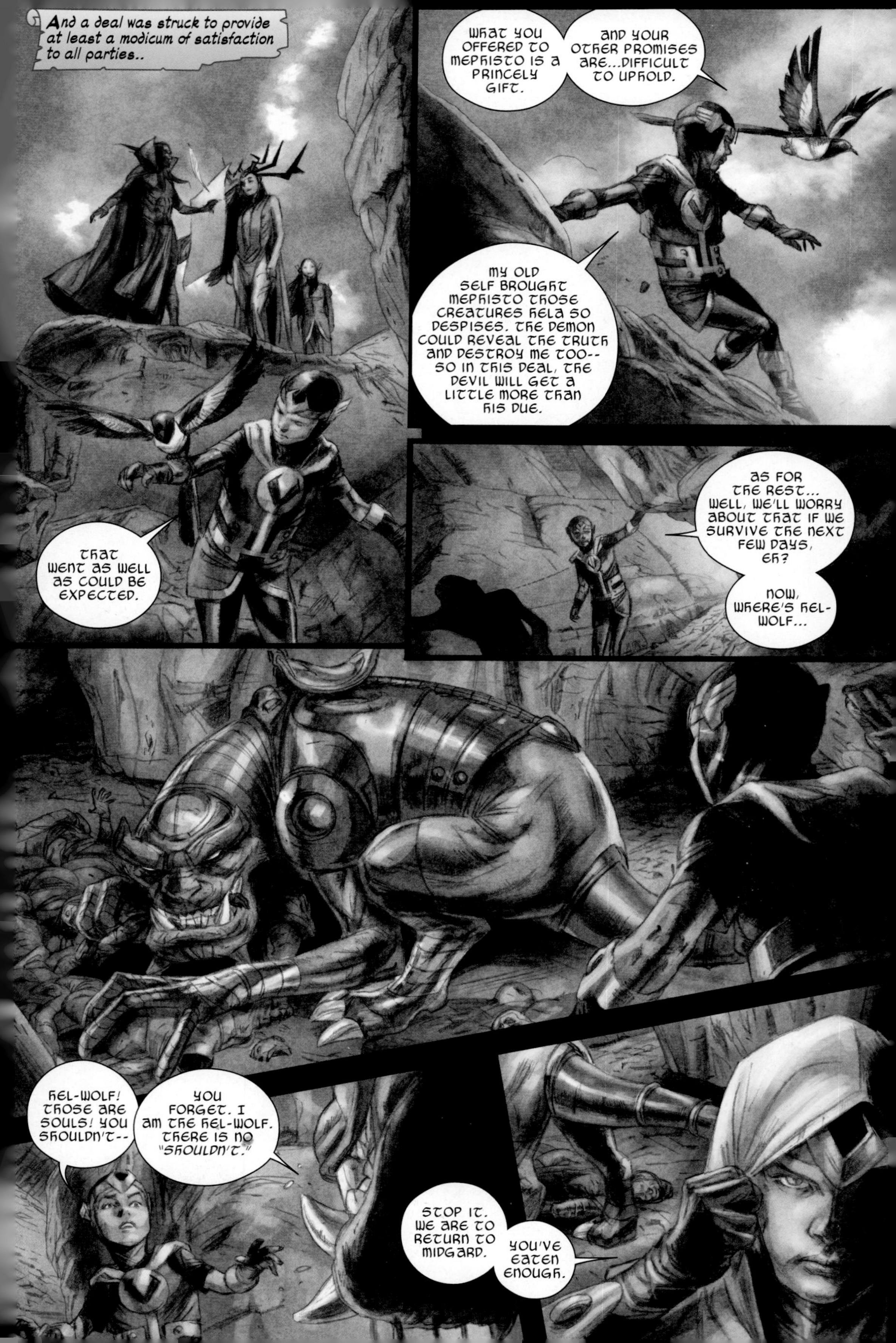
And a deal was struck to provide at least a modicum of satisfaction to all parties..
WHAT YOU OFFERED TO MEPHISTO IS A PRINCELY GIFT.
AND YOUR OTHER PROMISES ARE...DIFFICULT TO UPHOLD.
MY OLD SELF BROUGHT MEPHISTO THOSE CREATURES HELA SO DESPISES. THE DEMON COULD REVEAL THE TRUTH AND DESTROY ME TOO--SO IN THIS DEAL, THE DEVIL WILL GET A LITTLE MORE THAN HIS DUE.
THAT WENT AS WELL AS COULD BE EXPECTED.
AS FOR THE REST... WELL, WE'LL WORRY ABOUT THAT IF WE SURVIVE THE NEXT FEW DAYS, EH?
NOW, WHERE'S HEL-WOLF...
HEL-WOLF! THOSE ARE SOULS! YOU SHOULDN'T--
YOU FORGET. I AM THE HEL-WOLF. THERE IS NO "SHOULDN'T."
STOP IT. WE ARE TO RETURN TO MIDGARD.
YOU'VE EATEN ENOUGH.

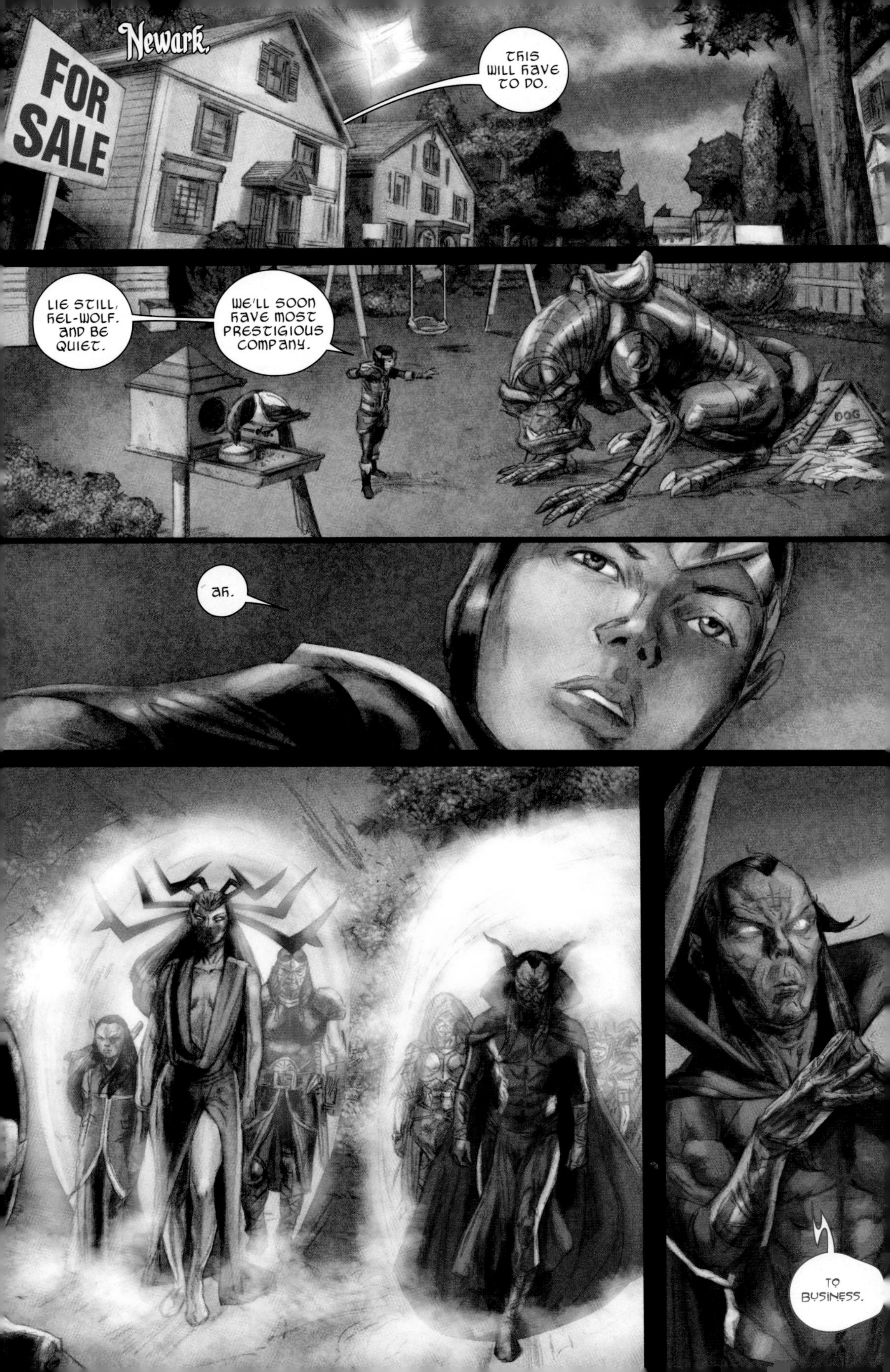
Newark.
FOR SALE
THIS WILL HAVE TO DO.
LIE STILL, HEL-WOLF. AND BE QUIET.
WE'LL SOON HAVE MOST PRESTIGIOUS COMPANY.
DOG
AH.
TO BUSINESS.

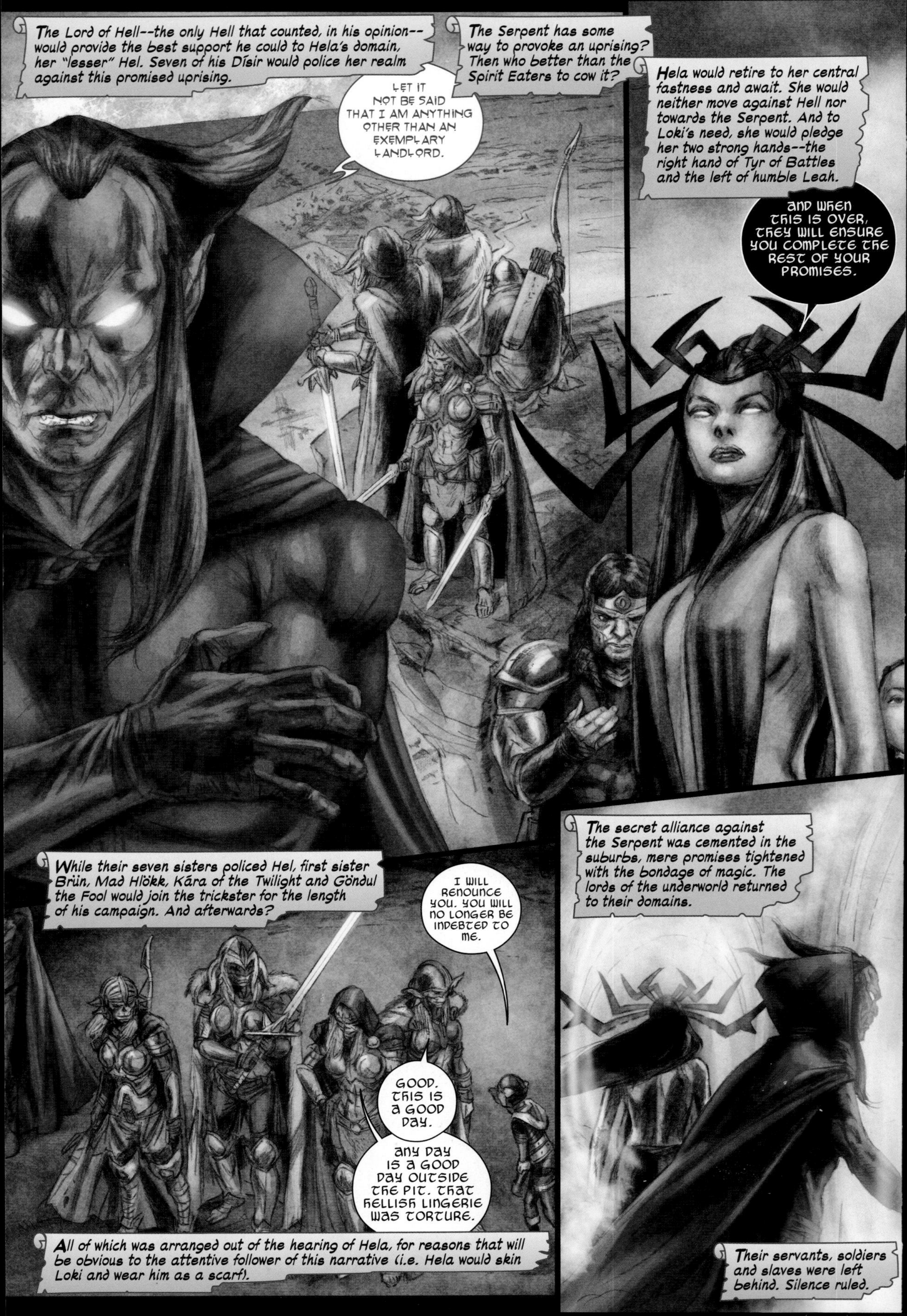

The Lord of Hell--the only Hell that counted, in his opinion--would provide the best support he could to Hela's domain, her "lesser" Hel. Seven of his Dísir would police her realm against this promised uprising.
LET IT NOT BE SAID THAT I AM ANYTHING OTHER THAN AN EXEMPLARY LANDLORD.
The Serpent has some way to provoke an uprising? Then who better than the Spirit Eaters to cow it?
Hela would retire to her central fastness and await. She would neither move against Hell nor towards the Serpent. And to Loki's need, she would pledge her two strong hands--the right hand of Tyr of Battles and the left of humble Leah.
AND WHEN THIS IS OVER, THEY WILL ENSURE YOU COMPLETE THE REST OF YOUR PROMISES.
While their seven sisters policed Hel, first sister Brün, Mad Hlökk, Kára of the Twilight and Göndul the Fool would join the trickster for the length of his campaign. And afterwards?
I WILL RENOUNCE YOU. YOU WILL NO LONGER BE INDEBTED TO ME.
GOOD. THIS IS A GOOD DAY.
ANY DAY IS A GOOD DAY OUTSIDE THE PIT. THAT HELLISH LINGERIE WAS TORTURE.
All of which was arranged out of the hearing of Hela, for reasons that will be obvious to the attentive follower of this narrative (i.e. Hela would skin Loki and wear him as a scarf).
The secret alliance against the Serpent was cemented in the suburbs, mere promises tightened with the bondage of magic. The lords of the underworld returned to their domains.
Their servants, soldiers and slaves were left behind. Silence ruled.

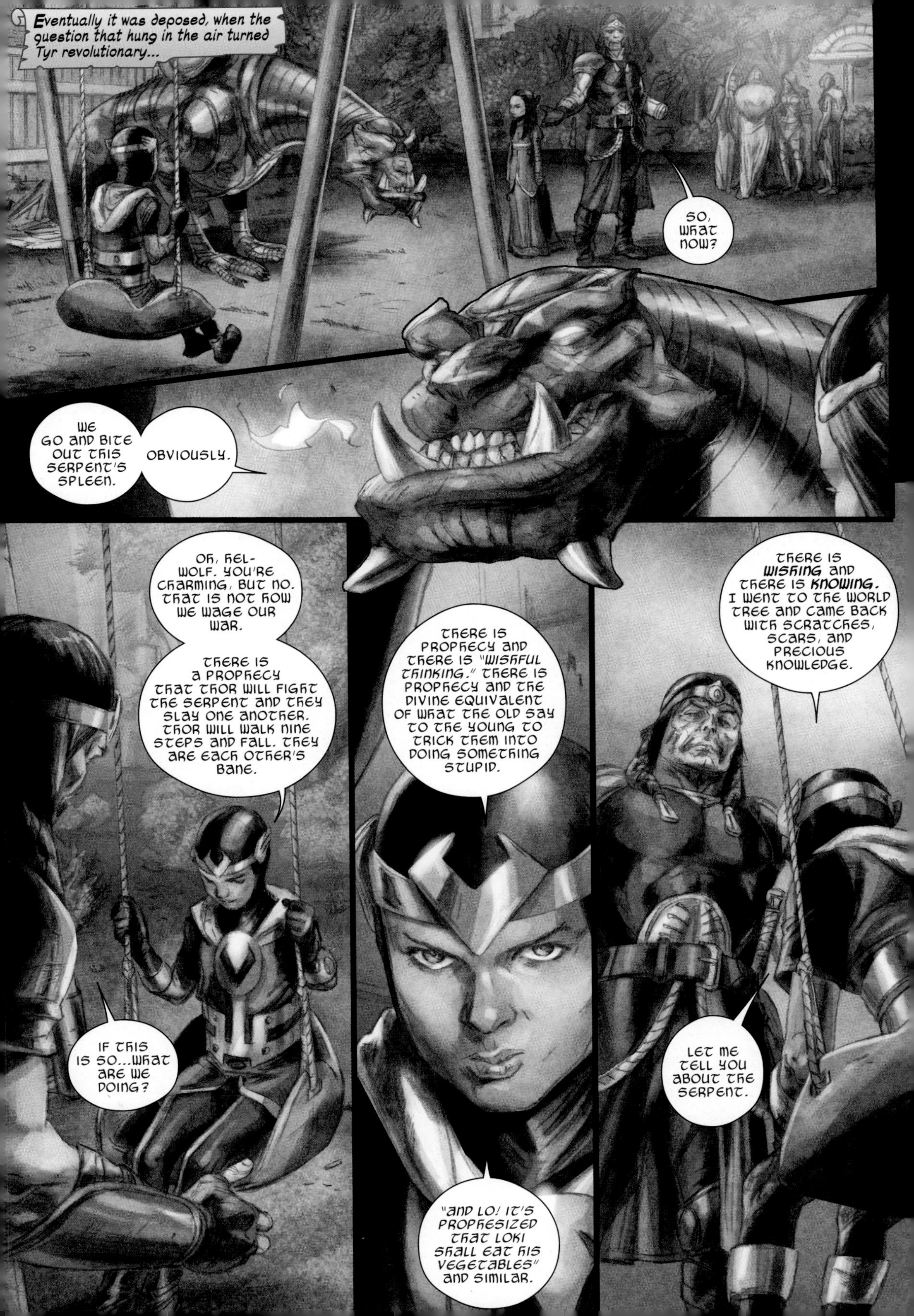

Eventually it was deposed, when the question that hung in the air turned Tyr revolutionary...
SO, WHAT NOW?
WE GO AND BITE OUT THIS SERPENT'S SPLEEN.
OBVIOUSLY.
OH, HEL-WOLF. YOU'RE CHARMING, BUT NO. THAT IS NOT HOW WE WAGE OUR WAR.
THERE IS A PROPHECY THAT THOR WILL FIGHT THE SERPENT AND THEY SLAY ONE ANOTHER. THOR WILL WALK NINE STEPS AND FALL. THEY ARE EACH OTHER'S BANE.
IF THIS IS SO...WHAT ARE WE DOING?
THERE IS PROPHECY AND THERE IS "WISHFUL THINKING." THERE IS PROPHECY AND THE DIVINE EQUIVALENT OF WHAT THE OLD SAY TO THE YOUNG TO TRICK THEM INTO DOING SOMETHING STUPID.
"AND LO! IT'S PROPHESIZED THAT LOKI SHALL EAT HIS VEGETABLES" AND SIMILAR.
THERE IS WISHING AND THERE IS KNOWING. I WENT TO THE WORLD TREE AND CAME BACK WITH SCRATCHES, SCARS, AND PRECIOUS KNOWLEDGE.
LET ME TELL YOU ABOUT THE SERPENT.

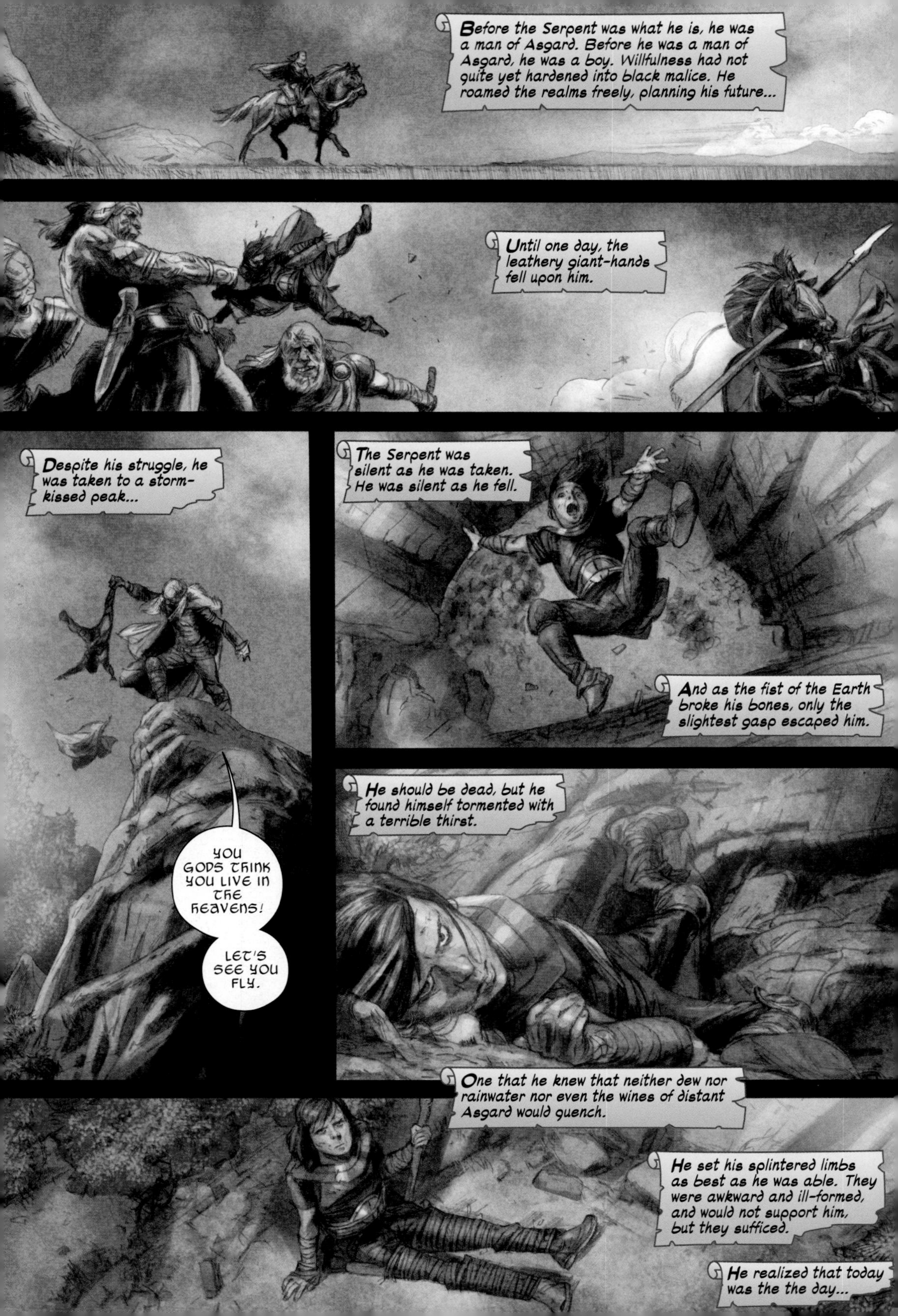
Before the Serpent was what he is, he was a man of Asgard. Before he was a man of Asgard, he was a boy. Willfulness had not quite yet hardened into black malice. He roamed the realms freely, planning his future...
Until one day, the leathery giant-hands fell upon him.
Despite his struggle, he was taken to a storm-kissed peak...
YOU GODS THINK YOU LIVE IN THE HEAVENS!
LET'S SEE YOU FLY.
The Serpent was silent as he was taken. He was silent as he fell.
And as the fist of the Earth broke his bones, only the slightest gasp escaped him.
He should be dead, but he found himself tormented with a terrible thirst.
One that he knew that neither dew nor rainwater nor even the wines of distant Asgard would quench.
He set his splintered limbs as best as he was able. They were awkward and ill-formed, and would not support him, but they sufficed.
He realized that today was the the day...

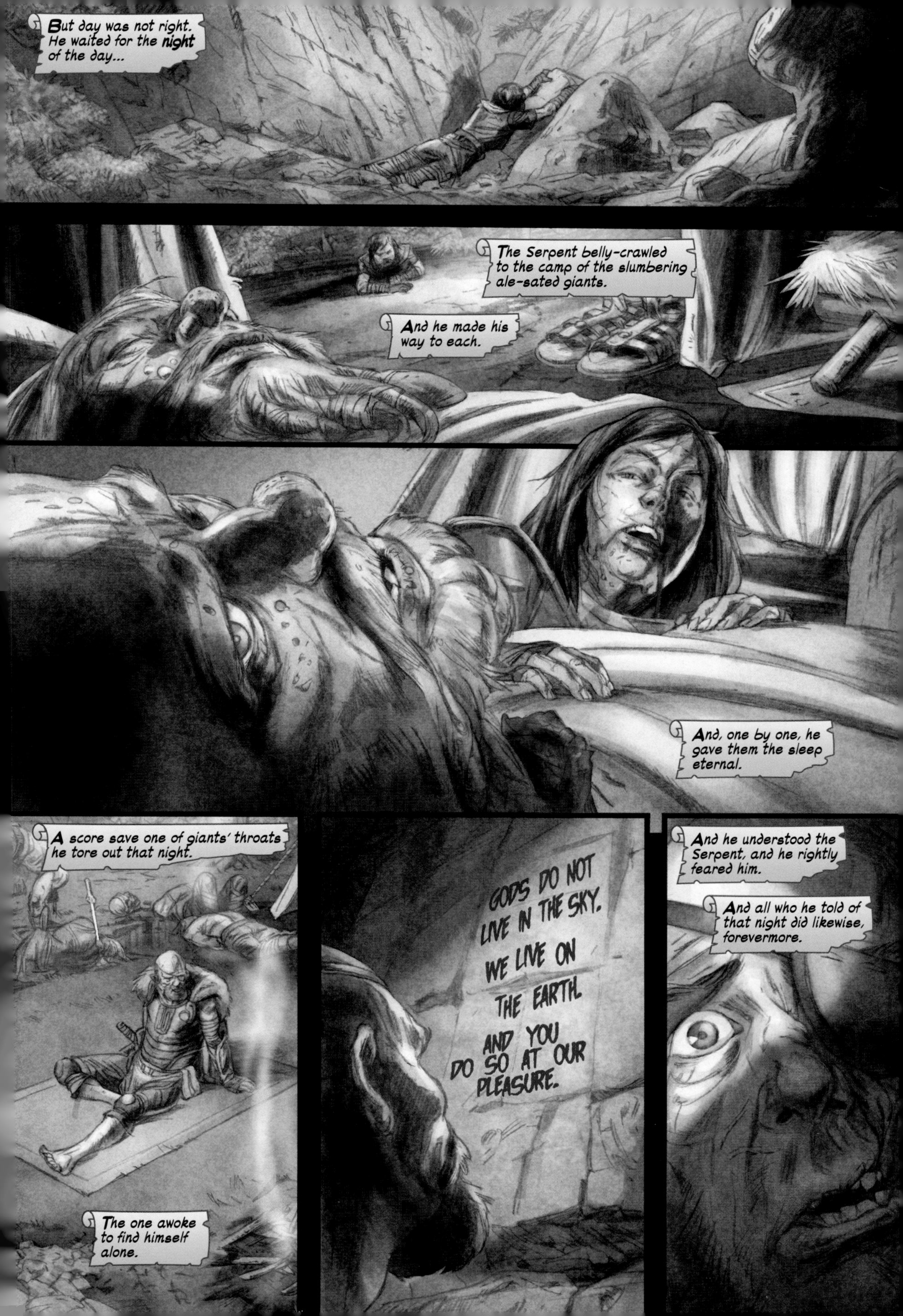

But day was not right. He waited for the night of the day...
The Serpent belly-crawled to the camp of the slumbering ale-sated giants.
And he made his way to each.
And, one by one, he gave them the sleep eternal.
A score save one of giants' throats he tore out that night.
The one awoke to find himself alone.
GODS DO NOT LIVE IN THE SKY. WE LIVE ON THE EARTH. AND YOU DO SO AT OUR PLEASURE.
And he understood the Serpent, and he rightly feared him.
And all who he told of that night did likewise, forevermore.

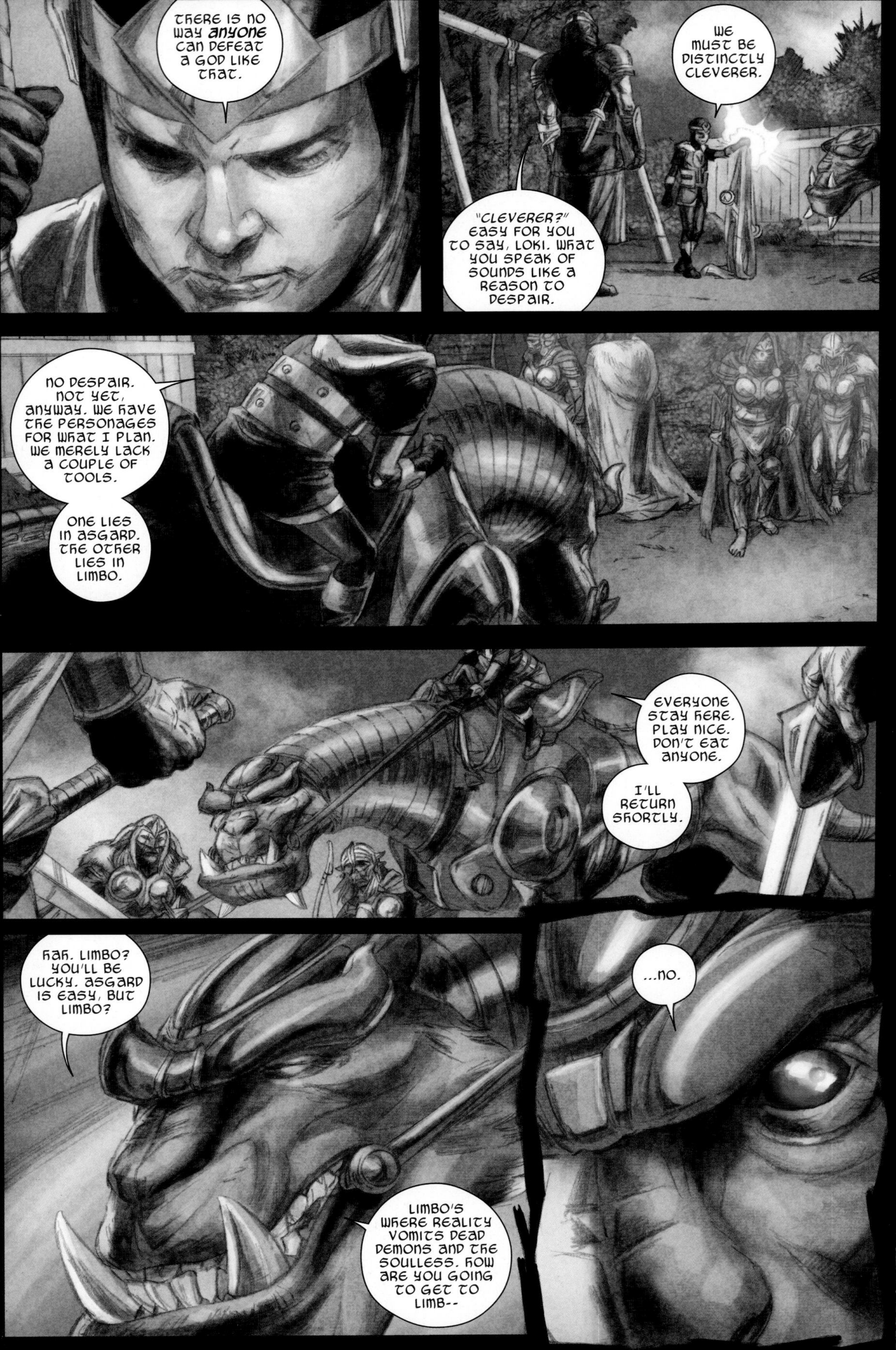
THERE IS NO WAY ANYONE CAN DEFEAT A GOD LIKE THAT.
WE MUST BE DISTINCTLY CLEVERER.
"CLEVERER?" EASY FOR YOU TO SAY, LOKI. WHAT YOU SPEAK OF SOUNDS LIKE A REASON TO DESPAIR.
NO DESPAIR. NOT YET, ANYWAY. WE HAVE THE PERSONAGES FOR WHAT I PLAN. WE MERELY LACK A COUPLE OF TOOLS.
ONE LIES IN ASGARD. THE OTHER LIES IN LIMBO.
EVERYONE STAY HERE. PLAY NICE. DON'T EAT ANYONE.
I'LL RETURN SHORTLY.
HAH. LIMBO? YOU'LL BE LUCKY. ASGARD IS EASY, BUT LIMBO?
LIMBO'S WHERE REALITY VOMITS DEAD DEMONS AND THE SOULLESS. HOW ARE YOU GOING TO GET TO LIMB--
...NO.

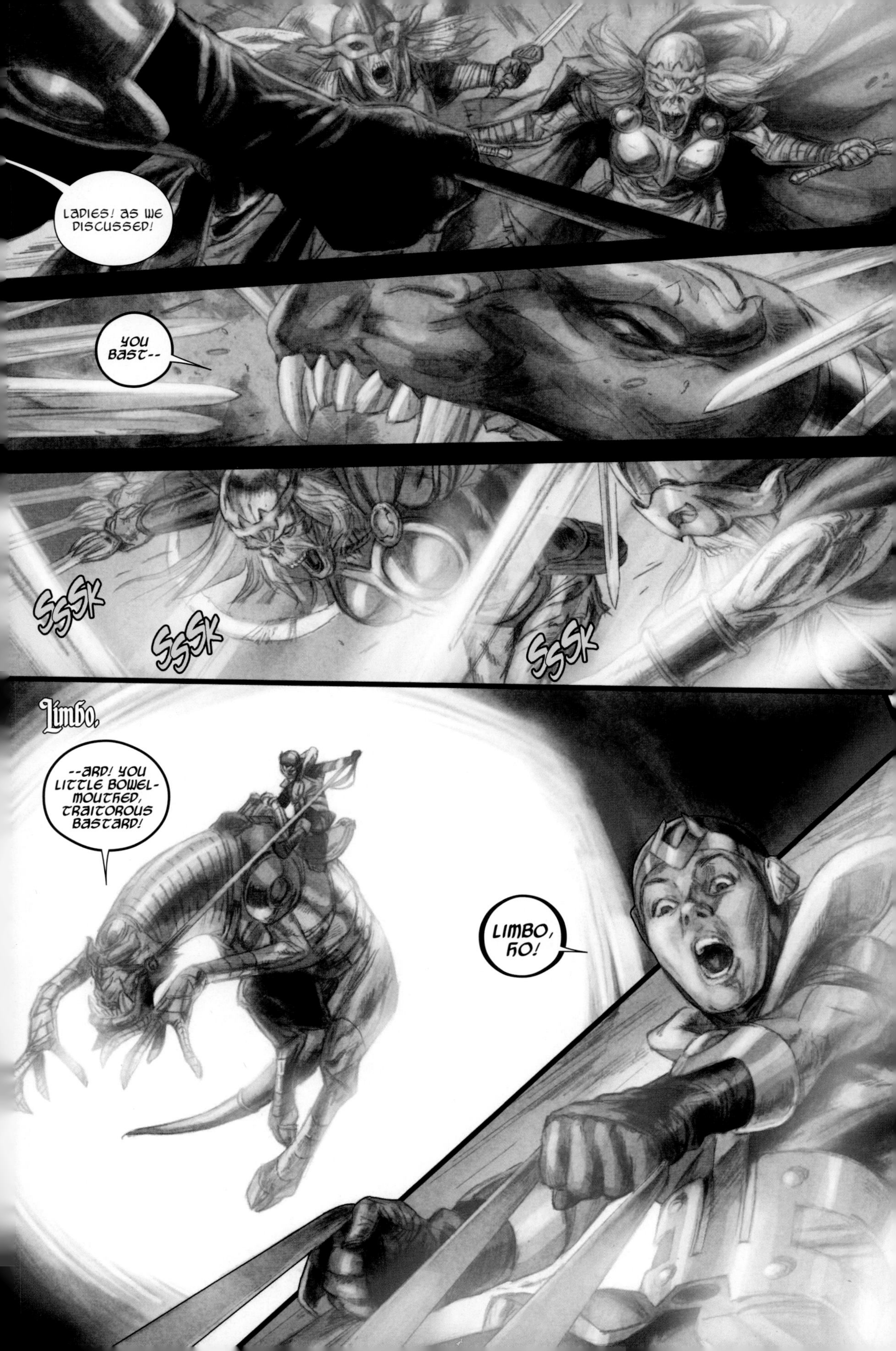
LADIES! AS WE DISCUSSED!
YOU BAST--
SSSK
SSSK
SSSK
Limbo,
--ARD! YOU LITTLE BOWEL-MOUTHED, TRAITOROUS BASTARD!
LIMBO, HO!

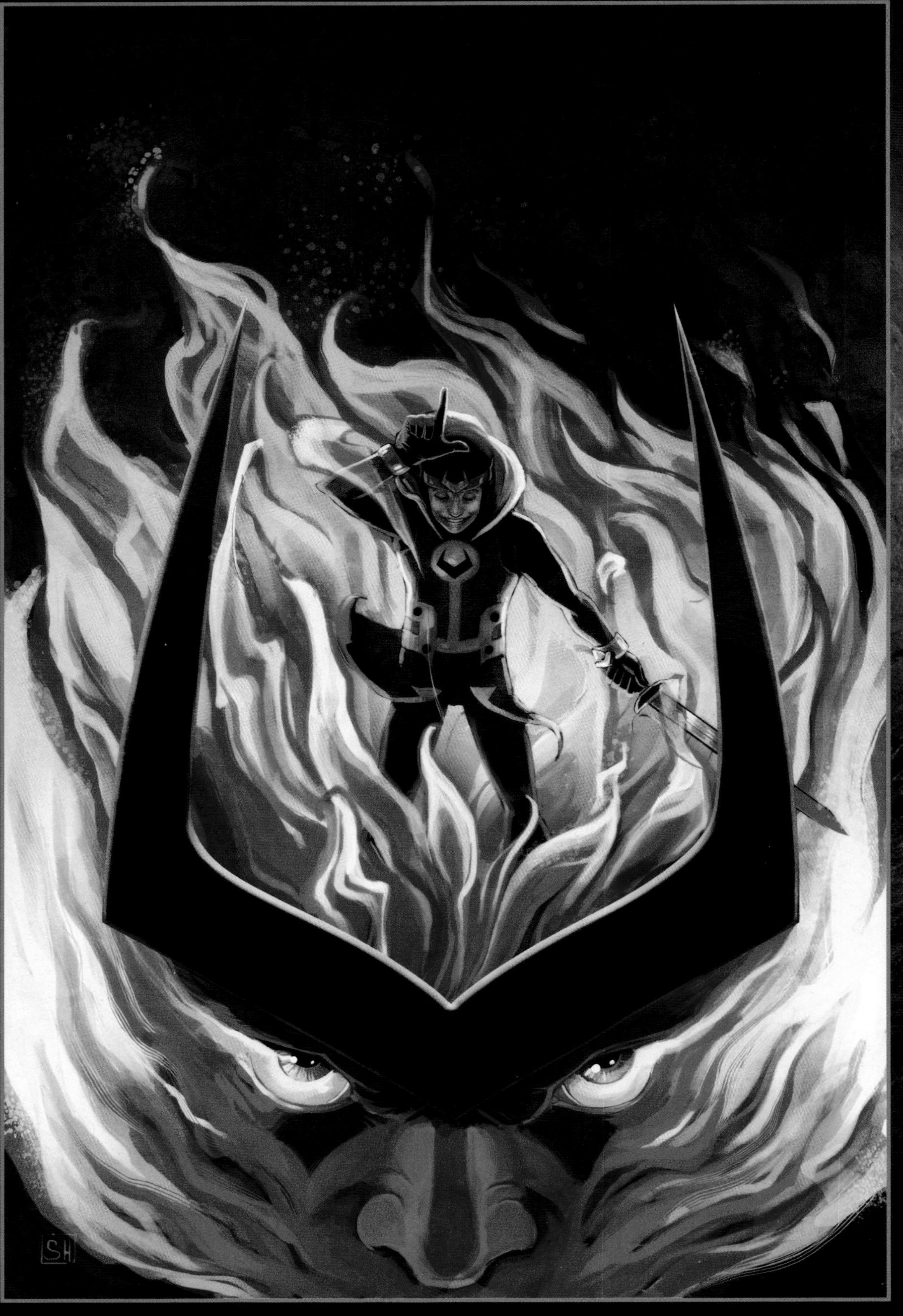
SH

JOURNEY INTO MYSTERY #626

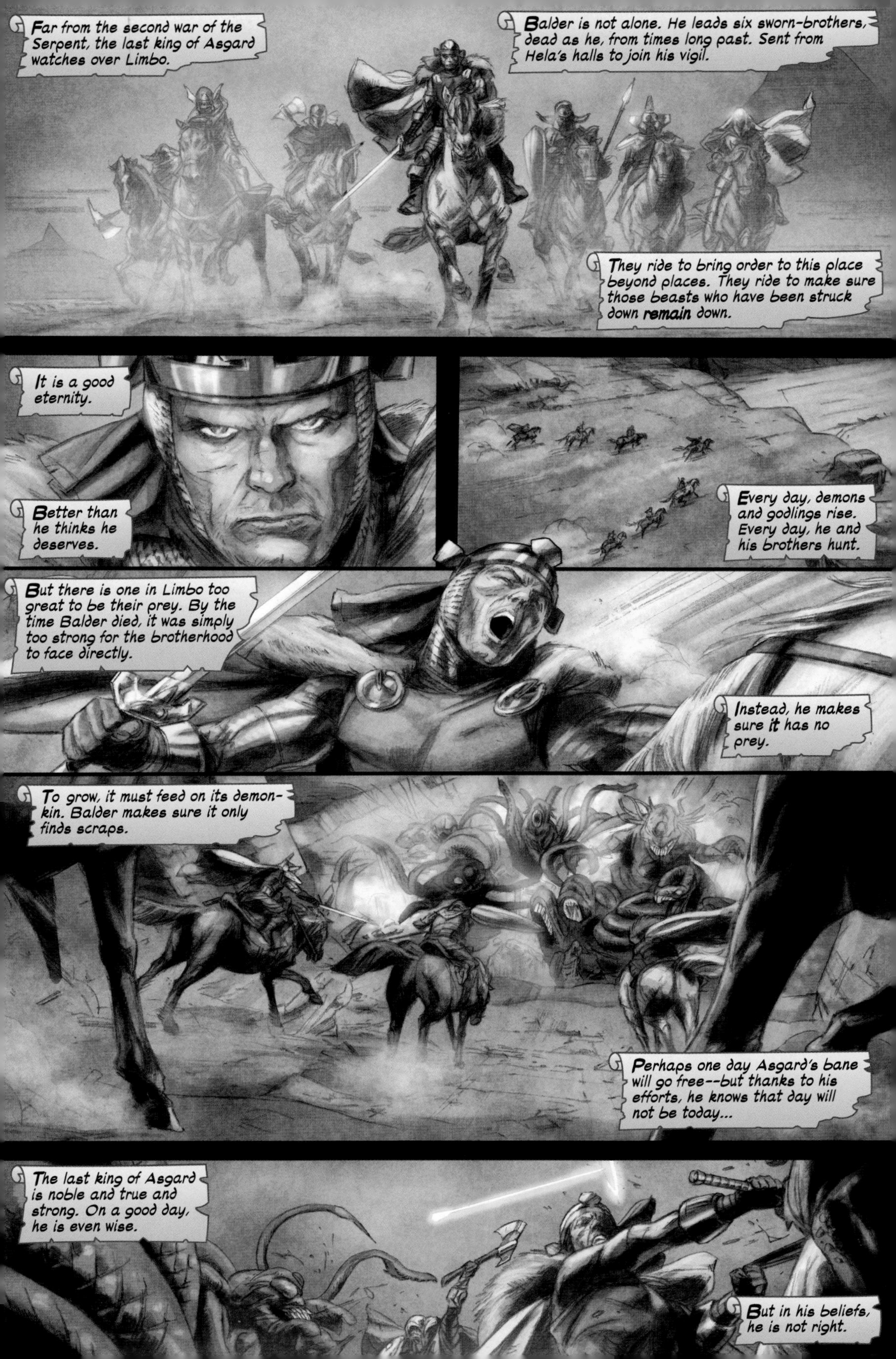
Far from the second war of the Serpent, the last king of Asgard watches over Limbo.
Balder is not alone. He leads six sworn-brothers, dead as he, from times long past. Sent from Hela's halls to join his vigil.
They ride to bring order to this place beyond places. They ride to make sure those beasts who have been struck down remain down.
It is a good eternity.
Better than he thinks he deserves.
Every day, demons and godlings rise. Every day, he and his brothers hunt.
But there is one in Limbo too great to be their prey. By the time Balder died, it was simply too strong for the brotherhood to face directly.
Instead, he makes sure it has no prey.
To grow, it must feed on its demon-kin. Balder makes sure it only finds scraps.
Perhaps one day Asgard's bane will go free--but thanks to his efforts, he knows that day will not be today...
The last king of Asgard is noble and true and strong. On a good day, he is even wise.
But in his beliefs, he is not right.

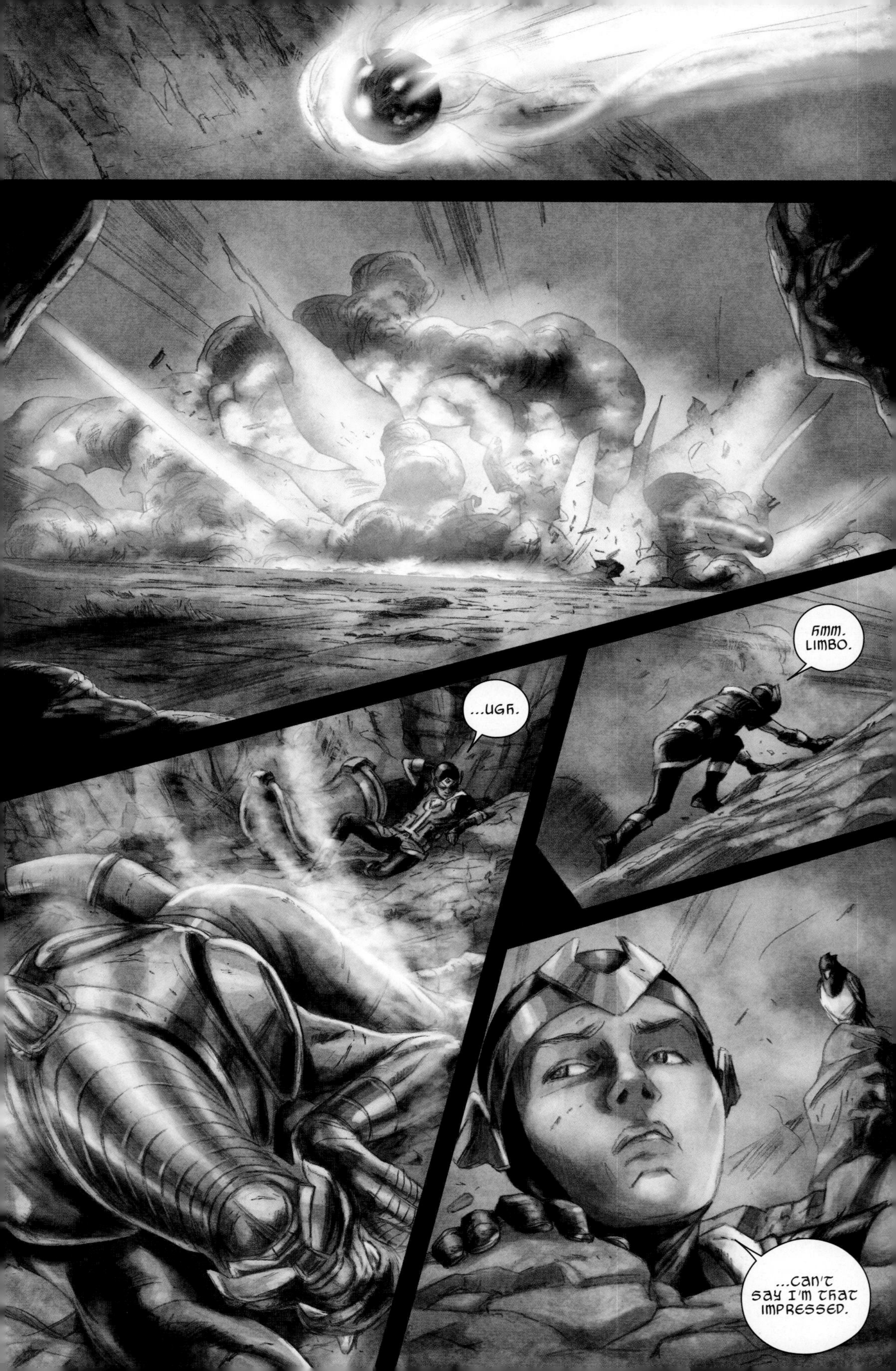

...UGH.
HMM. LIMBO.
...CAN'T SAY I'M THAT IMPRESSED.

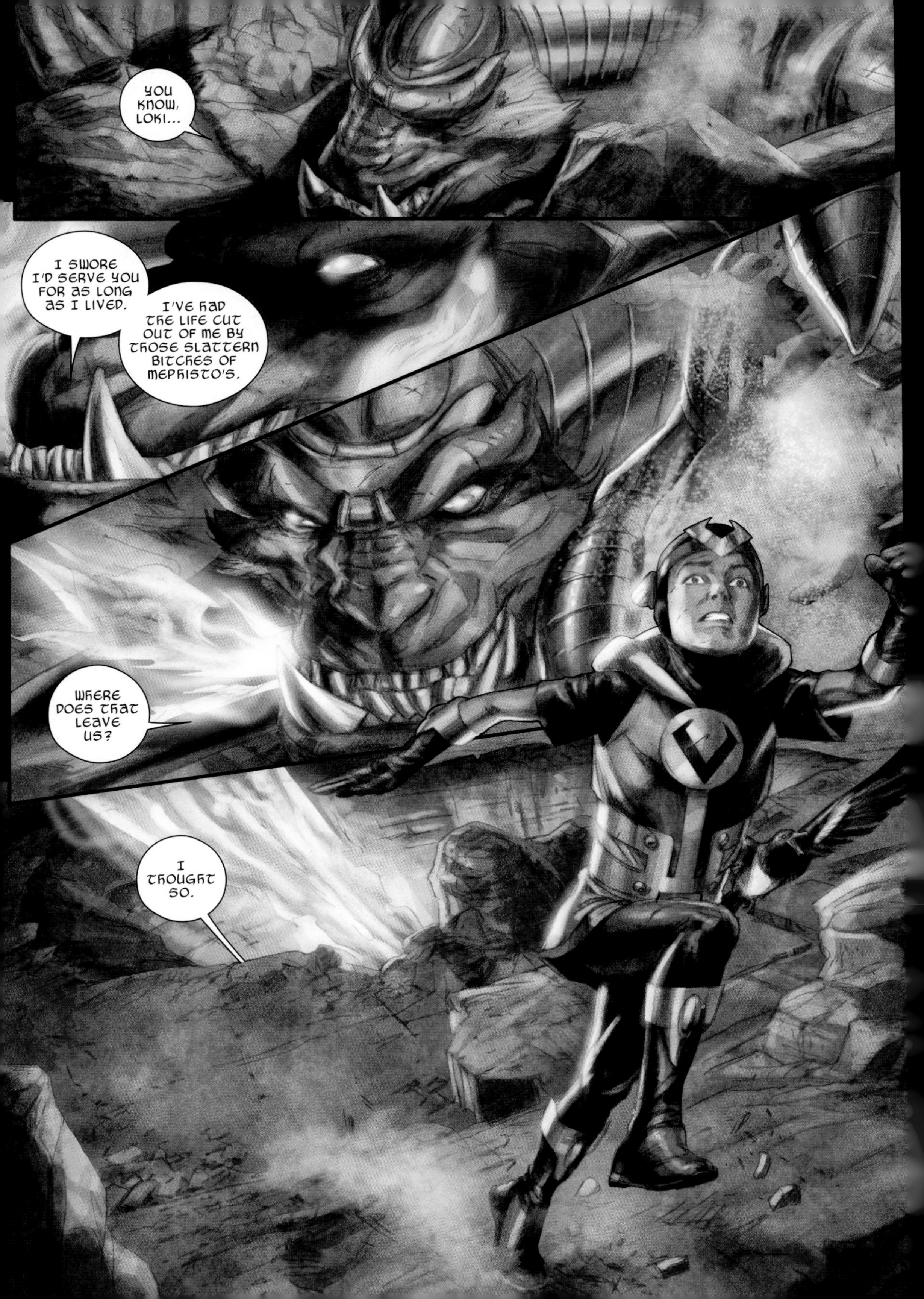
YOU KNOW, LOKI...
I SWORE I'D SERVE YOU FOR AS LONG AS I LIVED.
I'VE HAD THE LIFE CUT OUT OF ME BY THOSE SLATTERN BITCHES OF MEPHISTO'S.
WHERE DOES THAT LEAVE US?
I THOUGHT SO.

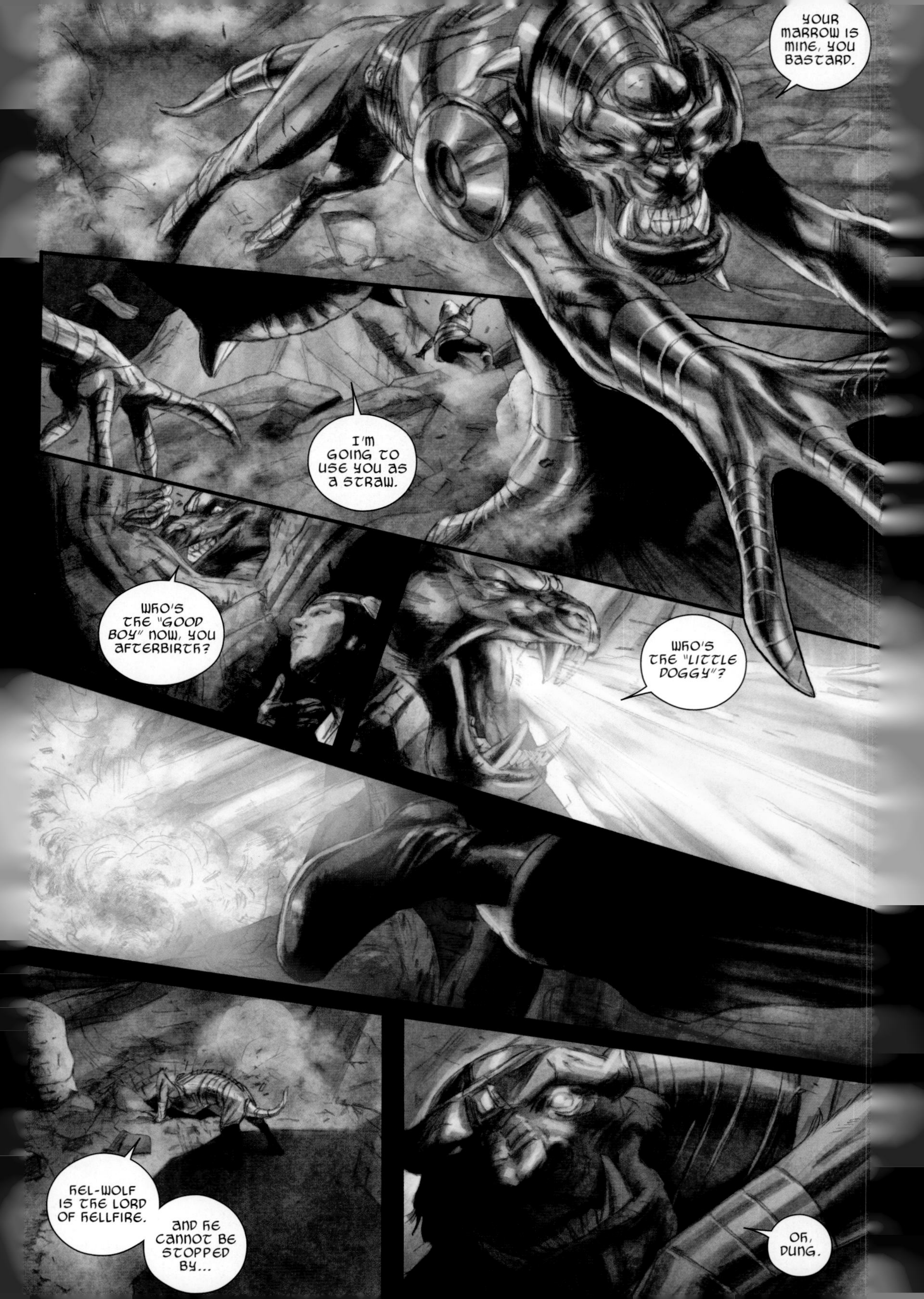
YOUR MARROW IS MINE, YOU BASTARD.
I'M GOING TO USE YOU AS A STRAW.
WHO'S THE "GOOD BOY" NOW, YOU AFTERBIRTH?
WHO'S THE "LITTLE DOGGY"?
HEL-WOLF IS THE LORD OF HELLFIRE.
AND HE CANNOT BE STOPPED BY...
OH, DUNG.

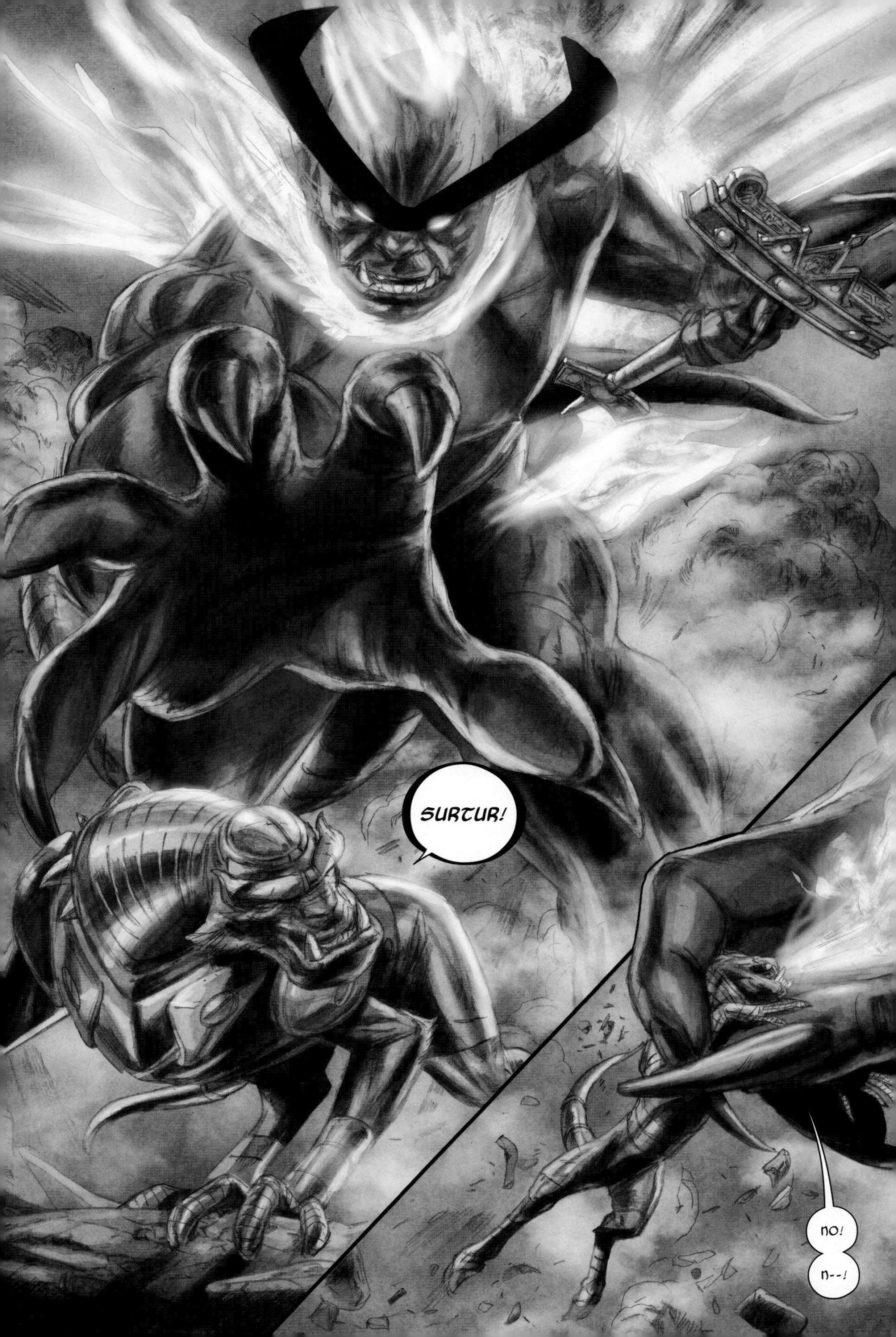
SURTUR!
NO!
N--!

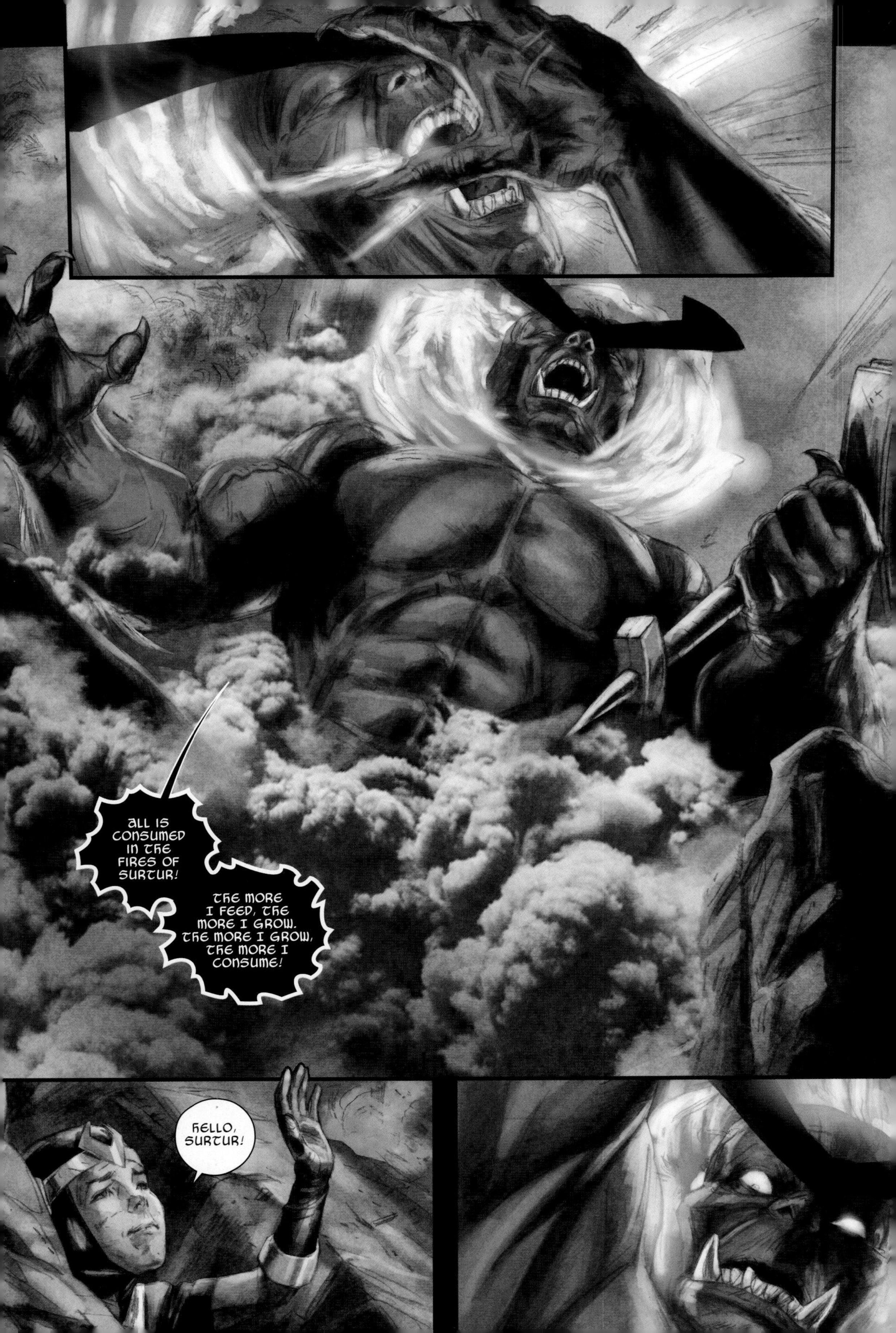
ALL IS CONSUMED IN THE FIRES OF SURTUR!
THE MORE I FEED, THE MORE I GROW. THE MORE I GROW, THE MORE I CONSUME!
HELLO, SURTUR!

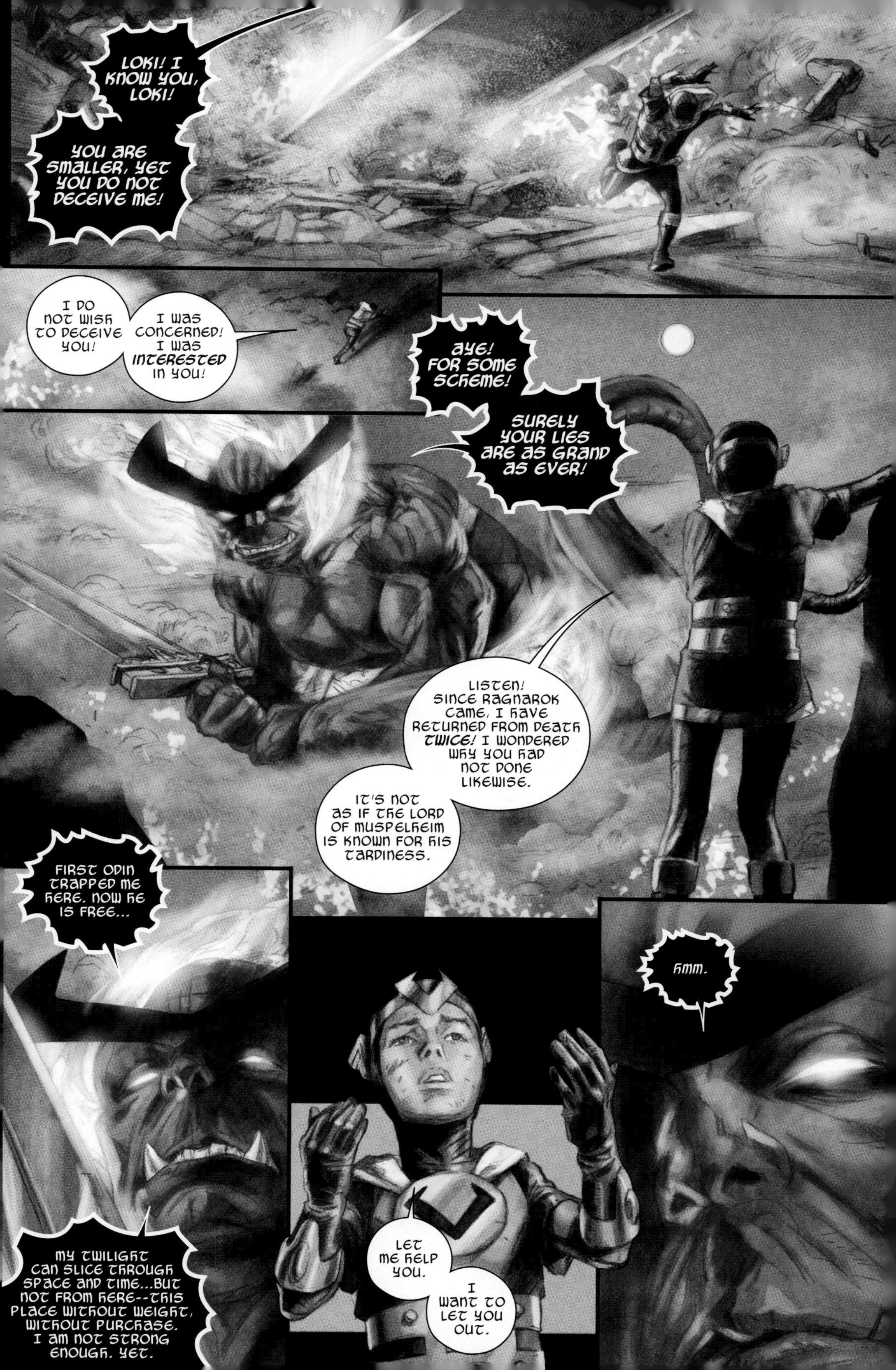
LOKI! I KNOW YOU, LOKI!
YOU ARE SMALLER, YET YOU DO NOT DECEIVE ME!
I DO NOT WISH TO DECEIVE YOU!
I WAS CONCERNED! I WAS INTERESTED IN YOU!
AYE! FOR SOME SCHEME!
SURELY YOUR LIES ARE AS GRAND AS EVER!
LISTEN! SINCE RAGNAROK CAME, I HAVE RETURNED FROM DEATH TWICE! I WONDERED WHY YOU HAD NOT DONE LIKEWISE.
IT'S NOT AS IF THE LORD OF MUSPELHEIM IS KNOWN FOR HIS TARDINESS.
FIRST ODIN TRAPPED ME HERE. NOW HE IS FREE...
MY TWILIGHT CAN SLICE THROUGH SPACE AND TIME...BUT NOT FROM HERE--THIS PLACE WITHOUT WEIGHT, WITHOUT PURCHASE. I AM NOT STRONG ENOUGH. YET.
LET ME HELP YOU.
I WANT TO LET YOU OUT.
HMM.

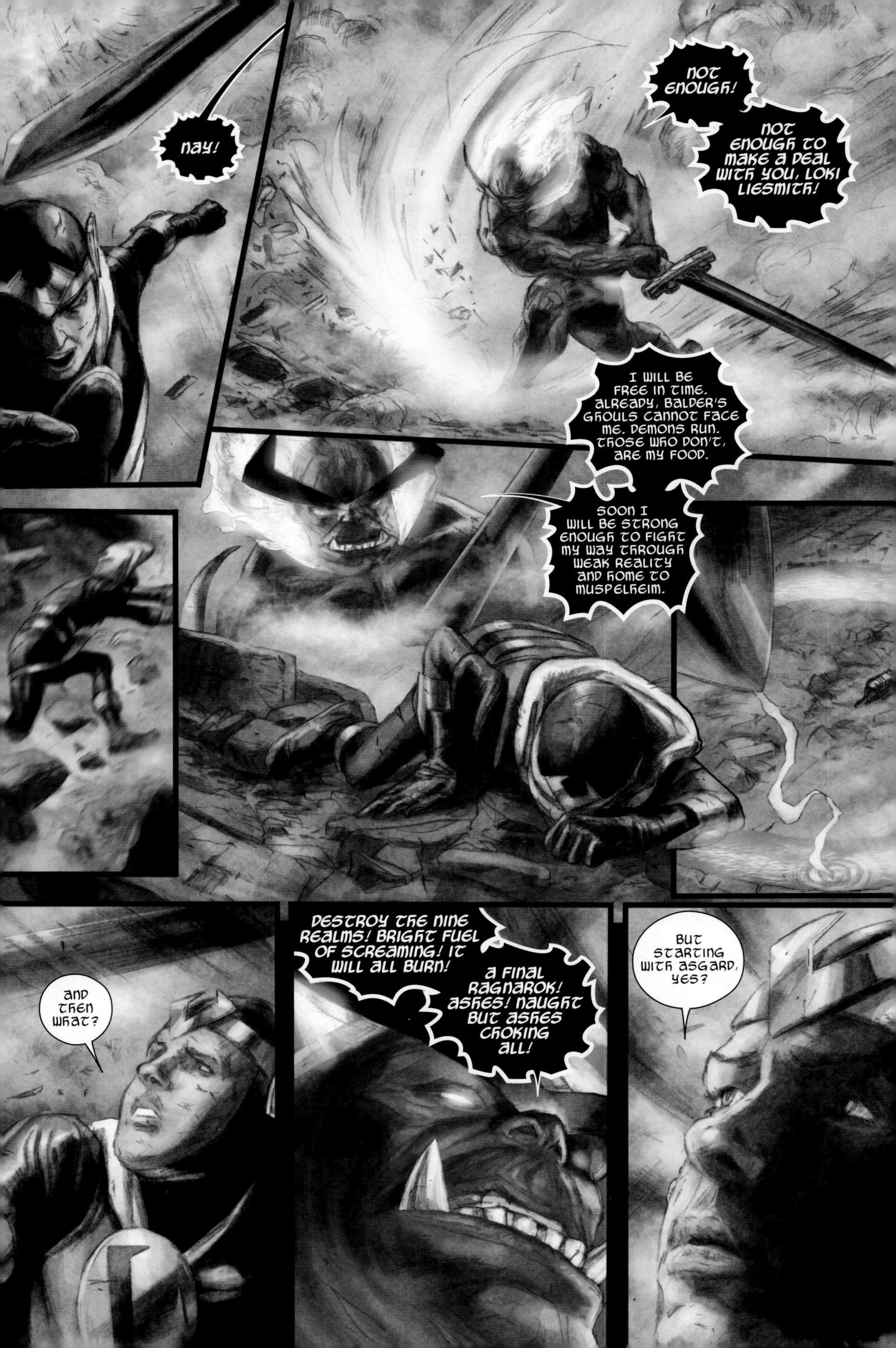
NAY!
NOT ENOUGH!
NOT ENOUGH TO MAKE A DEAL WITH YOU, LOKI LIESMITH!
I WILL BE FREE IN TIME. ALREADY, BALDER'S GHOULS CANNOT FACE ME. DEMONS RUN. THOSE WHO DON'T, ARE MY FOOD.
SOON I WILL BE STRONG ENOUGH TO FIGHT MY WAY THROUGH WEAK REALITY AND HOME TO MUSPELHEIM.
AND THEN WHAT?
DESTROY THE NINE REALMS! BRIGHT FUEL OF SCREAMING! IT WILL ALL BURN!
A FINAL RAGNAROK! ASHES! NAUGHT BUT ASHES CHOKING ALL!
BUT STARTING WITH ASGARD, YES?

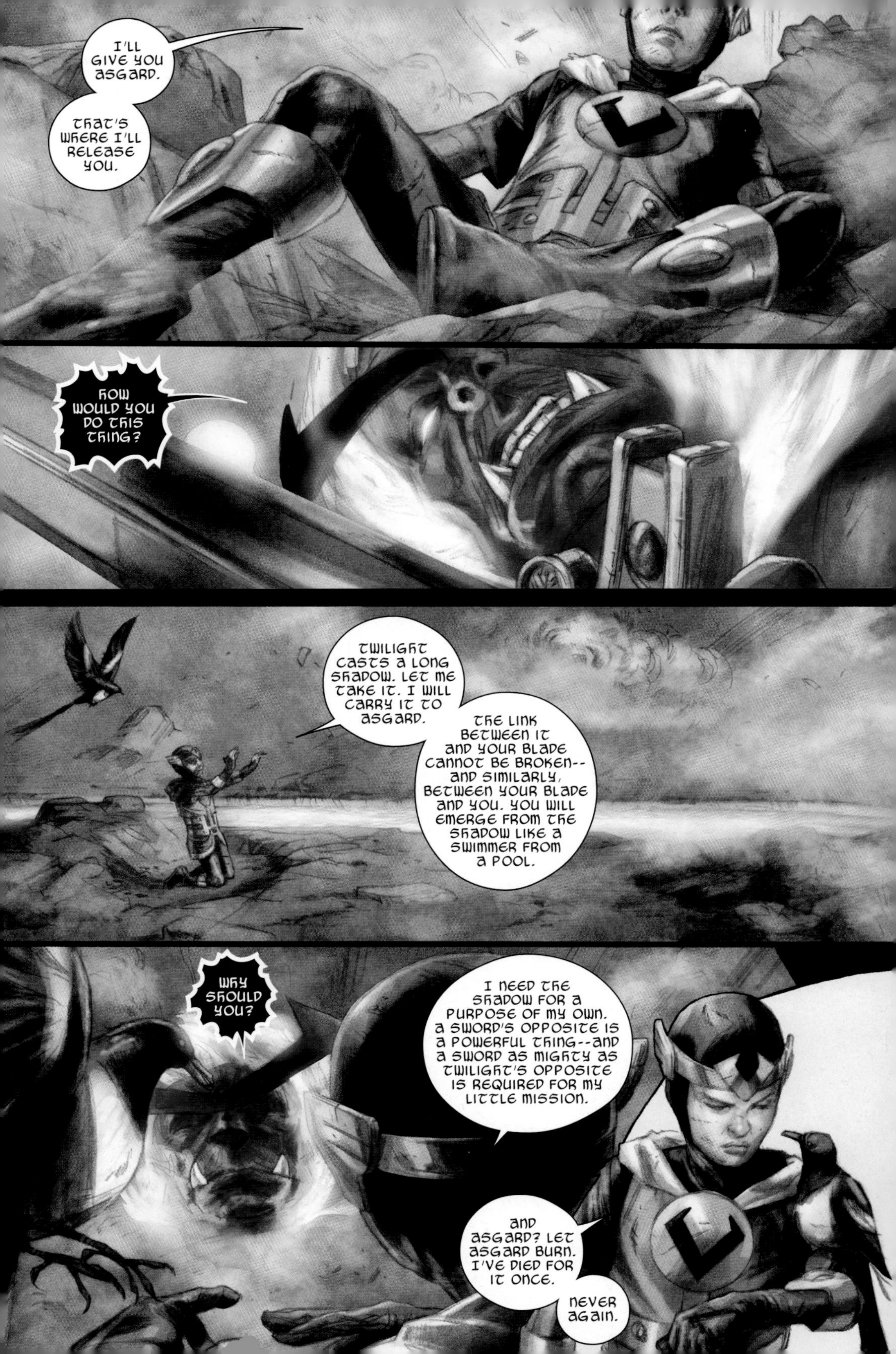
I'LL GIVE YOU ASGARD.
THAT'S WHERE I'LL RELEASE YOU.
HOW WOULD YOU DO THIS THING?
TWILIGHT CASTS A LONG SHADOW. LET ME TAKE IT. I WILL CARRY IT TO ASGARD.
THE LINK BETWEEN IT AND YOUR BLADE CANNOT BE BROKEN--AND SIMILARLY, BETWEEN YOUR BLADE AND YOU. YOU WILL EMERGE FROM THE SHADOW LIKE A SWIMMER FROM A POOL.
WHY SHOULD YOU?
I NEED THE SHADOW FOR A PURPOSE OF MY OWN. A SWORD'S OPPOSITE IS A POWERFUL THING--AND A SWORD AS MIGHTY AS TWILIGHT'S OPPOSITE IS REQUIRED FOR MY LITTLE MISSION.
AND ASGARD? LET ASGARD BURN. I'VE DIED FOR IT ONCE.
NEVER AGAIN.

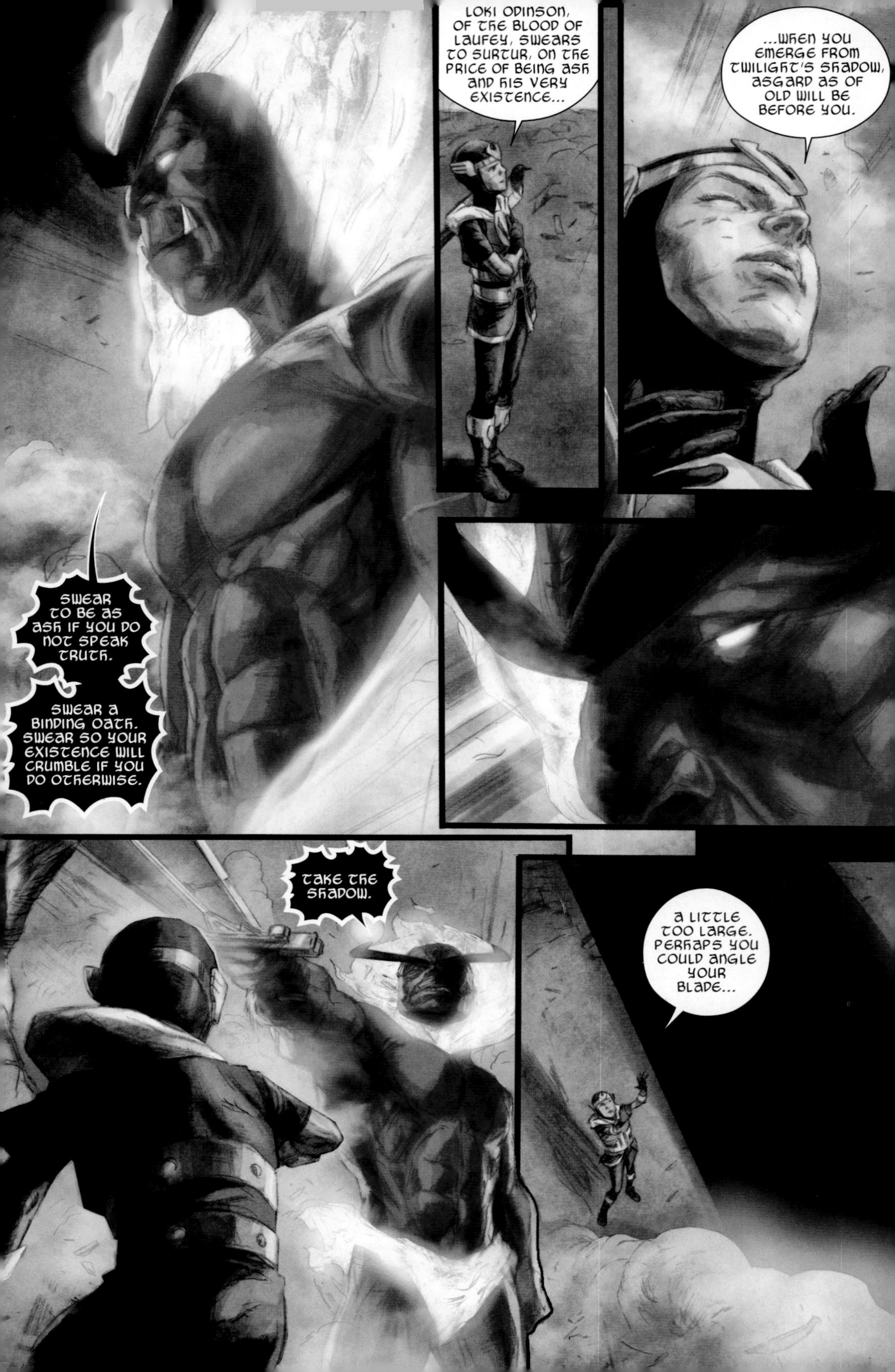
LOKI ODINSON, OF THE BLOOD OF LAUFEY, SWEARS TO SURTUR, ON THE PRICE OF BEING ASH AND HIS VERY EXISTENCE...
...WHEN YOU EMERGE FROM TWILIGHT'S SHADOW, ASGARD AS OF OLD WILL BE BEFORE YOU.
SWEAR TO BE AS ASH IF YOU DO NOT SPEAK TRUTH.
SWEAR A BINDING OATH. SWEAR SO YOUR EXISTENCE WILL CRUMBLE IF YOU DO OTHERWISE.
TAKE THE SHADOW.
A LITTLE TOO LARGE. PERHAPS YOU COULD ANGLE YOUR BLADE...

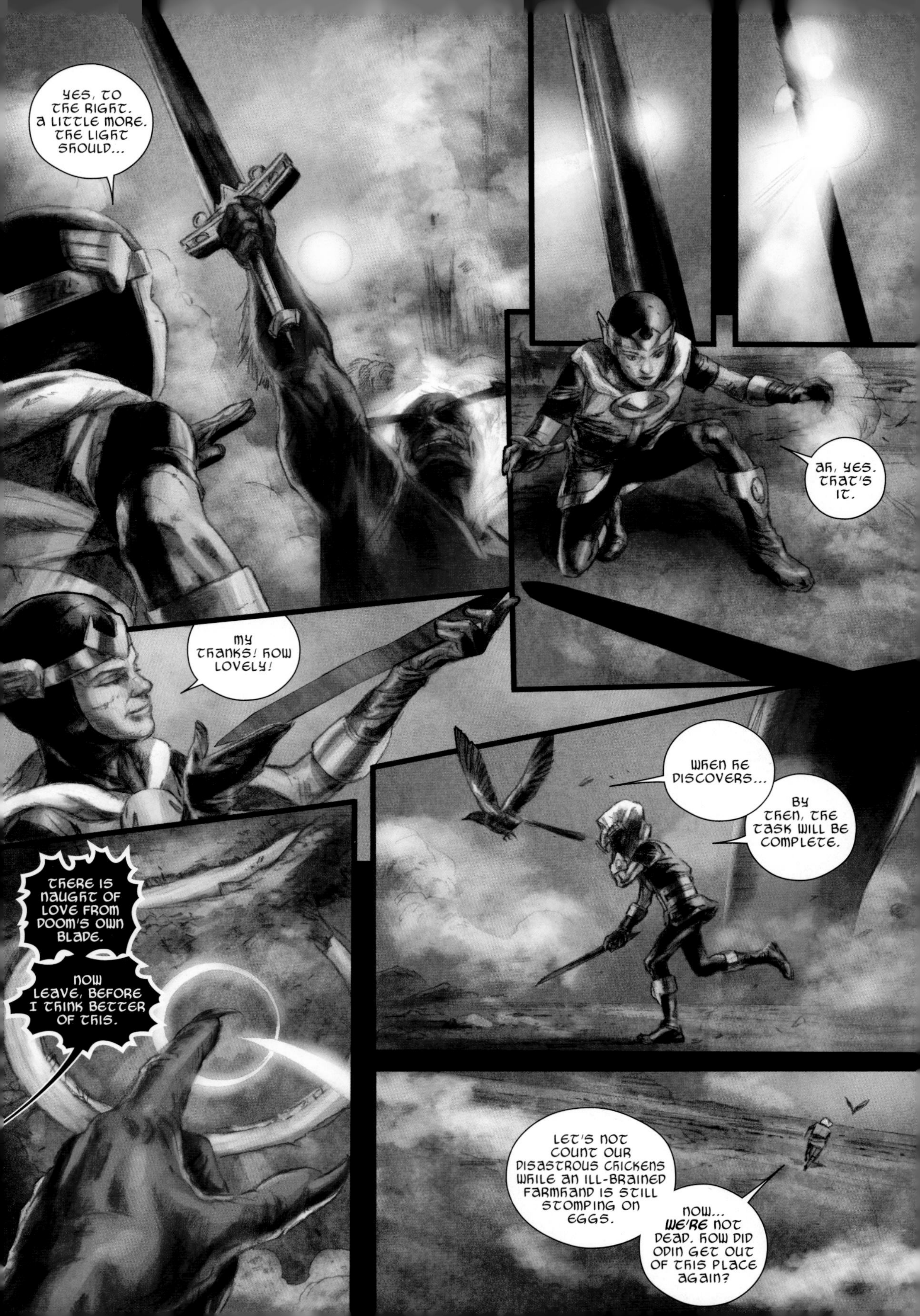
YES, TO THE RIGHT. A LITTLE MORE. THE LIGHT SHOULD...
AH, YES. THAT'S IT.
MY THANKS! HOW LOVELY!
WHEN HE DISCOVERS...
BY THEN, THE TASK WILL BE COMPLETE.
THERE IS NAUGHT OF LOVE FROM DOOM'S OWN BLADE.
NOW LEAVE, BEFORE I THINK BETTER OF THIS.
LET'S NOT COUNT OUR DISASTROUS CHICKENS WHILE AN ILL-BRAINED FARMHAND IS STILL STOMPING ON EGGS.
NOW... **WE'RE** NOT DEAD. HOW DID ODIN GET OUT OF THIS PLACE AGAIN?

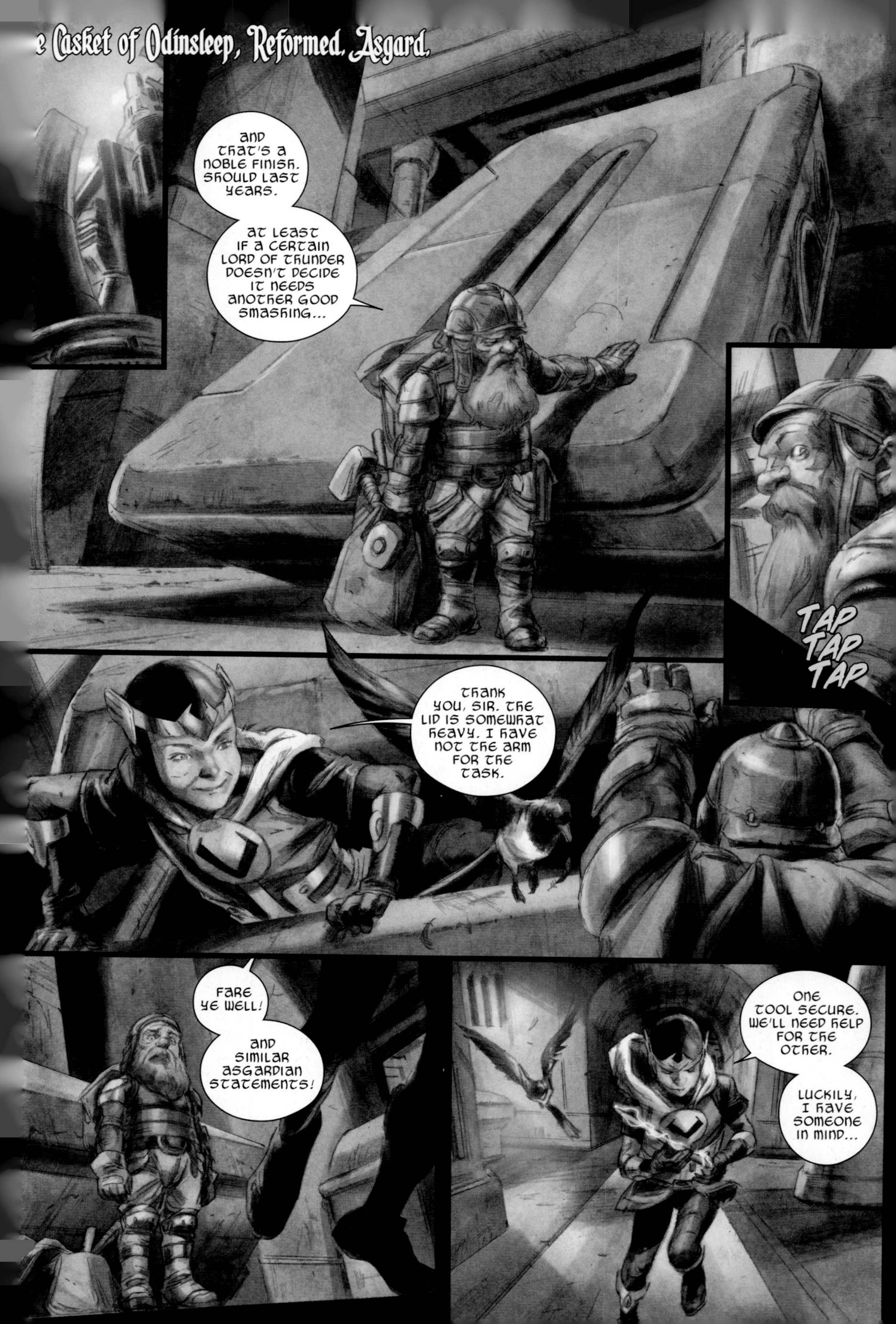
e Casket of Odinsleep, Reformed. Asgard.
AND THAT'S A NOBLE FINISH. SHOULD LAST YEARS.
AT LEAST IF A CERTAIN LORD OF THUNDER DOESN'T DECIDE IT NEEDS ANOTHER GOOD SMASHING...
TAP TAP TAP
THANK YOU, SIR. THE LID IS SOMEWHAT HEAVY. I HAVE NOT THE ARM FOR THE TASK.
FARE YE WELL!
AND SIMILAR ASGARDIAN STATEMENTS!
ONE TOOL SECURE. WE'LL NEED HELP FOR THE OTHER.
LUCKILY, I HAVE SOMEONE IN MIND...

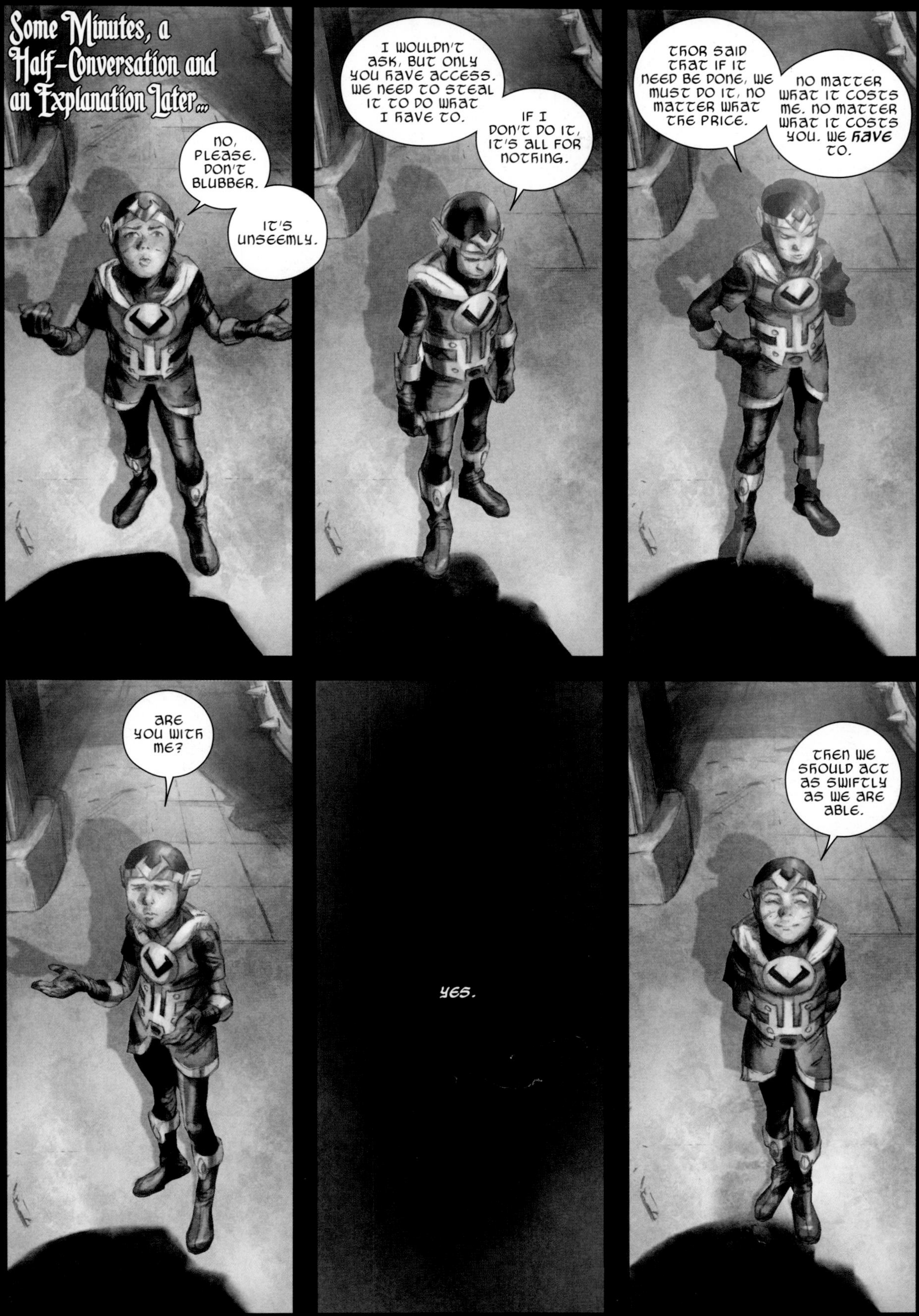
Some Minutes, a Half-Conversation and an Explanation Later...
NO, PLEASE. DON'T BLUBBER.
IT'S UNSEEMLY.
I WOULDN'T ASK, BUT ONLY YOU HAVE ACCESS. WE NEED TO STEAL IT TO DO WHAT I HAVE TO.
IF I DON'T DO IT, IT'S ALL FOR NOTHING.
THOR SAID THAT IF IT NEED BE DONE, WE MUST DO IT, NO MATTER WHAT THE PRICE.
NO MATTER WHAT IT COSTS ME. NO MATTER WHAT IT COSTS YOU. WE HAVE TO.
ARE YOU WITH ME?
YES.
THEN WE SHOULD ACT AS SWIFTLY AS WE ARE ABLE.

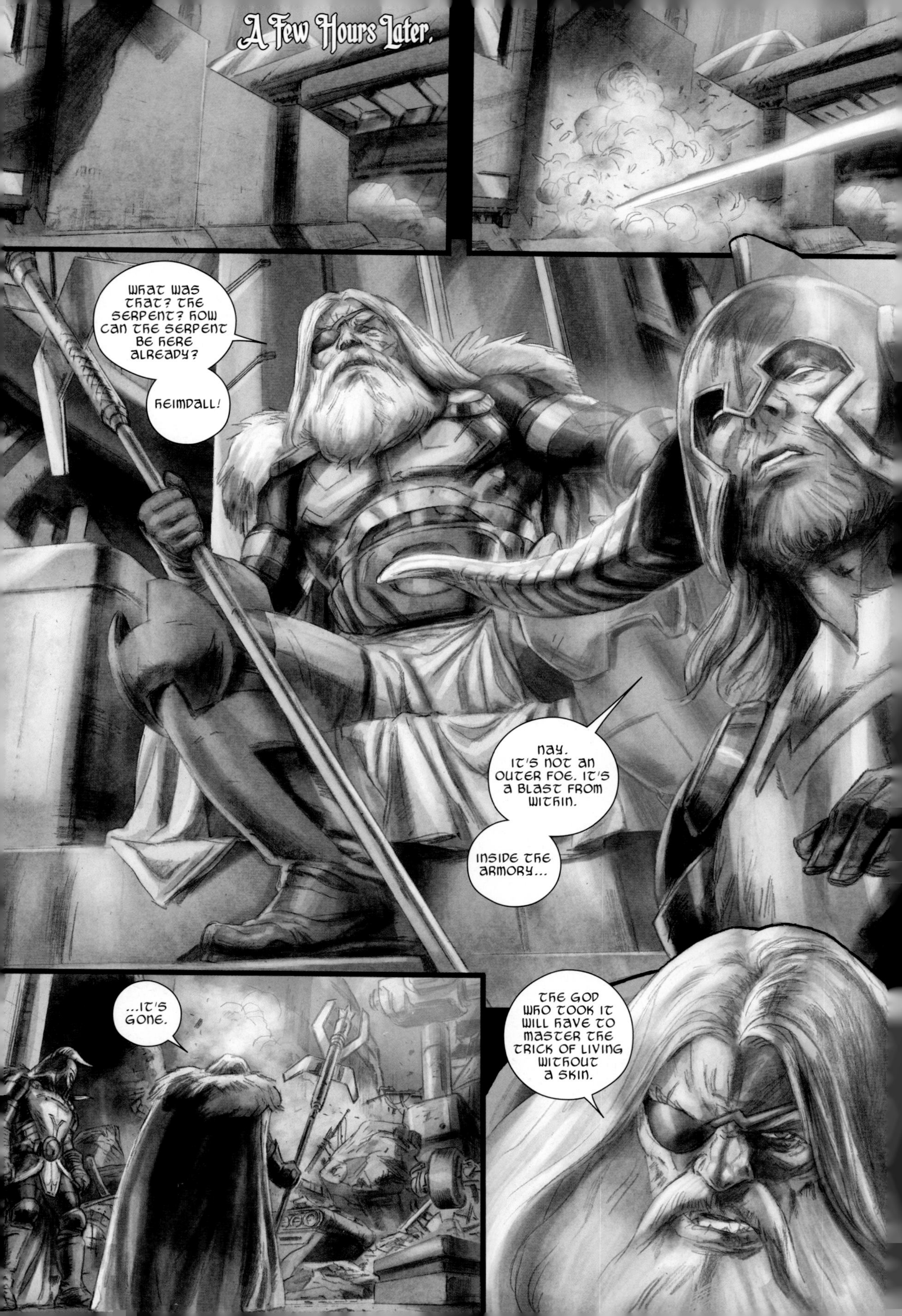
A Few Hours Later.
WHAT WAS THAT? THE SERPENT? HOW CAN THE SERPENT BE HERE ALREADY?
HEIMDALL!
NAY. IT'S NOT AN OUTER FOE. IT'S A BLAST FROM WITHIN.
INSIDE THE ARMORY...
...IT'S GONE.
THE GOD WHO TOOK IT WILL HAVE TO MASTER THE TRICK OF LIVING WITHOUT A SKIN.

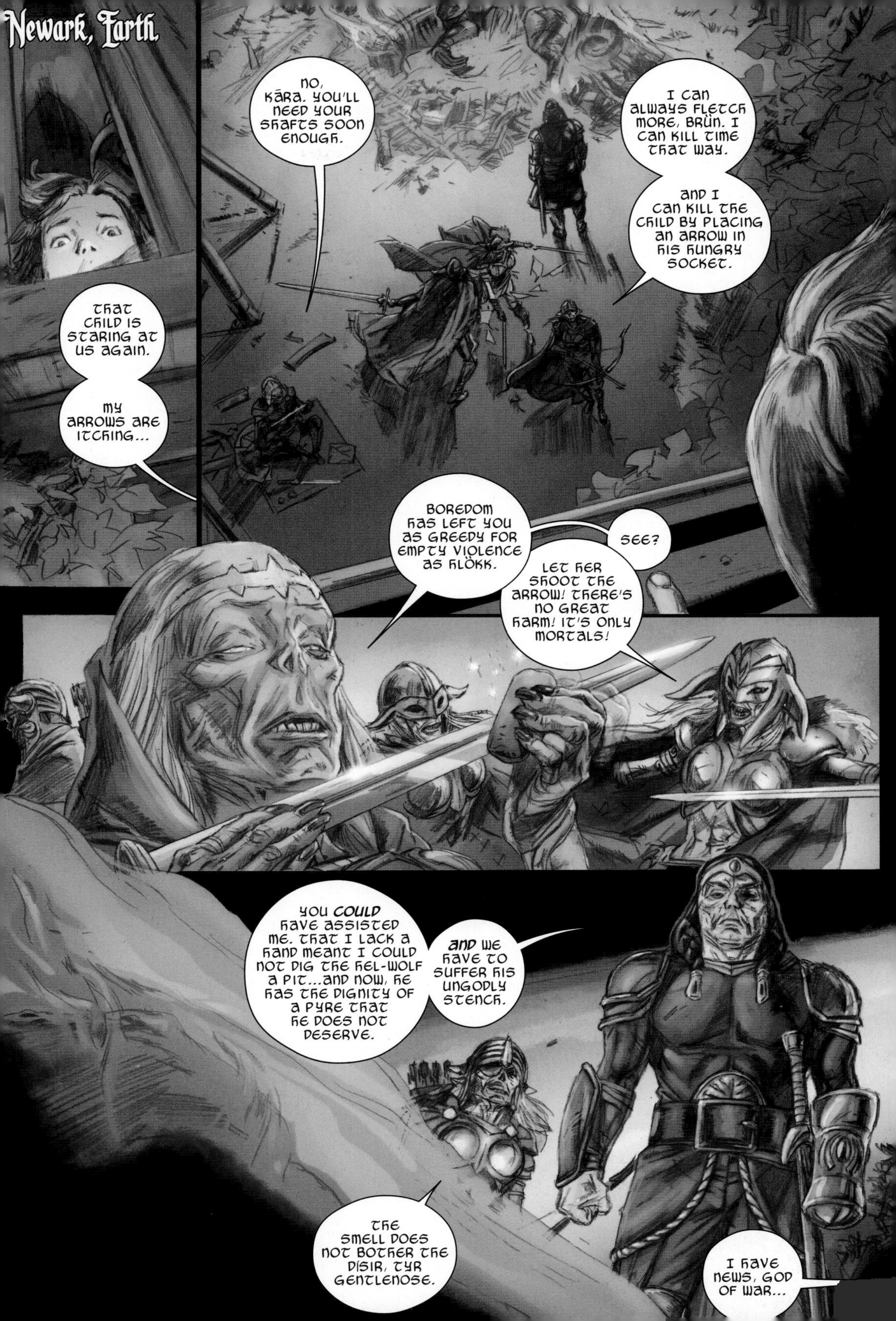
Newark, Earth.
That child is staring at us again.
My arrows are itching...
No, Kāra. You'll need your shafts soon enough.
I can always fletch more, Brün. I can kill time that way.
And I can kill the child by placing an arrow in his hungry socket.
Boredom has left you as greedy for empty violence as Hlökk.
See?
Let her shoot the arrow! There's no great harm! It's only mortals!
You could have assisted me. That I lack a hand meant I could not dig the Hel-wolf a pit...and now, he has the dignity of a pyre that he does not deserve.
And we have to suffer his ungodly stench.
The smell does not bother the Disir, Tyr Gentlenose.
I have news, God of war...

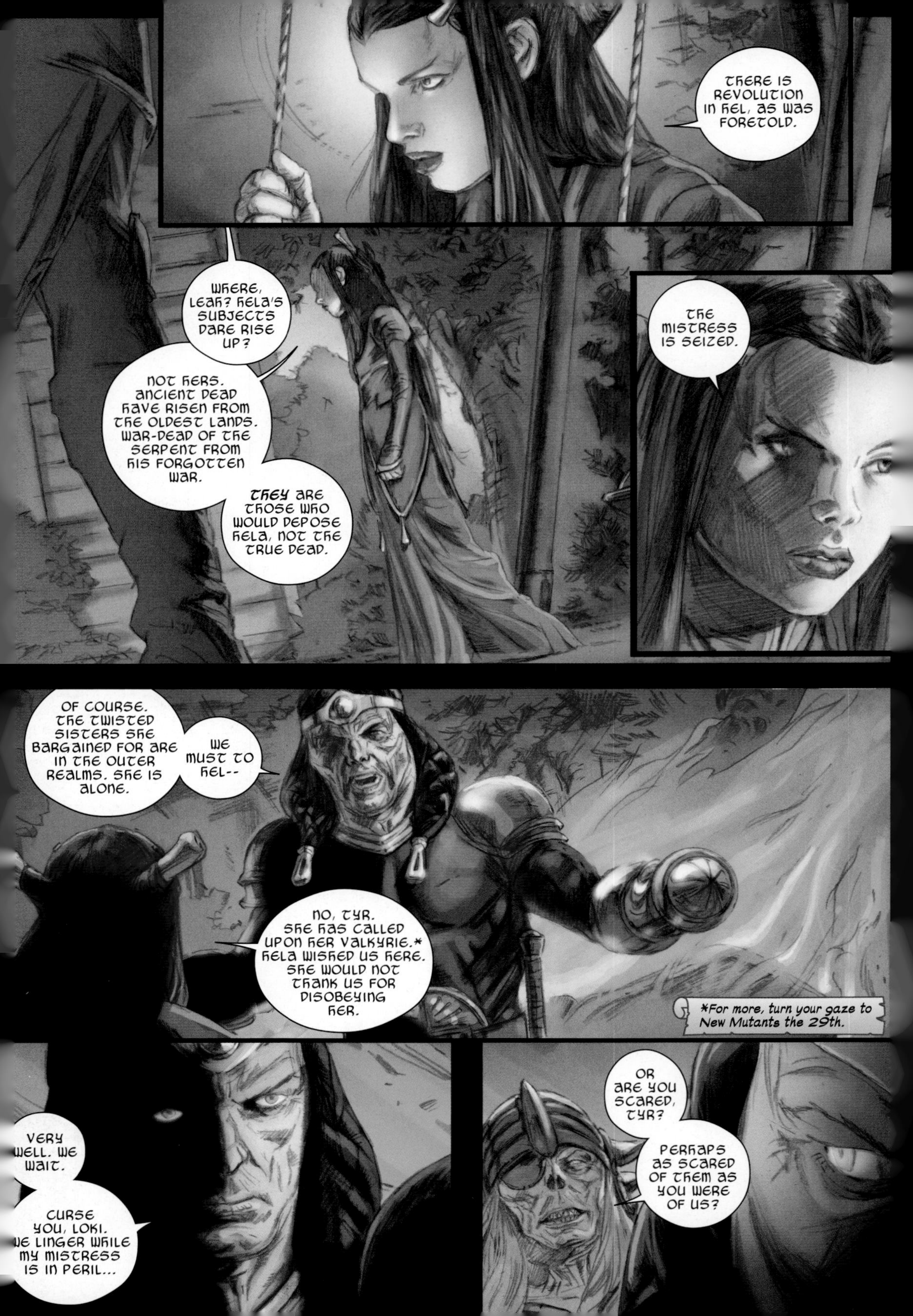

THERE IS REVOLUTION IN HEL, AS WAS FORETOLD.
WHERE, LEAH? HELA'S SUBJECTS DARE RISE UP?
NOT HERS. ANCIENT DEAD HAVE RISEN FROM THE OLDEST LANDS. WAR-DEAD OF THE SERPENT FROM HIS FORGOTTEN WAR.
THEY ARE THOSE WHO WOULD DEPOSE HELA, NOT THE TRUE DEAD.
THE MISTRESS IS SEIZED.
OF COURSE. THE TWISTED SISTERS SHE BARGAINED FOR ARE IN THE OUTER REALMS. SHE IS ALONE.
WE MUST TO HEL--
NO, TYR. SHE HAS CALLED UPON HER VALKYRIE.* HELA WISHED US HERE. SHE WOULD NOT THANK US FOR DISOBEYING HER.
*For more, turn your gaze to New Mutants the 29th.
VERY WELL. WE WAIT.
CURSE YOU, LOKI. WE LINGER WHILE MY MISTRESS IS IN PERIL...
OR ARE YOU SCARED, TYR?
PERHAPS AS SCARED OF THEM AS YOU WERE OF US?

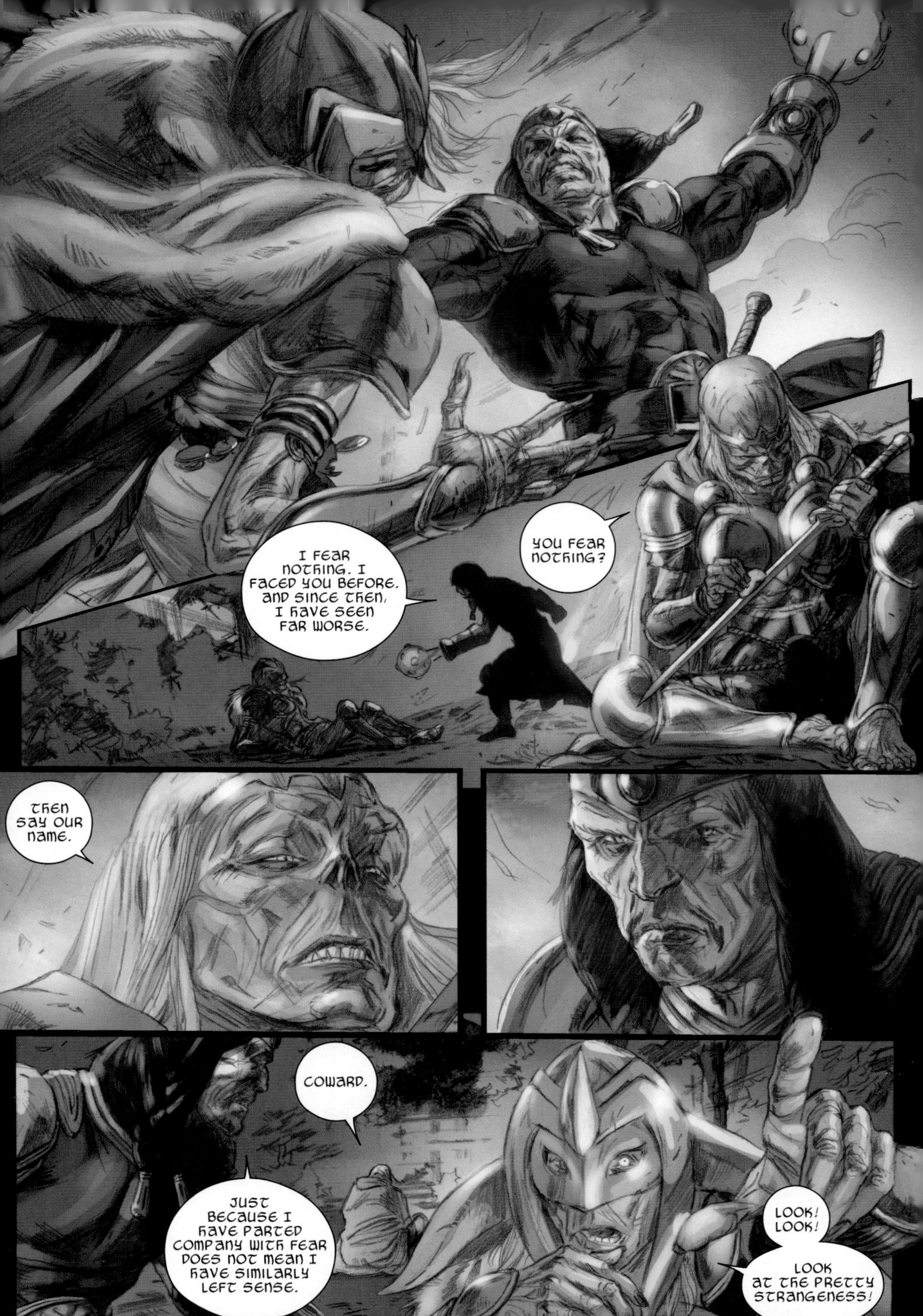
I FEAR NOTHING. I FACED YOU BEFORE. AND SINCE THEN, I HAVE SEEN FAR WORSE.
YOU FEAR NOTHING?
THEN SAY OUR NAME.
COWARD.
JUST BECAUSE I HAVE PARTED COMPANY WITH FEAR DOES NOT MEAN I HAVE SIMILARLY LEFT SENSE.
LOOK! LOOK!
LOOK AT THE PRETTY STRANGENESS!

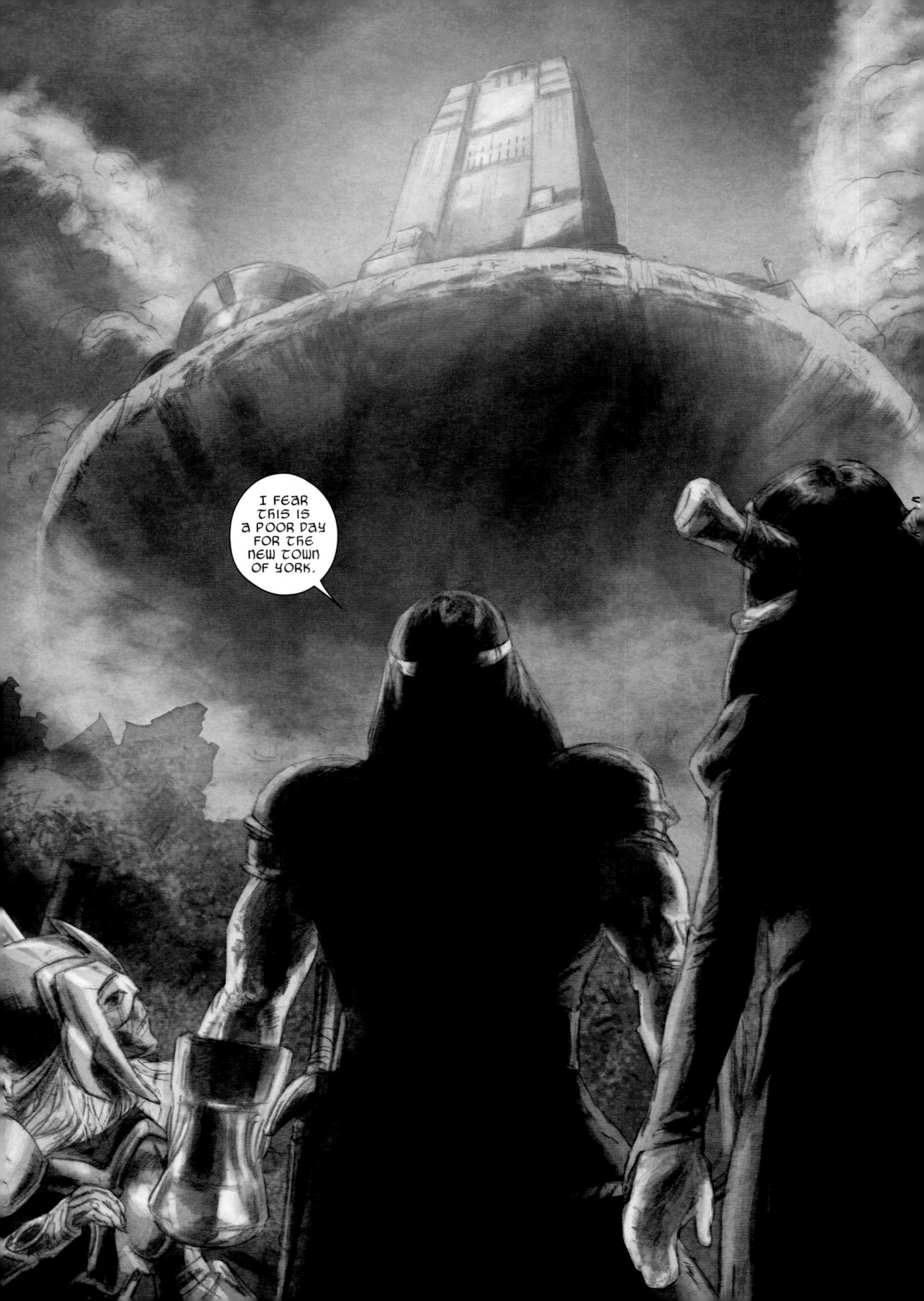
I FEAR THIS IS A POOR DAY FOR THE NEW TOWN OF YORK.

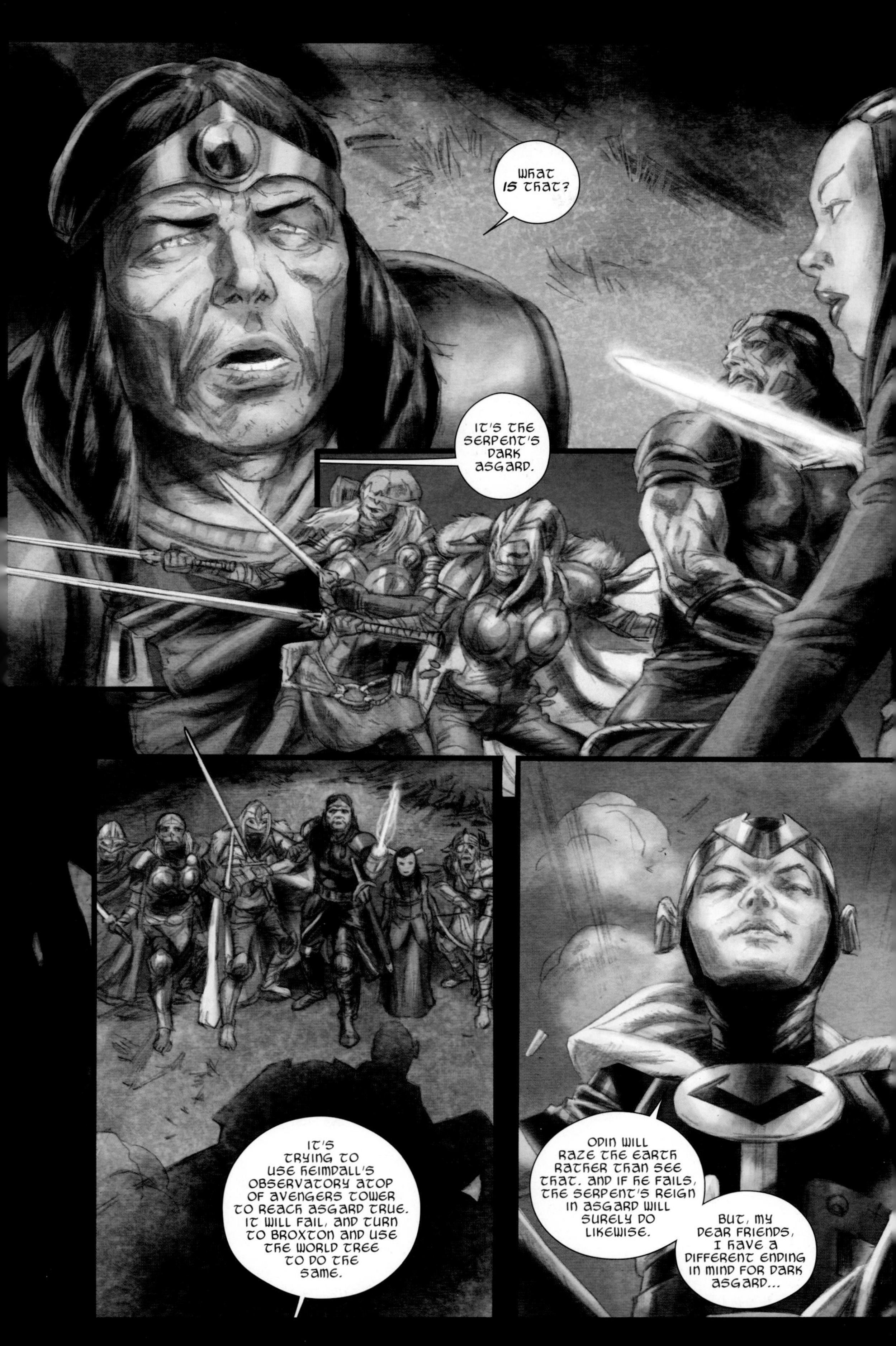
WHAT IS THAT?
IT'S THE SERPENT'S DARK ASGARD.
IT'S TRYING TO USE HEIMDALL'S OBSERVATORY ATOP OF AVENGERS TOWER TO REACH ASGARD TRUE. IT WILL FAIL, AND TURN TO BROXTON AND USE THE WORLD TREE TO DO THE SAME.
ODIN WILL RAZE THE EARTH RATHER THAN SEE THAT. AND IF HE FAILS, THE SERPENT'S REIGN IN ASGARD WILL SURELY DO LIKEWISE.
BUT, MY DEAR FRIENDS, I HAVE A DIFFERENT ENDING IN MIND FOR DARK ASGARD...

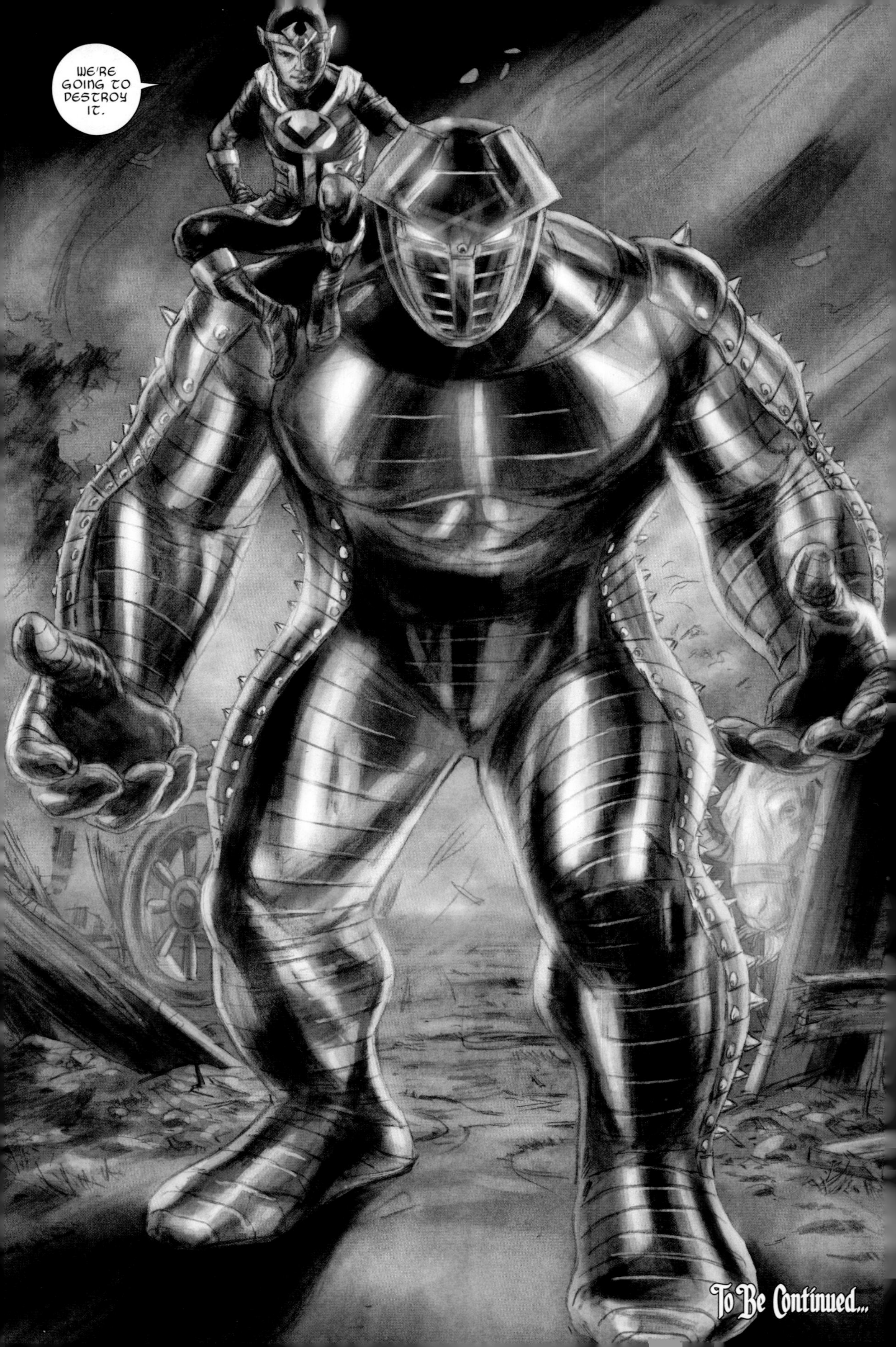
WE'RE GOING TO DESTROY IT.
To Be Continued...

THOR

It was the end of times. Asgard had fallen at last.

Writer: **DANA PERKINS**   Designer: **SPRING HOTELING**

With the cycle fashioned by Those Who Sit Above In Shadow broken, the final battle — the ultimate Ragnarok — had occurred, and the denizens of the Golden Realm were no more. Thor, the last Lord of Asgard, had sailed off into sweet oblivion, adrift in such things as dreams are made of.

But even the slumber of the gods must end, especially when events are set in motion by dark forces intent on disturbing the sleep of the just. Such was the case when Latveria's imprisoned ruler, Victor Von Doom, saw opportunity in the form of Thor's mighty hammer Mjolnir as it rent the fabric of the Hell in which Doom was imprisoned. Absorbing some of the essence of Thor and the Asgardians as they fell in battle, Doom flung himself in the hammer's wake as it passed him on its post-Ragnarok flight throughout the myriad dimensions. Although unable to grasp the mystic mallet in his effort to possess it, Doom nonetheless was able to breach his infernal prison and return to Earth.

Meanwhile, Mjolnir had landed far from the fields it knew: in the plains of Oklahoma, to be precise. While covert U.S. forces tried to excavate the weapon, Doom again attempted to gain the power of the Thunder God. After a battle between an army of Doombots and the Fantastic Four, Doom himself arrived. Grasping the handle of the storm hammer, Doom made an unsuccessful bid to raise the weapon aloft. At his contact, however, eldritch energies from Mjolnir shot forth to the heavens and lit up the night for miles around. This supernatural spotlight served as a beacon for a person with the initials D. B. on his suitcase tag.

At this mystery man's touch, both he and the hammer vanished in an explosion of light and thunder.

Thus, even at the end of times, the story would begin anew.

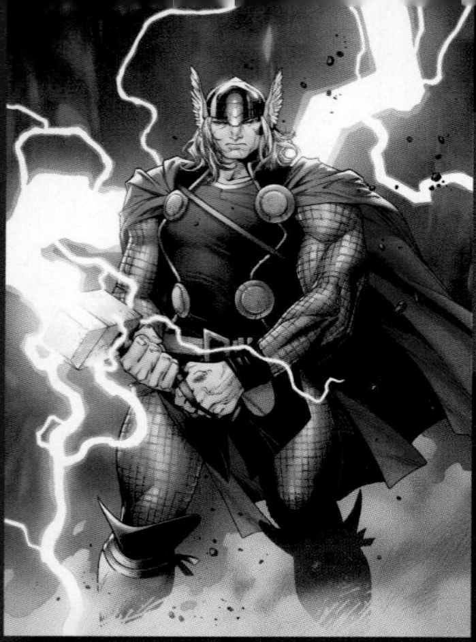

During his spiritual sojourn within the Void, Thor encountered the spirit of the long-absent Dr. Donald Blake. The Thunder God's former alter ego inspired him that he was still needed — and that the Asgardians lived on in the hearts and souls of mortals. Armed once more with Mjolnir, Thor fought his way through a host of demons that sought to keep him from returning to the mortal plane; newly garbed and empowered with the Odinforce, he returned to Earth.

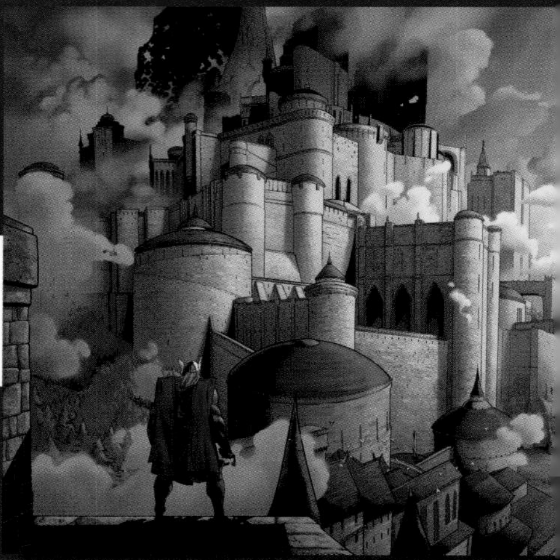

After setting up residence in the town of Broxton, Oklahoma, as Blake, Thor traveled miles into the arid flatland. Once there, he used his incredible power to open up a gateway between the worlds and brought the city of Asgard to settle upon the desert plains.

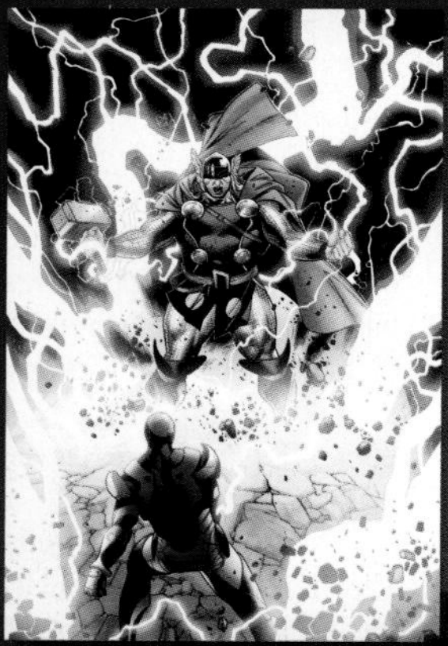

After sorting out the legalities of such actions, including raising Asgard so it remained hovering above the ground, Thor walked the city's abandoned halls. The echoes of his lonely footfalls inspired him to seek out the other Asgardians. His initial quest brought him to New Orleans, where he encountered his former ally Iron Man. After an impassioned exchange both verbal and physical, a battered Tony Stark suggested Asgard be granted diplomatic immunity.

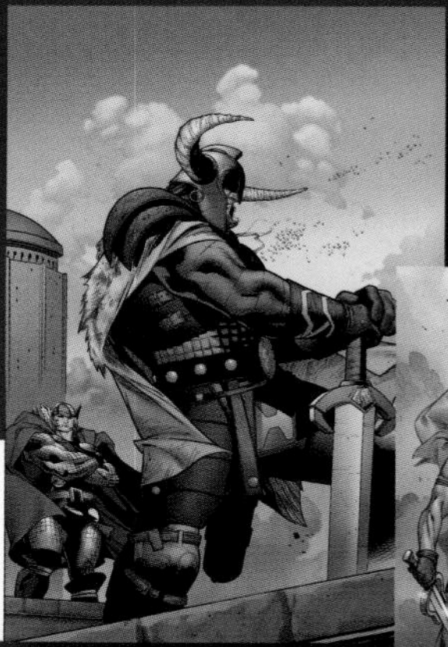

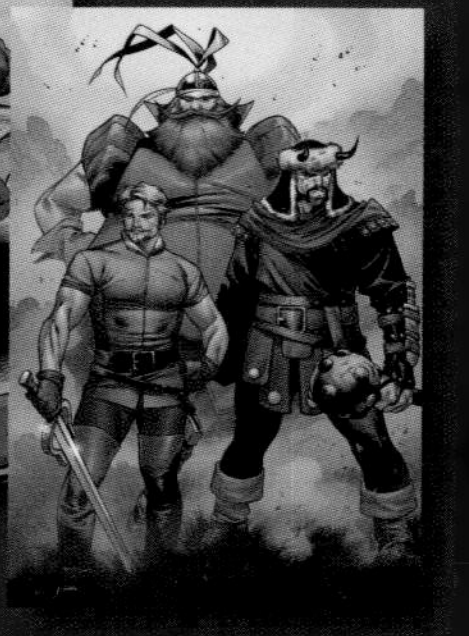

After Stark departed, Thor found the mortal host of Heimdall, faithful guardian of Bifrost, and brought forth his Asgardian aspect. From that point on, the hosts of Asgard were quickly reinstated to their former glory — beginning with the Warriors Three.

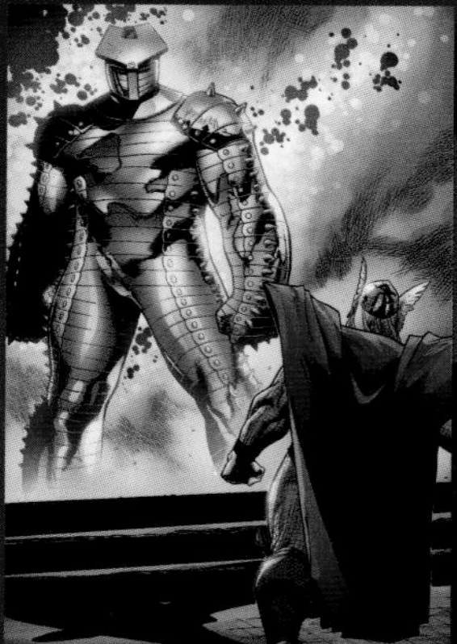

Soon after, Heimdall informed Thor of a gathering darkness in the desert between Nevada and New Mexico. Flying to an abandoned fallout bunker, Thor found dozens of human hosts who had been kidnapped from throughout the world by the Asgardian engine of destruction known as the Destroyer. Among them was a beautiful, raven-tressed young woman who claimed she knew Thor.

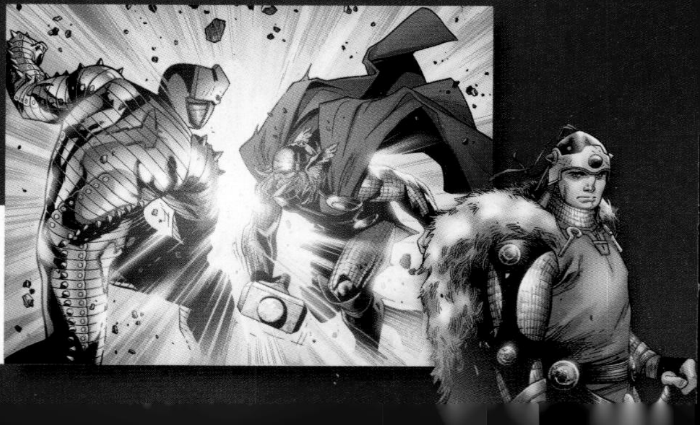

After Thor defeated the Destroyer with a lightning blast that freed the Asgardians, the force behind the Destroyer armor was revealed: Balder the Brave. Balder told Thor it was his anger at failing to prevent Ragnarok that had drawn him into the armor

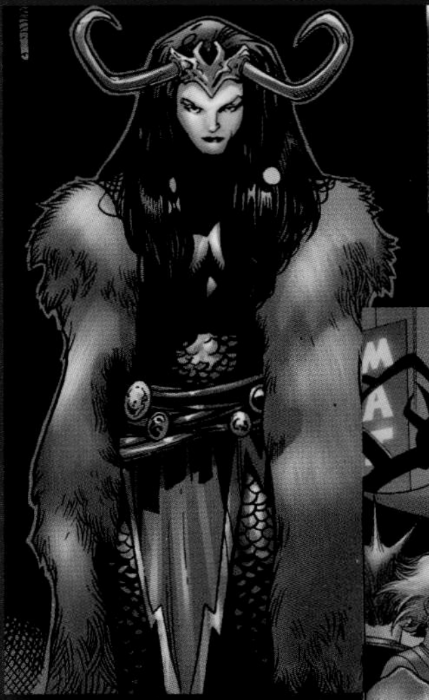

Along with Balder, there was another surprise awaiting Thor within the confines of that desert bunker. The dark-haired beauty who claimed to know Thor was not Sif as he had expected. It was his foster brother, Loki, returned to life in the body of a woman! After Loki insisted this was a new start for all of them, and that she was trustworthy, Thor reluctantly granted his brother a chance to prove him — or rather — *her*self.

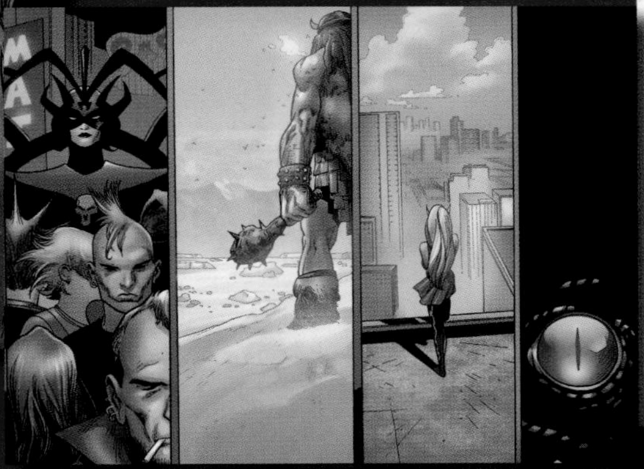

Loki, alas, showed her true colors almost immediately. While Thor debated with the essence of Donald Blake regarding returning the souls of all the departed Asgardians — including Odin, who Thor feared might desire to stay Asgard's new course — Loki reminisced on a plan he had devised with Doctor Doom. The first layer of an increasingly intricate plot would cause the return of such beings as Frost Giants, Trolls, and evil-natured Asgardians such as Hela and the Enchantress.

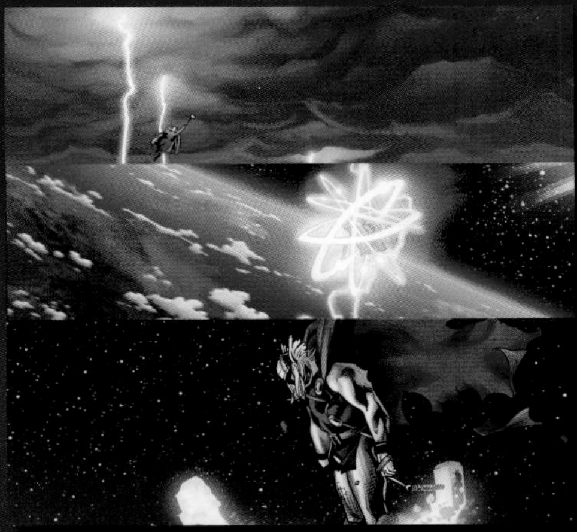

With an explosion of sheer power on the cosmic scale, Thor blanketed Earth with divine lightning. All the trapped Asgardians were freed, except for those unwilling or unable to be called back — such as Odin and Sif.

The expenditure of such energy depleted Thor's power, and he was placed within the Odincasket so he could replenish his strength via the Odinsleep.

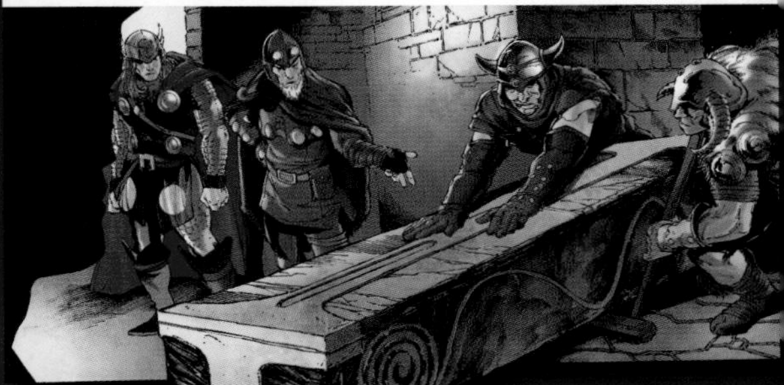

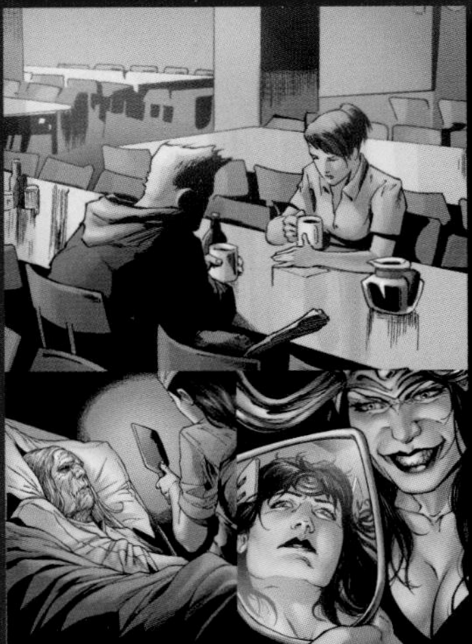

Once Thor entered this place between life and death, Don Blake materialized and traveled to New York City to see Dr. Jane Foster. Jane had once shared a bond with Sif that was similar to his link with Thor, and Blake hoped Jane could aid him in his search for the missing goddess. There, he encountered one of Dr. Foster's patients: a frail old woman who had been made to host Sif's spirit so Loki could use the goddess' body as his own.

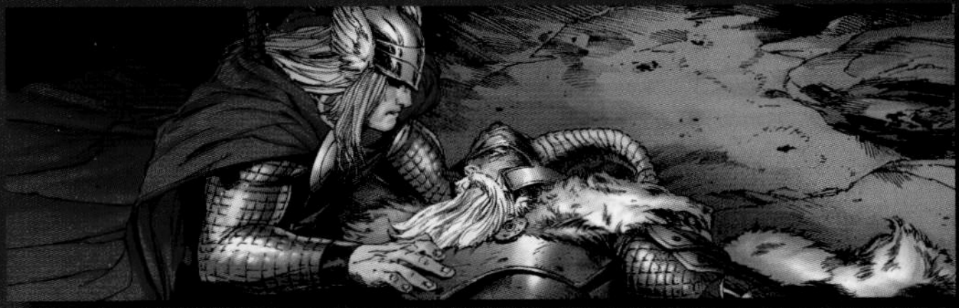

While wandering this Limbo-like realm, Thor found Odin engaged in eternal battle with Surtur. Each day, a wounded Surtur would flee while Odin would die from his wounds, only to be born again the next day. Odin also informed Thor of his awareness of his son's reluctance to call him back from the dead.

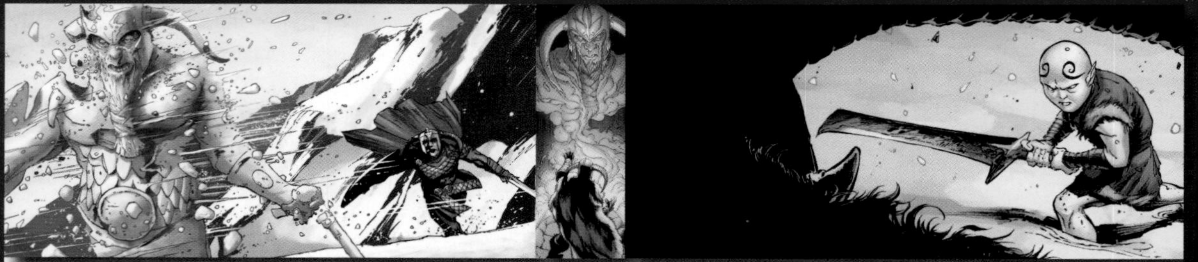

Over Thor's protests, Odin told a tale of Asgard from long ago in which a mysterious and powerful sorcerer had turned Thor's grandfather, King Bor, to living snow. Odin had chosen to ignore Bor's pleas for help so he could lead the Asgardians without paternal interference. Odin was then cursed by what he believed to be Bor's spirit, who compelled him to adopt the son of an enemy slain by his own hand: Loki Laufeyson.

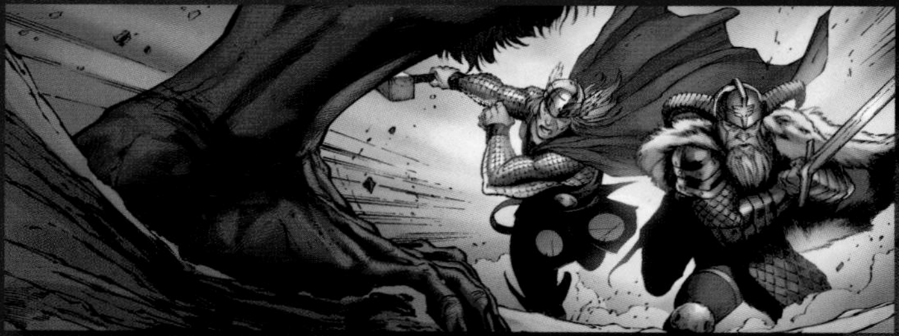

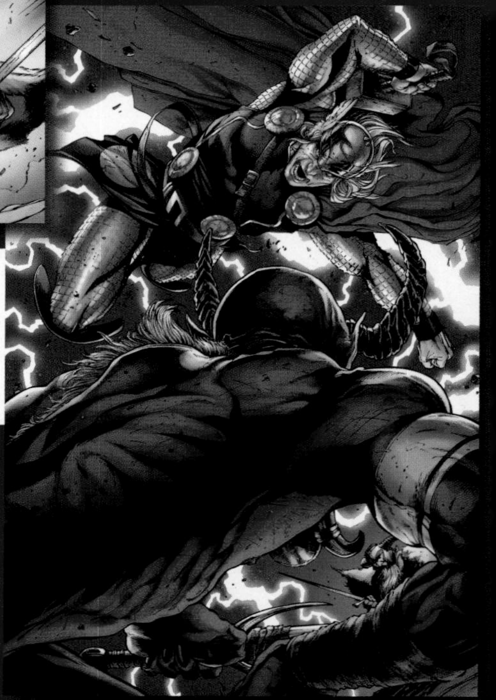

Armed with this knowledge, Thor offered to return Odin to the land of the living. Although thankful, Odin refused, resolute in keeping Surtur from escaping into the world once more. Before returning home, Thor fought alongside Odin. Together, father and son vanquished the fire demon. For one day, at least, Odin did not have to experience death.

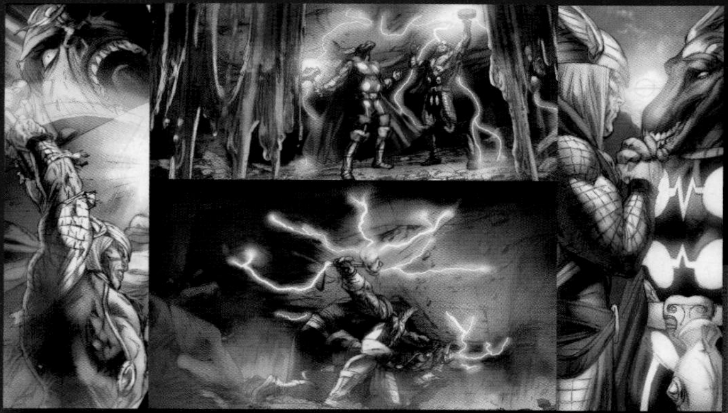

Upon waking, Thor emerged from the Odincasket and announced that all the Asgardians who could have been brought back had returned, and that it was time to begin building Asgard's future. This noble goal was put to an immediate test by the shape-shifting Skrulls' invasion of Earth. Aligned with his oath brother, Beta Ray Bill, Thor led the Asgardians to victory in battle against the alien attackers.

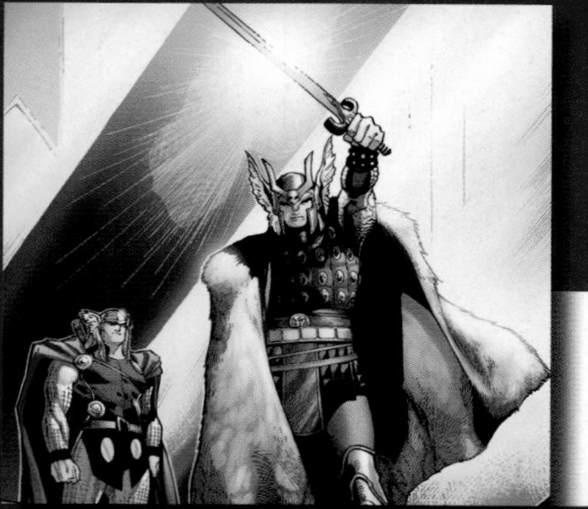

Meanwhile, the Mistress of Mischief had been up to her old tricks by sowing seeds of discord among the Asgardians. At Loki's insistence, Balder confronted Thor about the truth of his heritage — and learned he, too, was Odin's son. This news prompted a coronation at which Balder was crowned a prince of Asgard.

The duplicity of the Trickster had never contrasted greater with the Thunder God's nobility than on the evening of the first anniversary of Captain America's death. While Loki stirred the proverbial hornets' nest by telling Balder the Asgardians' adventurous natures were being held in check by Thor's desire to control, Thor summoned forth the spirit of the Sentinel of Liberty in New York City. During their meeting, Thor told Cap that while he had lived many ages and the life spans of many men, the greatest honor he had known had been fighting by Cap's side and calling him his friend.

After honoring Cap with a worldwide minute of silence, Thor returned to Asgard. Due to Loki's meddling, Balder confronted Thor about the unrest in Asgard. The Trickster was just getting started, however, and next paid a visit to her daughter Hela in Las Vegas. Hela helped Loki travel to the distant past, where it was revealed that Loki had played the part of the enchanter who had turned Bor into snow. Also, it was Loki — disguised as Bor's spirit — who had commanded Odin to take the son of a king killed by him in battle to make amends for not returning Bor to the living. After further time travel, Loki then met with his younger self and gave instructions on how to act in front of Odin once his father Laufey was killed.

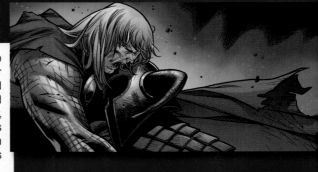

The pieces of her grand plan now in place, Loki returned to the present and summoned forth Bor from the snow. Bor materialized in modern-day New York, his senses hampered by a spell cast by Loki that caused all to appear and sound distorted and monstrous in his eyes. Alerted by Jane Foster, Thor engaged Bor in a tremendous battle that resulted in Bor's death and the breaking of Mjolnir. Loki timed his arrival with Balder so they came upon the scene too late to stop Thor; as such, Thor was exiled for killing the first lord of Asgard.

Upon Thor's exile, Balder was proclaimed king. At Loki's urging, Balder met with Dr. Doom. The villain invited the Asgardians to take up residence in Latveria, a clime more suited to them. Balder accepted. Among the relocated Asgardians was Bill, an Oklahoman romantically involved with the lovely goddess Kelda.

Meanwhile, as Thor began his exile, Jane Foster learned the true state of Sif's spirit and informed Thor. The sorcerer Dr. Strange helped Thor repair Mjolnir using part of the Thunder God's own essence; now, the two are tied together more closely than ever.

Thor made it to the hospital in time to call forth Sif before her aged human host expired. Thor and Sif returned to Oklahoma and joined the Warriors Three, who had exiled themselves to remain with Thor.

Meanwhile, in Latveria, Loki reassumed his old male form, and he and Doom discussed their insidious plans. After Doom sent several Doombots — refitted to hide their true origin — to assassinate Don Blake, Loki provided Doom with a hapless Asgardian warrior so he could begin his experiments on Asgardians via vivisection to discover what provided them with their godly essence.

Bill the Oklahoman learned of their sinister stratagems and attempted to warn King Balder, but not before a group of disloyal Asgardians intercepted him and wounded him unto death. Balder rode up in time to learn of the wicked plan, and he defeated Loki's henchmen. Before he died, Bill saved Balder from one of the Trickster's minions and asked Balder to tell Kelda of his love for her. Learning of Bill's death, Kelda sought vengeance against Latveria's despot. Upon entering Doom's laboratory, Kelda was caught up in the grip of a familiar, massive armored being. As she struggled in vain, Doom explained to her that he would use her divine energies for his own wicked purpose — whereupon her heart was torn out of her body.

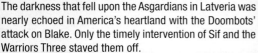

The darkness that fell upon the Asgardians in Latveria was nearly echoed in America's heartland with the Doombots' attack on Blake. Only the timely intervention of Sif and the Warriors Three staved them off.

After Heimdall sounded the Gjallerhorn to summon the Asgardians to war, Balder led his forces against Castle Doom. Doom sent his Asgardian abominations, vivisected cyborg monstrosities, against their former comrades and kin. While a horrified Balder and his host battled the monsters, Thor arrived and confronted Doom, who threw Kelda's body down from the stronghold's ramparts. As the appalled warriors looked upon the dead goddess, Loki informed them he could revive her if her heart was returned to her body in time.

As the battle continued, a lightning blast by Thor charged a Destroyer battle suit — the armored figure that had caught Kelda in its unbreakable grip. Kelda's attack on Doom had not fully energized the monstrosity; Thor's lightning granted it full power. Climbing into the armor, Doom attacked Thor. At the same time, Balder retrieved Kelda's heart and destroyed the remaining Asgardian experiments held in stasis. As Thor defeated Doom, who magically disappeared before the Thunder God could land his final blow, Kelda was revived — although still heartbroken due to Bill's death.

Thor and the Asgardians returned to Broxton and Asgard, respectively, only to learn of more disastrous news. For some time, Loki had been influencing Norman Osborn, director of the peacekeeping task force H.A.M.M.E.R., convincing him Asgard was a potential threat that did not belong in the United States. Using Volstagg as a scapegoat, Loki and Osborn sent a group of super villains against the adventuring Asgardian, which caused a deadly explosion that destroyed a sports stadium and killed hundreds of spectators — setting the stage for Osborn's siege of Asgard. Although not at fault, Volstagg was blamed for the destruction; he made his way back to Broxton, where he gave himself up to local police.

This news was only the first herald of disaster, for the Asgardian seer Knut then prophesied Asgard's fall on the morrow. Ever the mischief-maker, Loki dismissed Knut's prophecy and later killed the aged seer. To prevent the ever-vigilant Heimdall from giving warning, Loki magically transferred Heimdall's chambers to the depths of Asgard. After much effort, Heimdall made his way to the surface — but not in time to warn Balder of the impending siege, which had begun with the super-powerful Sentry's destruction of Heimdall's watchtower.

Osborn's dogs of war had been loosed — but just when things looked their darkest, the Asgardians found themselves aided by a group of assembled heroes including Nick Fury, Iron Man and the recently returned Captain America.

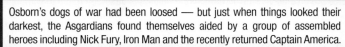

With the madness of war surrounding them, Loki — without revealing his whole part in the affair — stated Thor was not truly at fault for killing Bor, as sorcery had been at work distorting reality. As victory slipped from his grasp, Osborn commanded the Sentry to lay waste to all Asgard. With a streak of gold, the home of the gods had fallen once more.

Without Osborn to keep him in check, the Sentry reverted to his dark incarnation, the Void. Even Loki was taken aback at the carnage surrounding him, and he sacrificed himself in combat with the Void. With Osborn's forces defeated — among them the clone of Thor, Ragnarok, who was buried when Asgard fell — the Thunder God delivered the final blow and sent the Void to oblivion.

With sorrow at the loss of a once-great hero who had lost his way, Thor gently delivered the Sentry's body into the sun.

In the aftermath of the Siege of Asgard, Balder ended Thor's exile and offered him the kingship once more. Thor refused. With the city's reconstruction under way, the Thor clone was discovered among the ruins. Thor destroyed Ragnarok in battle, thus erasing a lingering taint from the super-hero Civil War. With this dark chapter in the Book of the Nine Worlds finished, a new Heroic Age dawned upon Thor and his people. Along with his closest companions, Thor appeared before the recently reformed Avengers to give thanks for their help, and proclaimed Asgard and Earth to be eternal allies. As a symbol of this newly forged alliance, Heimdall's watchtower was placed atop Avengers Tower.

And as a last reassurance, Thor announced that if the call "Avengers Assemble!" rang forth, he would answer.

Yet as the casualties from the Siege were burned on funeral pyres, a warning from Hela cast a somber pall over Asgard. She spoke of a dreadful evil that had returned from ancient times: the Dísir, the cursed Valkyries of Bor, who feast upon the souls of the Asgardian dead.

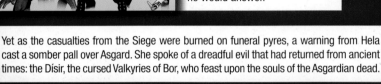

Since the displacement of Asgard, Asgardian souls had been made to wander; such homeless souls were in danger of ultimate annihilation at the hands of the Dísir. Due to the machinations of Loki, Mephisto had granted to Hela a region in his domain over which she could rule the dead. But the Dísir had approached the ever-untrustworthy Mephisto and had been granted access to Hela's dominion, thus endangering the Asgardian spirits.

Determined to deliver the threatened souls from this evil, Thor and the war god Tyr were transported to Hela's infernal realm. Upon arriving, Tyr remained with Hela to command her troops, while Thor made his way through Hell to find a weapon suitable for dealing with the Dísir: the sword Eir-Gram. After many trials, Thor arrived at Mephisto's throne and found Eir-Gram locked in stone. Thor called out to the Dísir, and three answered his summons. After freeing the sword, Thor slew them — but not before one of them admitted to being an oath breaker, which resulted in the death of all the Dísir. Hela's realm and the Asgardian dead were saved.

But an even greater threat would soon emerge: the World Eaters. For with the absence of Asgard from its place atop the Nine Worlds, a void has been created that must be filled, and the earthbound Asgard is overrun with those surviving denizens of the remaining Nine Worlds — all of which have fallen to the World Eaters.

Faced with foes more ruthless than any before encountered, it will take the most drastic actions of all — including the return of Loki and Odin — to prepare Thor and his people for the unimaginable challenge that lies before them. But no matter the outcome, one thing is ordained: Thor and the Asgardians will face it with unmatched courage and the promise of future songs of glory in their hearts. VERILY!

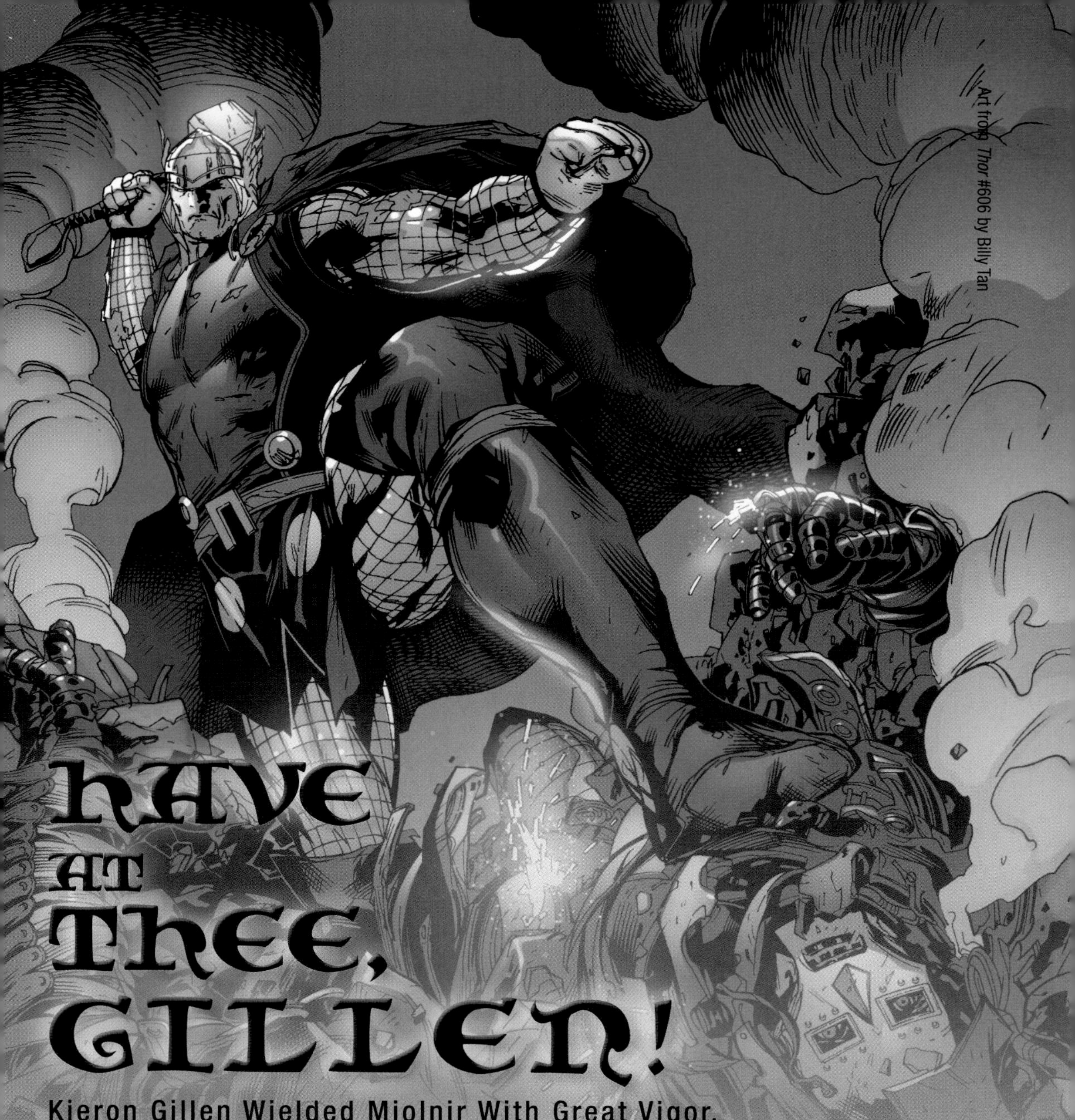

Art from *Thor* #606 by Billy Tan

HAVE AT THEE, GILLEN!

Kieron Gillen Wielded Mjolnir With Great Vigor. We Take A Look Back — And Forward — With The Worthy Writer.

BY JESS HARROLD DESIGN BY SPRING HOTELING

WHEN fan-favorite writer J. Michael Straczynski took his leave from a Thor title he had revitalized, it required a brave man to step into the Thunder God's knee-high, leather-strap boots. Step forward British writer and music and videogame journalist Kieron Gillen. Initially slated as a fill-in writer, Kieron ultimately delivered a popular and critically acclaimed run that lasted for almost a year, setting the scene nicely for his friend Matt Fraction to take over. With Kieron now juggling Uncanny X-Men with Generation Hope, you'd be forgiven for thinking he'd abandoned the Hallowed Halls for Utopia. While you can take the boy out of Asgard, you can't take Asgard out of the boy. The increasingly busy writer is all set to scratch his mythological itch once more — and revive a classic Marvel title, to boot — with Journey Into Mystery. Spotlight dragged Kieron away from his mounting pile of scripts and asked him to bring the thunder. And verily, he doth bring it.

SPOTLIGHT: You took over _Thor_ after one of its most revered runs in years, by one of comics' most popular writers, in the lead-up to the most high-profile Asgard storyline of all time. So, no pressure, right?

KIERON: After a few days of panicked vomiting and crying, I got over it. Mostly.

SPOTLIGHT: And then how did you feel? Daunted? Inspired? All a-tingle?

KIERON: I presumed my appointment was due to a clerical error deep in the machinery of Marvel that they'd eventually realize. They'd then drag me out, stick me in a pillory and throw sodden back issues at my head. I would be reduced to a papier-mâché statue that would be hoisted up before the entryway to the Marvel offices, as a warning to all and sundry. While I was intimidated, in some perverse way, it almost helped that it was such a big, revered run that had ended so abruptly. In a typical piece of hilariously melodramatic British pessimism, I went into it assuming that no matter what I did, people would hate me just because I wasn't J. Michael Straczynski. And that actually totally frees you. You don't need to worry about whether anyone is going to like it or not. You just worry about the story, and making it as good as you can. And after you get over the flicker of intimidation, you can't help but grin. Thor and his supporting cast are fantastic characters. And I got to sprinkle a little Doctor Doom over the top, just for taste.

SPOTLIGHT: And — the destruction of Asgard on your watch aside — the Thunder God was in safe hands. Your initial fill-in really turned into the little _Thor_ run that could, right?

KIERON: It just wouldn't stop. It was originally only going to be five issues. Then six. Then they added

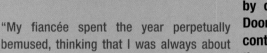

"My fiancée spent the year perpetually bemused, thinking that I was always about to finish this job which never seemed to actually end."

— Writer Kieron Gillen on his year-long "fill-in" run on _Thor._

the tie-in issue _Siege: Loki_, which basically means seven. And then we added a _Siege_ aftermath to tie up a few plots for Matt. Then, after the _Thor_ office had another look at Pascqual Ferry's deadlines, they figured it would be safer if I did another short arc. Add the _New Mutants_ issue I did to tie into _Siege_, which uses Tyr and the Valkyries, and that's thirteen issues. My fiancée spent the year perpetually bemused, thinking that I was always about to finish this job which never seemed to actually end. That's the other thing that made it less nerve-wracking, actually. At any one moment, what I had to concentrate upon was relatively limited. And one of the things I'm most pleased about is that, despite the fact it did expand, the whole thirteen issues absolutely have their own closed themes: the fall and rise of Tyr; Balder facing the duties of kingship; Kelda's grief for Bill; and, of course, the duplicity of Loki cascading toward his death. I don't think it feels like something I was constantly expanding. Also, on a really basic level, I'm happy it sold as well as it did. Capitalism wins!

SPOTLIGHT: You made the transition pretty seamless, building on what had come before, by developing Loki and Doom's relationship, and continuing Kelda's story throughout your run. Was that sense of continuity particularly important to you on this project?

KIERON: It's an ongoing book. I wanted it to absolutely feel like that. I knew what Matt was planning to do. I knew where JMS had left us. With those two landmarks on the terrain, I wanted to plot a route between the two that resolved JMS' directions while preparing the ground for Matt's adventures. Those plots had so much energy left in them that I'd have felt like a bad caretaker of _Thor_ without having resolved them. Kelda storming off furiously in the last of JMS' issues is something that needed to be continued. There was so much

Writer Kieron Gillen

momentum there, I'd have felt terrible to ignore it. And you try and leave some toys for the writers after you. Reintroducing Tyr was fun, and I'm enjoying seeing Matt play with him, too.

"...Loki seems to have an emotional need for what he does. Mephisto's just working his way up and down the list of deadly sins, like a tasting menu."
— Gillen comparing Loki and Mephisto.

SPOTLIGHT: You really delivered some major character development with those two characters, as well as Loki and Balder, particularly when "Stormin'" Norman Osborn came a-calling. Your book was very much the Asgardian face of *Siege*. The devastation of that story was a great backdrop for you to show the very human qualities of these gods.

KIERON: Absolutely. Since Thor was so involved in the main crossover, I thought it had the opportunity to focus on the supporting cast and how they respond to this tragedy. It's the invasion of Asgard, and *Thor* became the book where you got to see how the Asgardians actually felt about it. The theme beneath it all was basically how all the cast feel they compare to Thor. Thor's the gold standard for Asgardians, in many ways. The arc showed how they all ended up either living up to that paragon or not. That's one reason why I brought Ragnarok in and had him fight Volstagg. On one hand, you've got someone with all the power of Thor and none of the heart. On the other, you've got someone who's nothing but heart. In the end, despite the beating he took, Volstagg is far truer to what really matters than Ragnarok with all his power.

SPOTLIGHT: And you got to crush that dastardly Thor clone, which must have been fun.

KIERON: The job needed doing. *Siege* was the end of the last five years of the larger story of the Marvel Universe, and Ragnarok is one of the biggest symbols of the era. Thor smashing Ragnarok was him bringing the hammer down on everything he represented, as hard as he can. The time for things like him was definitely over.

SPOTLIGHT: Post-*Siege*, you delivered a storyline that not only had two of Marvel's best villains, Mephisto and Hela, plotting and counter-plotting against each other courtesy of the machinations of a third, Loki, but also introduced some devastating new baddies, right out of myth: the god-soul-eating Dísir. They're a great addition to Thor's rogues' gallery, and one we will surely see again.

KIERON: Hopefully. I suspect they're thinking "hopefully," too. Ending up on the ring finger of Mephisto in eternal torment has got to be the sort of thing ladies like the Dísir would want to get out of as soon as possible. They were sort of inspired by necessity. I wanted something to threaten the dead Asgardians in *Siege*, so Dani Moonstar can go and do her Valkyrie thing again. Some kind of anti-Valkyrie seemed logical. So what would they do? Like the time I found myself trapped on

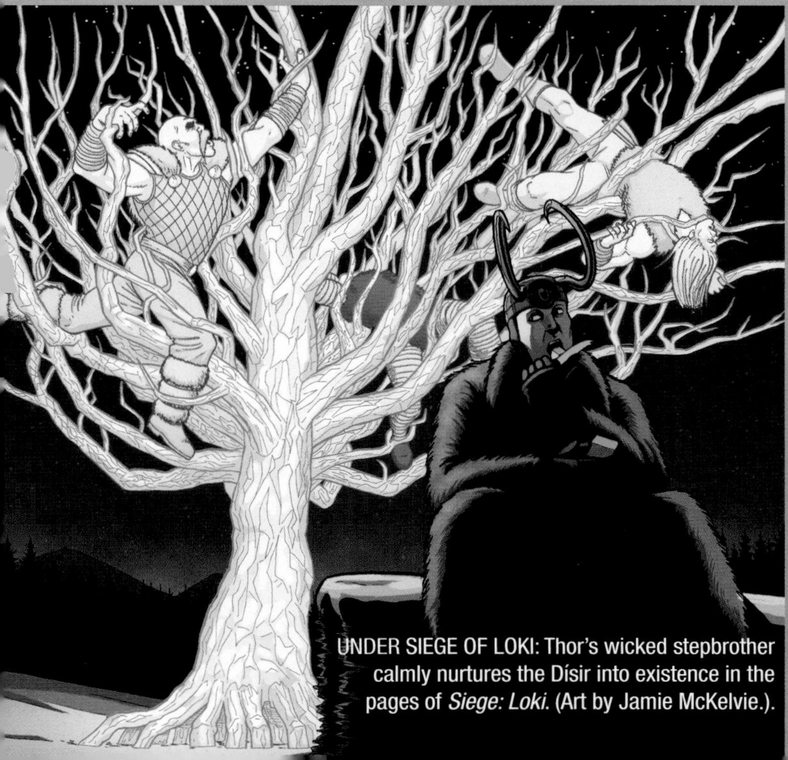

UNDER SIEGE OF LOKI: Thor's wicked stepbrother calmly nurtures the Dísir into existence in the pages of *Siege: Loki*. (Art by Jamie McKelvie.).

a camping holiday with no food, I soon turned to cannibalism. I decided to call them the Dísir — a conflicted, old general Norse term for ancestor spirits — because I hit upon a line saying that there's some research which argues "Dísir" is actually what they used to call Valkyrie before the word was invented. It struck me that instead of making that linguistically true, we could have some fun if we made that *mythlogically* true. As in, before the Valkyrie, there were the Dísir. Also: Nazgûl Valkyrie. That's an image. So I developed them, including a fair bit of their military organization, for their two appearances in the *Siege* tie-ins, barely any of which was on the page. When I was asked to do another four issues, it struck me as a chance to really let the ladies take center stage. That I'd left them in the ever-supple hands of Mephisto suggested the rest. (I love Mephisto. One of my favorite stories I've done for Marvel is a one-off Doctor Strange tale I did with Frazer Irving that has him being similarly sardonically wicked. He's just a very bad man. At least Loki seems to have an emotional need for what he does. Mephisto's just working his way up and down the list of deadly sins, like a tasting menu.)

SPOTLIGHT: Yum. Judging by both your *Thor* book and your *Ares* series, you know your mythology and your history. What is your background on this stuff, and with *Thor*?

KIERON: My background is basic common-or-garden teenage geek. I read mythology as a child, and what I didn't read I ripped off from role-playing-game manuals. My

GENERATION GILLEN

In his continuing quest to become Marvel's busiest writer, Kieron Gillen's *Journey Into Mystery* launch will take his tally to three ongoing series. This may be *Thor Spotlight*, but we'd be remiss if we didn't also fill you in on *Uncanny X-Men* and *Generation Hope*. Oh, and a certain one-shot that's bound to "leap" off the shelves.

SPOTLIGHT: How are you enjoying your time with the X-Men? Is Utopia all it's cracked up to be?

KIERON: It's the world's greatest undiscovered holiday resort. Every room has its beachfront view. No Sentinel attacks for at least a week. Perfect.

SPOTLIGHT: And how was working with Matt Fraction? Are you guys more Logan and Kurt or Logan and Scott?

KIERON: It was delightful. Generally speaking, though, we're less Logan, Kurt or Scott and more Dazzler and Pixie.

SPOTLIGHT: Now, you're going solo, and one of the most challenging aspects of writing *Uncanny X-Men* must be making it reader-friendly with such a huge cast.

KIERON: Yeah, that's the thing. When people leave the Avengers, they leave the Avengers. But once an X-Man, always an X-Man. On the other hand, that's a strength. "There are only a few mutants, and they mostly live on this island" is a fairly easy setup to explain. Matt's traditional method has been giving each character an introduction caption whenever they appear. Looking forward, I'm trying to structure stories so that we can absolutely frontload the introductions and have a "roster" for the story in question.

SPOTLIGHT: For all those Gillen completists out there checking out *Uncanny X-Men* for the first time: What one thing do they absolutely need to know, and what can they expect from the book?

KIERON: Their enemies gathered and tried to purge the last mutants from the face of the Earth. The X-Men made a stand, and they wor The question is: What do they dc now? They've got what's basicall a small nation, a model communit They've fought for this. They've survived. They won a war. Can the now win a peace? They need t learn to *live*.

SPOTLIGHT: Hope and the Five Lights. Not a crime-solving cartoon pop group, but th saviors of mutantkind and stars of your *Generation Hope* series How is mutant life treating them so far?

KIERON: As you may expect, they're sort of adjusting to the "hated and-feared" thing. Hope has this almost religious compulsion to save mutants, and they all fee compelled to follow. They're basically the flip of X-Force X-Force is a black-ops squac Generation Hope is a search-and rescue team, midwife to a nev generation. They are also engaging in teenage bonding exercises lik trying to make out with each othe

SPOTLIGHT: And just because we love him, Batroc. *Captain Americ and Batroc #1*. March. Ongoing series a foregone conclusion n'est-ce pas?

KIERON: I'll break the news here 2012's big crossover is *'Tach Wars*, where Stark, Batroc and al the other great cultivators of upper lip fuzz go facial hair-to-facial hai in the Mighty Marvel Manner. — J

Cover to *Generation Hope #1* by Olivier Coipel.

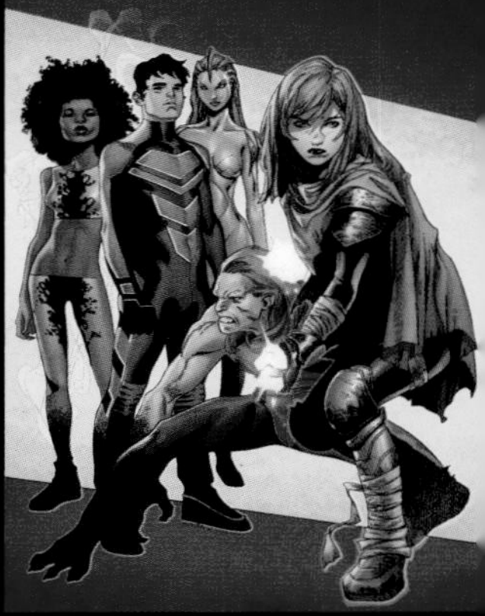

first Marvel comic I ever read was a *Thor* 1960s reprint, introduction of the Wrecker, which gave me my abiding interest in the man with the head-swaddling and the crowbar.

SPOTLIGHT: The world is about to discover Marvel's Thor. If a non-comics fan asked you what his deal is, what would you tell them?

KIERON: He's about the duality of the mortal and the divine. He's about reintroducing classic myth into the modern world, and gaining all the crazed and furious energy from contrasting them. He's the most important direct line between the modern super hero and the ancient proto-superhumans. They've been telling stories about Thor for 1,200 years now. We're not going to stop.

SPOTLIGHT: Now, as of April, you're the bona fide *Uncanny X-Men* writer. *(See sidebar.)* It's fair to say your Marvel career is going pretty well at this point.

KIERON: DON'T JINX IT!

SPOTLIGHT: Sorry! But while you have your hands full keeping track of the myriad merry mutants on Utopia, you still have some spare time to spend in Asgard. Word on the street is you're reviving a famous Marvel title of old. What tales to astonish of amazing fantasy will you be suspensefully crafting in the pages of *Journey Into Mystery*?

KIERON: The easiest way to describe *Journey Into Mystery* is that if *Thor* is *Avengers*, then *Journey Into Mystery* is *Secret Avengers*. While *Thor* is acting in bright daylight, *Journey Into Mystery* works by night. It's driven by Loki, using all his considerable wit and intelligence to keep the Nine Realms safe — or, at least, a suitable playground for his own kinds of mischief. And to do that, he recruits allies, or manipulates foes, to do what needs to be done — ideally, without anyone ever realizing he's doing it. Black ops, Norse-myth style. The first issue starts with one of the biggest mysteries in the modern Marvel Age: "Why did Loki do it?" What was Loki up to with *Siege*? You can see motivation within motivation set up there. If you read it closely, you can see parts of his plan. But...really, what was Loki trying to do by sacrificing himself? If that's been nagging at you, then all is laid out in our first issue. I think people will be surprised. He really thought of everything. Not an entirely stupid man, our Loki. But what's most important isn't what he was thinking, but what he was feeling. And then we go directly into young Loki pulling his team together to do what he has to do in *Fear Itself*. (*For more on Marvel's upcoming epic, see* Fear Itself Spotlight *in March! — Ed.)* Loki's saving the world, and no one will ever know.

"It's driven by Loki, using all his considerable wit and intelligence to keep the Nine Realms safe."

— Gillen on his new *Journey Into Mystery* title

SPOTLIGHT: In recent years Loki has been a man, a woman and a teen! Teen Loki — that's enough reason to pick up the book right there.

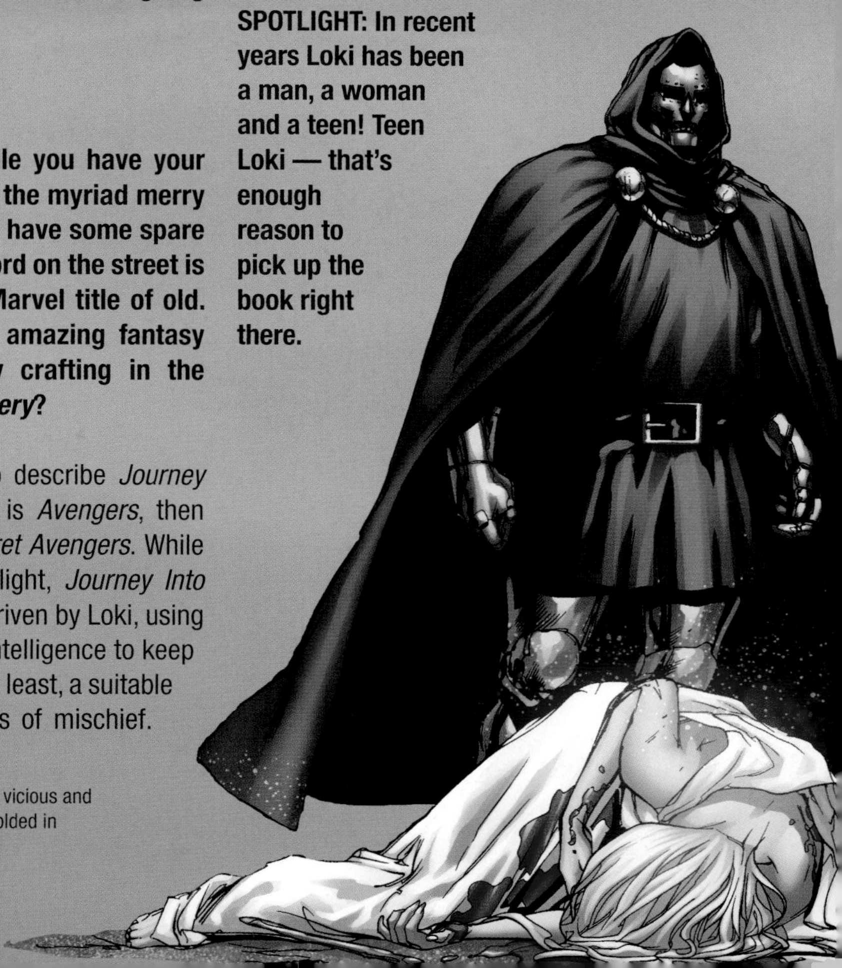

DOOM UNLEASHED: One of Doom's most vicious and murderous plots in his sordid history unfolded in Gillen's "Latverian Prometheus." (Art from *Thor #604* by Billy Tan.)

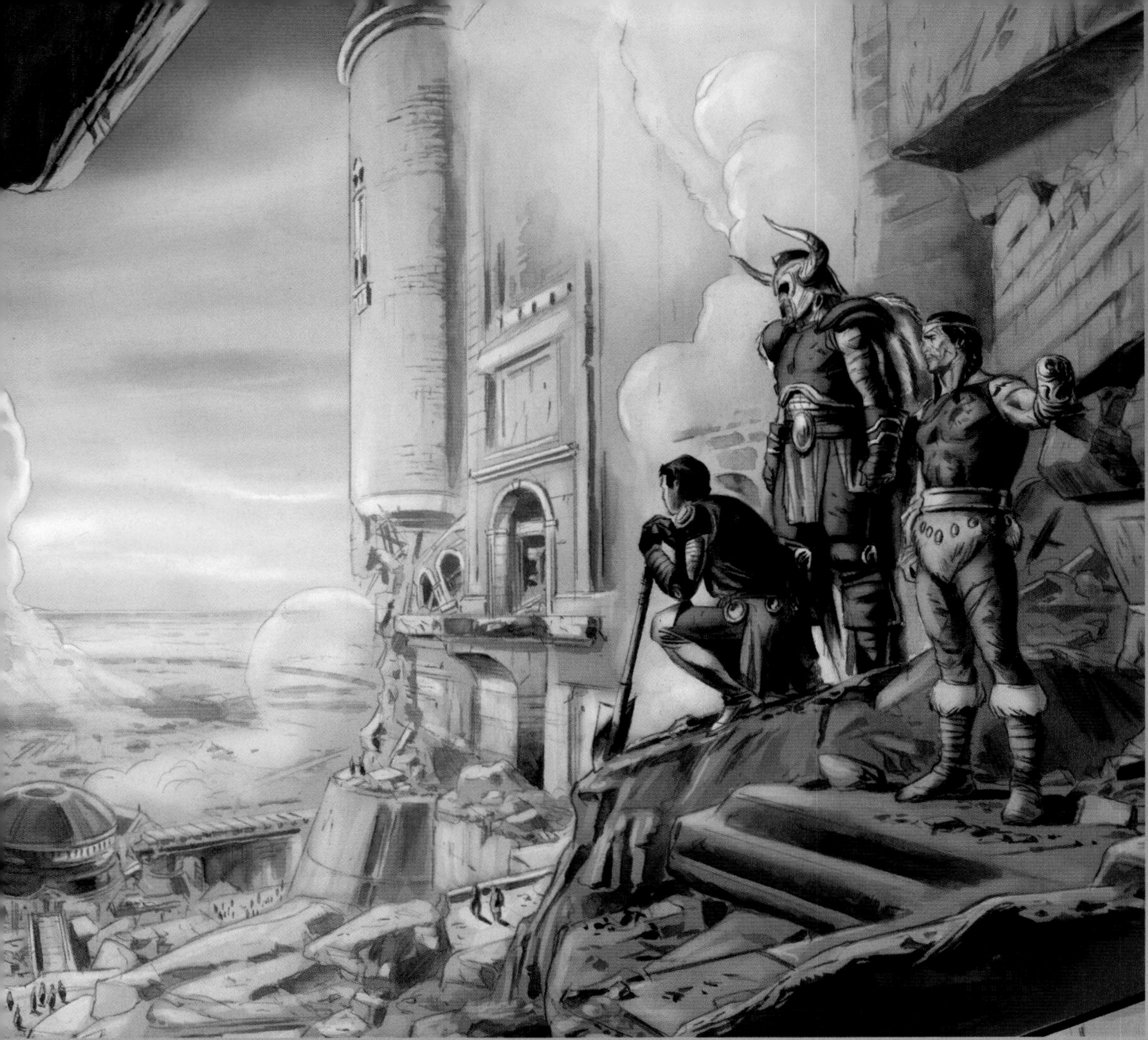

SIEGE COMPLETE: Balder, Tyr and Heimdall survey the damage brought by the Sentry's onslaught. (Art from *Thor #610* by Doug Braithwaite.)

KIERON: He works really well as a teen. Loki's always been the god of mischief, which generally speaking has been read in his god-of-evil-aspect. Teen Loki is exploring another way Loki was used mythologically — as in, the boyish trickster. You can have him acting in what's clearly a Loki way, but without the pure force of malice there. In fact, the malice is more aimed *at* him. Understandably, no one trusts Loki. If it wasn't for Thor, you suspect certain Asgardians would have throttled the boy the second he reappeared in Asgard. Immediately, we've got this great underdog dynamic, and tricksters are always best when they're underdogs.

SPOTLIGHT: Who else can we expect to see popping up?

KIERON: Old, dead Loki in issue #1, for a start. Bar him? Anyone and everyone from the mystic realms — and bordering areas — of the Marvel Universe. Long term, that's what *Journey of Mystery* is about: the shadow war between all the mythologies and arcane parts of the Marvel Universe. All the core Asgardians. Some of the Asgardians you won't expect. Norse mythology. Hela and Loki have unfinished business. Tyr. Mephisto. The Dísir. And it's been a while since we've seen Surtur, hasn't it? Looking forward? Dormammu? Strange? Ares? One of the joys of *Journey Into Mystery* is going to be seeing who Loki's going to be dragging in next, while knowing it's a book with a distinct end-point. It's heading somewhere, and when it gets there — well, the book would have to change utterly to continue. It's a big *vision thing*. I kind of got some of the core thoughts of *Journey Into Mystery* from that final arc of *Thor*, "The Fine Print." The idea of doing a book that can mash all these magical and mythological aspects together, and tell of this secret Machiavellian war that influences everything else. The deals that Hela and Mephisto make, beneath the table. And in Loki, we have a character that is a little more flexible ethically than most heroes, so we're able to slip between all these worlds. One part *Tintin*; one part *I, Claudius*; one part *Magnificent Seven*; one part *Sandman*; one part *Queen & Country*; all parts spangly. That's *Journey Into Mystery*. I know it's a clichéd thing for a writer to say, but I think *Journey Into Mystery* is the strongest book I've done for Marvel. There's nothing quite like it out there, I think.

SPOTLIGHT: With you writing both *Uncanny* and *JIM*, is there any chance of some interaction down the line? "Mutants in Asgard" has worked pretty well before.

KIERON: And with Asgard on Earth, it's certainly easier to do. They just need to take a plane ride to get to Broxton. I've certainly got ideas, but nothing in the immediate future.

SPOTLIGHT: And just so we know where your true loyalties lie: Thor vs. Wolverine. Only one can walk away. Who wins, and how?

KIERON: Thor would win — because it's hard to defeat someone who can destroy the planet you're standing on if they put their mind to it — but Wolverine would lose in a very cool way.

Kieron Gillen's work on Thor *can be found in a series of three trade paperbacks.* (See sidebar.) *Catch up on those — and, before you know it,* Journey Into Mystery *will be on comic-store shelves! ! Journey Into Mystery #622 — picking up the numbering of Fraction and Ferry's Thor — is written by Gillen and drawn by Secret Invasion: Thor artist Doug Braithwaite!*

ThOR

By Kieron Gillen

CHECKLIST 2010

Kieron Gillen's short history on the title between runs by heavyweights J. Michael Straczynski and Matt Fraction shouldn't be overshadowed by either!

MARVEL
THOR
LATVERIAN PROMETHEUS
GILLEN TAN

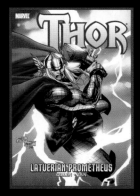

1. THOR: LATVERIAN PROMETHEUS TP

Collects *Thor (2007) #604-606, Sif #1* and more!

By Kieron Gillen, Billy Tan, Kelly Sue DeConnick and more

Doctor Doom makes his move in a horrifying tale of murder and evil!

SIEGE
THOR
GILLEN • TAN • ELSON
MCKELVIE • BRAITHWAITE
HENRICHON
MARVEL

2. SIEGE: THOR HC/TP

Collects *Thor (2007) #607-610, Siege: Loki* and *New Mutants (2010) #11*

By Kieron Gillen, Billy Tan, Niko Henrichon and more

The Asgardians face the battle of their lives on Midgard against Norman Osborn and the Sentry! Plus, behind the scenes on Loki and Dani Moonstar's return to Asgard!

MARVEL
THOR
SIEGE AFTERMATH
GILLEN • ELSON • BRAITHWAITE

3. THOR: SIEGE AFTERMATH TP

Collects *Thor (2007) #611-614*

By Kieron Gillen, Richard Elson and Doug Braitwhaite

Mephisto unleashes the scourge of the Disir upon fallen Asgard!

FEAR, LOATH

Writers Kieron Gillen, Robert Rodi And Roger Langridge Explicate Marvel's Trickster God

By Mike Conroy
Design by Michael Kronenberg

He's the Trickster God, Thor's adopted brother and deadly rival, one of Asgard's most villainous residents and a major player in *Fear Itself*. He's Loki, a Norse deity who's spread malice and mischief throughout the Marvel Universe ever since Stan Lee and Jack Kirby introduced him in 1962's *Journey into Mystery #85*.

With *Fear Itself* looming, a brain trust of Marvel writers with recent ties to Odin's adopted offspring offered their opinions on what makes this son of a Frost Giant such a terrifying threat and an apt player in an event that's bringing dread to the M.U.

"Loki was always God of Mischief," said Kieron Gillen, who's spotlighting Loki's involvement in *Fear Itself* beginning in the April-shipping *Journey into Mystery #622*. "Fear is one of the prime tools in his toolbox. Even in the most benevolent mischief – a practical joke – it's fear that gives it the spice, and the removal of fear is its punch line. And as anyone who's been reading

Cover art to *Journey into Mystery #623* by Stephanie Hans.

Marvel comics across the recent decades knows, it's rare that Loki's doing anything toward that end of mischief. But I think the greatest use of fear that Loki has is that his peers don't fear him *enough*.

"They know he's bad," said the British writer, who followed J. Michael Straczynski with a highly acclaimed year-long run on *Thor*. "They know he's done terrible things. But he's always found a way to wriggle free and come off cleaner than any sane mind would expect. He's a magical liar; the world is his web, and everyone was caught in it – and they never realized it. They should fear him more, and that's an incredible reason for why we should be afraid of what he could do.

"That's our older Loki," said Gillen, who also takes over the reins of *Uncanny X-Men* in April in tandem with artist Carlos Pacheco. "With our reincarnated, younger Loki, there's an element of irony. While his older self died in a moment of glory in a disaster, it was a disaster he precipitated. Now that he's returned, everyone *does* fear Loki, thinking it's a scheme of some kind. If Thor wasn't there, Loki would be dead in the night when some aggrieved Asgardian did the sensible thing. He's more actively feared and vulnerable than he has been at any point in his history, which is one of the things I think that makes Loki such a compelling lead.

"The twist is they're right. As the first issue of *Journey*

NG aND LOKi

reveals, it *is* all a scheme. Just one entirely unlike anyone could imagine, and it sets Loki on his path of using fear and mischief against *Fear Itself*."

Robert Rodi's credentials for opining on Thor's sibling rival relate to *Loki*, a four-parter he wrote in 2004; more recently, he has authored *Thor: For Asgard* and *Astonishing Thor*.

"What makes Loki so fearsome a figure is that he embodies the principle of misrule: He exists only to subvert...disrupt...destroy. Civilization is a fragile construct, and there are always cracks in its veneer; Loki represents all the forces that threaten to turn those cracks into chasms.

"He exists to unleash everything we strive to suppress, to tear down what we've built, to stir up what we've settled," the *Identity Disc* writer explained. "And he does all this while laughing; that's possibly the most frightening thing about him. He sows ruin and chaos and death, and he delights in it. For him, mayhem means mirth. He can't ever be reasoned with, or even understood. He can only be avoided.

"Except when he can't," cautioned Rodi, whose Mike Choi-penciled *Astonishing Thor* five-parter concludes in May. "Then, God help us."

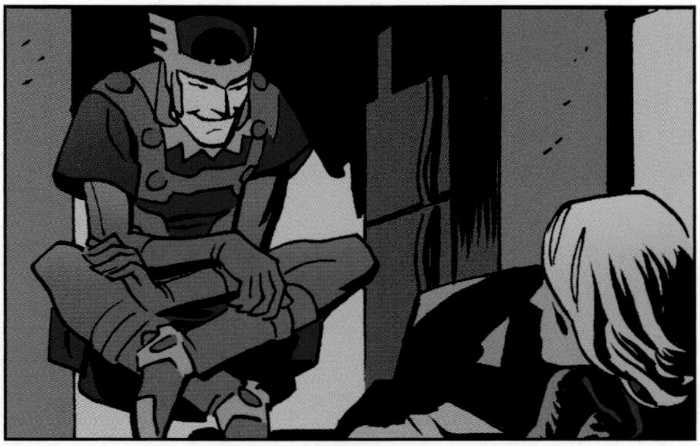

Art from *Thor: The Mighty Avenger #3* by Chris Samnee.

Offering a slightly different perspective was Roger Langridge, a New Zealander now based in England. "'My' Loki, from *Thor: The Mighty Avenger*, isn't quite the same character as the regular Marvel Universe Loki. With that caveat in mind, though...

"My first thought is that the title, *Fear Itself*, is a contraction of FDR's famous phrase, – 'We have nothing to fear but fear itself' – which is another way of saying that our greatest enemy is a trick our mind plays upon us. A trick...a trickster...aha! (You see where I'm going with this?) So there's that.

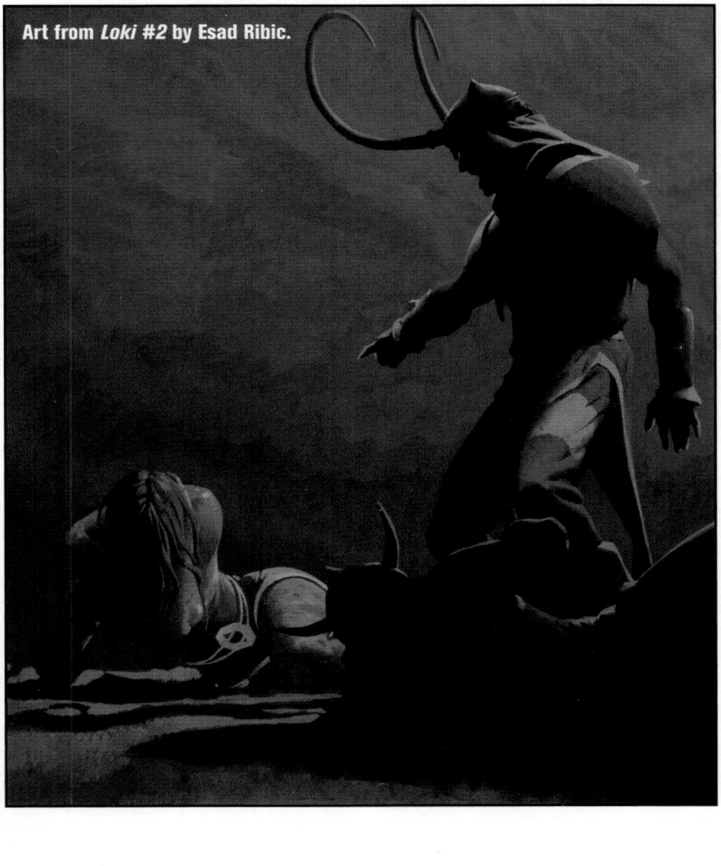

Art from *Loki #2* by Esad Ribic.

"On a more basic level, there's the simple fact that Loki is a character from mythology, with all the dark baggage that goes along with that," the New Zealander continued. "Have you read any of those Norse myths? Deeply disturbing stuff. Baby-eating, incestuous, evil-goat-devouring weirdness. Loki is part of a terrifying world. Furthermore, he's the wild card in that context. He has the potential to transgress the already-transgressive rules of his world. And there's nothing more frightening than something that is totally unpredictable.

"So, yeah. He's so crazy it just might work," concluded Langridge, who wrote and drew 2008's four-issue *Fin Fang Four*.

However you look it, everybody agrees terror accompanies Loki wherever he goes. And Odin's adopted son definitely won't be out of place in an event known as *Fear Itself*. •

Come With Us

Since 1952, Those Three Words Have Enticed Readers Onto The Unimagined Roads Of Marvel.

By Robert Greenberger
Design by Michael Kronenberg

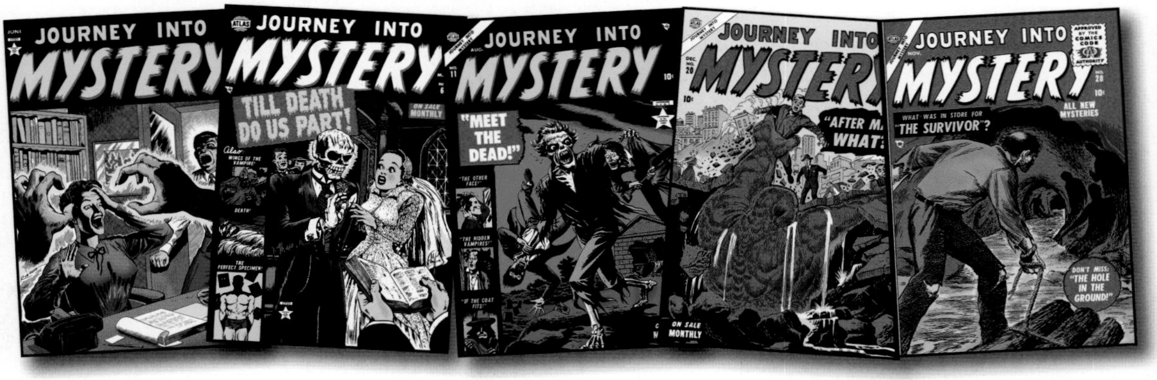
JOURNEY INTO MYSTERY
JOURNEY INTO MYSTERY
TILL DEATH DO US PART!
JOURNEY INTO MYSTERY
"MEET THE DEAD!"
ON SALE MONTHLY
JOURNEY INTO MYSTERY
JOURNEY INTO MYSTERY
WHAT WAS IN STORE FOR "THE SURVIVOR"?
ALL NEW MYSTERIES
DON'T MISS: "THE HOLE IN THE GROUND!"

As the Golden Age of comics was drawing to a close during the late '40s, the most popular genres appeared to be war, Western, crime and – bringing up the rear – horror. Timely Comics, which was evolving into Atlas Comics, continued its tried and true method of figuring out what was popular with readers and flooding the market with such titles. Atlas already was publishing several mystery series, including *Strange Tales,* with short thrills and twist endings when it launched *Journey into Mystery* in June 1952. Russ Heath's cover to the debut issue was noteworthy for its complete lack of cover copy, a rarity.

Journey into Mystery chugged along for most of the next ten years, with dollops of O. Henry-style stories; ghouls, goblins and monsters; and studies on the human psyche. Edited and largely written by Stan Lee, the book boasted an impressive array of artistic talents – including Gene Colan, Russ Heath, John Romita, Jerry Robinson, Dick Ayers, Joe Maneely, Tony Dipreta, Jack Abel, Paul Reinman, John Forte, Mort Lawrence, Sam Kweskin, Jay Scott Pike, Howard Post, Carl Hubbell, Dick Briefer, Bill Everett, Don Perlin, George Tuska, Myron Fass, Vince Colletta, and Doug Wildey.

Journey into Mystery was a casualty when the line contracted in 1957, but was back a little more than a year later; taking one of the precious eight slots the company was allotted by distributor Independent News.

As Lee ushered in the Marvel Age in the fall of 1961 with *Fantastic Four*, he was encouraged to create other heroes, each of whom needed a berth. Lee chose to make Thor the lead feature in *JIM*, beginning with issue #83. The book's hammer-hurling star grew so popular anthology stories running behind the Thor feature – monster fare mostly written by Stan's brother, Larry Leiber – were jettisoned as of issue #97 in favor of the *Tales of Asgard* feature. It was in these pages readers not only met Thor, but also Odin, Loki, Balder the Brave, the Warriors Three, Sif, Surtur, the Destroyer, Ulik and Hela. Longtime Marvel foes the Absorbing Man, Cobra, Mr. Hyde, the Grey Gargoyle, the Lava Men and Radioactive Man all made their first appearances in *JIM*, further marking it as a noteworthy title. There was but one *Journey into Mystery Annual*, a 1965 offering that introduced readers to Stan and Jack Kirby's concept of Hercules and Mount Olympus. And lo, another hero was born. As of issue #126, though, Lee took the

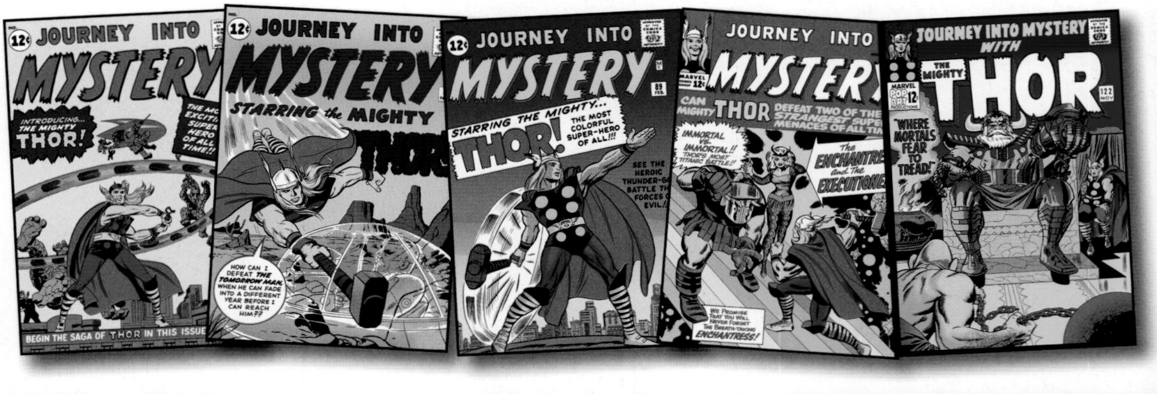
JOURNEY INTO MYSTERY
INTRODUCING... THE MIGHTY THOR!
BEGIN THE SAGA OF THOR IN THIS ISSUE
JOURNEY INTO MYSTERY
STARRING the MIGHTY
HOW CAN I DEFEAT THE TOMORROW MAN WHEN HE CAN FADE INTO A DIFFERENT YEAR BEFORE I CAN REACH HIM?!
JOURNEY INTO MYSTERY
STARRING THE MIGHTY... THOR!
THE MOST COLORFUL SUPER-HERO OF ALL!!!
JOURNEY INTO MYSTERY
IMMORTAL VS. IMMORTAL!! THOR'S MOST TITANIC BATTLE!!
WE PROMISE THAT YOU WILL NEVER FORGET THE BREATH-TAKING ENCHANTRESS!
JOURNEY INTO MYSTERY WITH THE MIGHTY THOR
"WHERE MORTALS FEAR TO TREAD!"

n A JOURNEY INTO MYSTERY

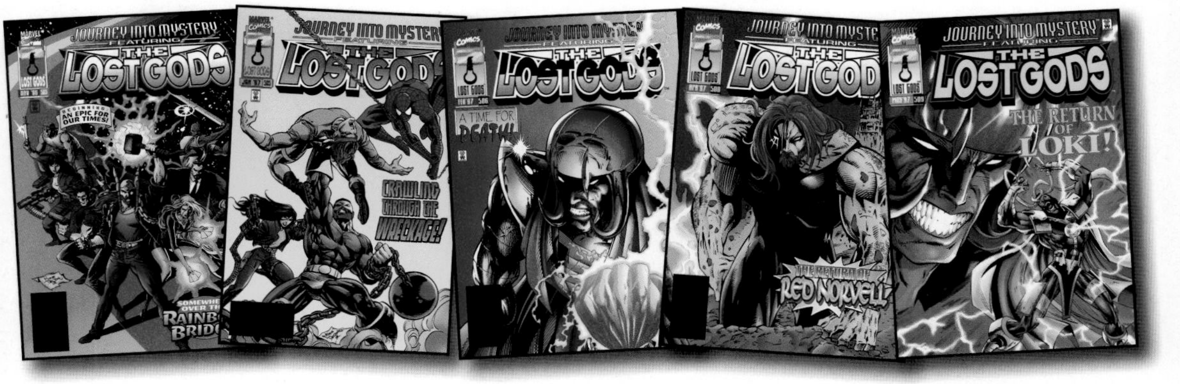
JOURNEY INTO MYSTERY
FEATURING
THE LOST GODS
BEGINNING AN EPIC FOR OUR TIMES!
CRAWLING THROUGH THE WRECKAGE!
A TIME FOR DEATH!
THE RETURN OF RED NORVELL
THE RETURN OF LOKI!

unprecedented step of changing the book's title to *Thor*, which it remained into the mid-1990s.

As the Comics Code Authority revamped its guidelines during the early 1970s, it ushered in a new era of horror. Marvel obliged the pent-up demand with *Chamber of Chills, Tower of Shadows* and a revived *Journey into Mystery* in October 1972. Along with original terror tales and reprints, the new series adapted works from Robert E. Howard, Robert Bloch and H.P. Lovecraft. Writers included Roy Thomas, Steve Englehart, Steve Gerber, Ron Goulart, and George Alec Effinger; among the artistic contributors were Gil Kane, Jim Starlin, Tom Palmer, Ralph Reese, Billy Graham and Gene Colan, who was also represented in the first incarnation. After five issues, *JIM* switched to all reprints before ending with #19.

Everything changed in 1996 as Thor was among several heroes to vanish at the end of the Onslaught event. Toward the end of the year, *Journey into Mystery* returned with issue #503 and a feature known as "The Lost Gods." Written by Tom DeFalco and illustrated by Deodato Studios, the story focused on the Asgardian gods minus their memories, now living on Earth. The World Tree Yggdrasil had been lulled into thinking Ragnarok had occurred, and that a new cycle of gods was to begin. For the next year, readers saw Sif, Balder, Ulik the Troll, the Warriors Three and the Enchantress slowly regain their knowledge of the past and forge a future for themselves without Asgard to call home. Red Norvell gathered them to prepare them to do battle with Set, the Egyptian God of the Dead.

With issue #614, *Journey into Mystery* became an anthology, its focus shifting to other heroes from the Marvel Universe such as Shang-Chi, Master of Kung-Fu; Black Widow; and Hannibal King.

Thor returned in 1998, but received his own title and a new #1 under writer Dan Jurgens and artist John Romita Jr. After 85 issues, that title faded; a new *Thor* series began in 2007. It was at this point the Marvel mathematicians took a look back all the way to *Journey into Mystery*'s 1952 origins. They learned that once you counted up the 521 issues of the original run of *JIM/Thor* and added in the second *Thor* series, you were rapidly approaching a 600th issue. So it was that in 2009, *Thor* reverted to the original series numbering. This new status quo remained in place until issue #621, when the God of Thunder left for a new series titled *The Mighty Thor*.

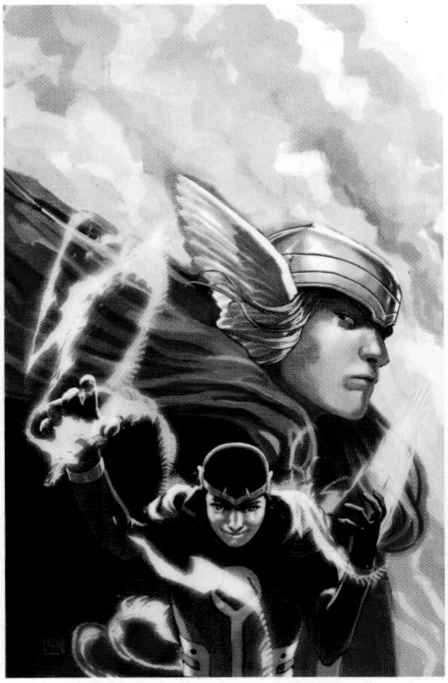

But what of the long-lived moniker *Journey into Mystery*? With issue #622, Marvel handed the reins to writer Kieron Gillen and artist Doug Braithwaite; their focus will be on the newly resurrected young Loki and his relationship with Thor. And so, 59 years after those three words appeared on newsstands, *Journey into Mystery* still has life in it yet! •

Journey into Mystery Collections

- *Marvel Masterworks: Atlas Era Journey into Mystery Vols. 1-3*, collecting *Journey into Mystery (1952) #1-30*
- *Marvel Masterworks: Thor Vols. 1-4*, collecting *JIM #83-125* and *JIM Annual #1*
- *Thor: The Lost Gods*, collecting *JIM (1996) #503-513*

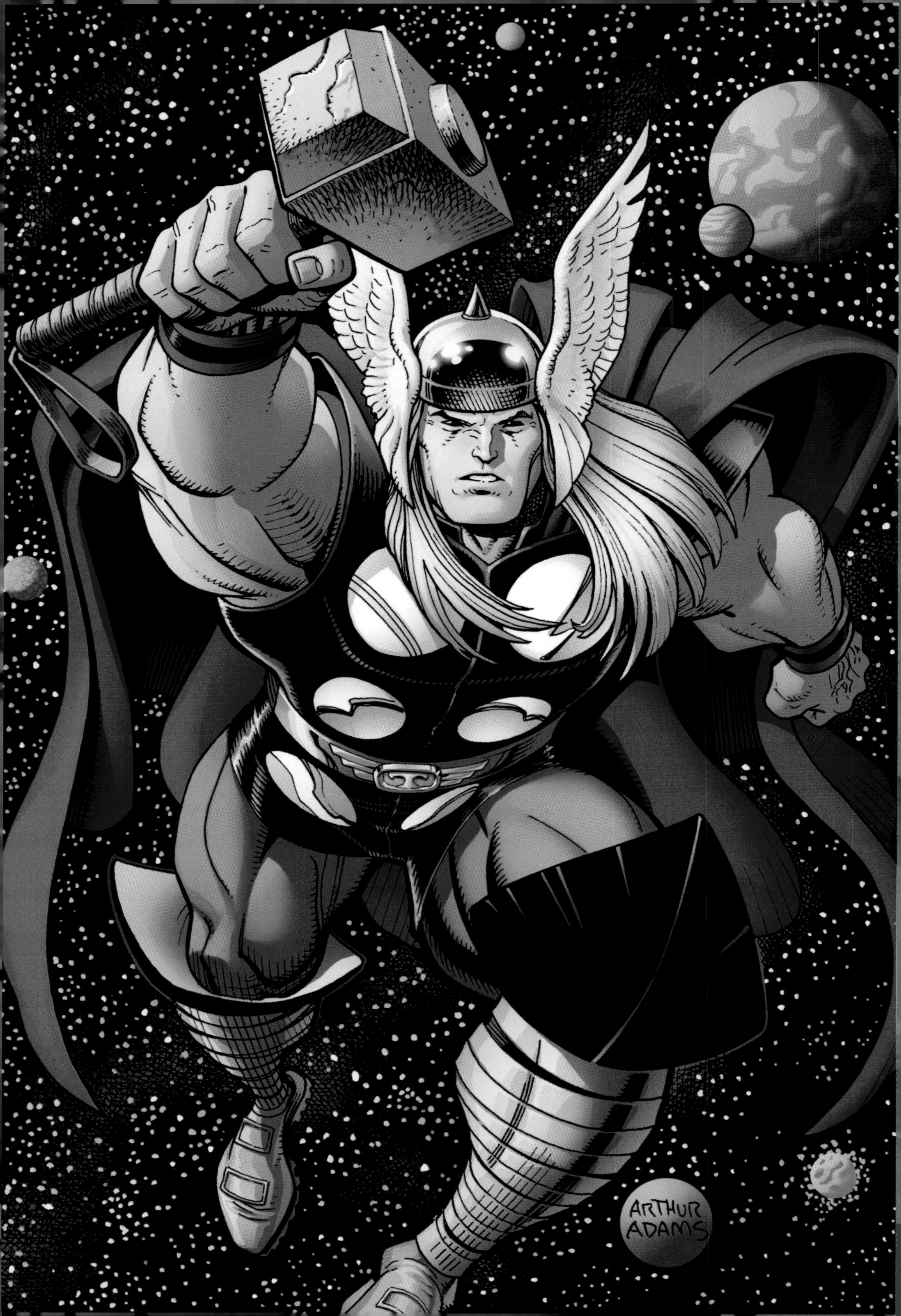
ARTHUR
ADAMS

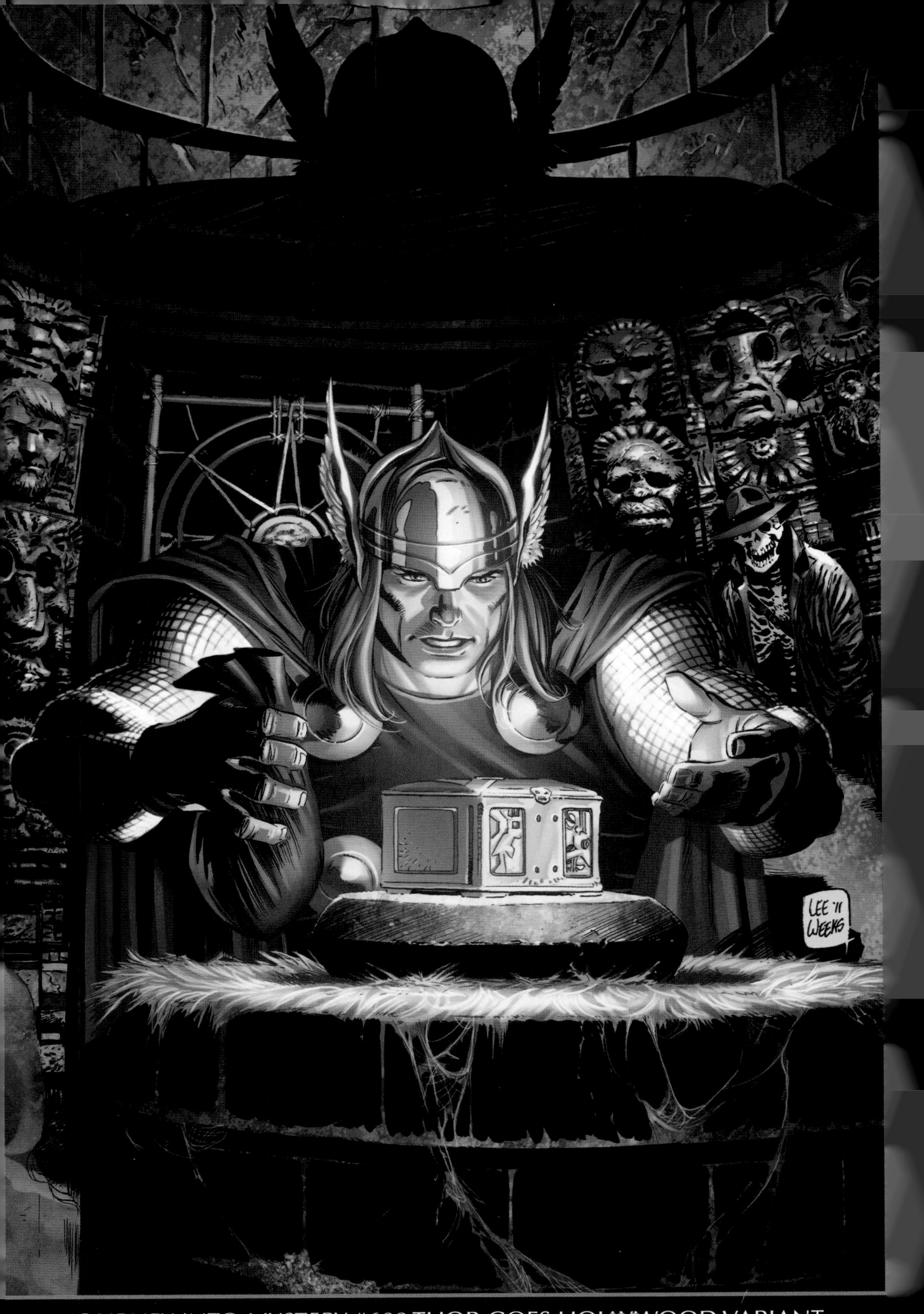
LEE '11
WEEKS

JOURNEY INTO MYSTERY #622 THOR GOES HOLLYWOOD VARIANT

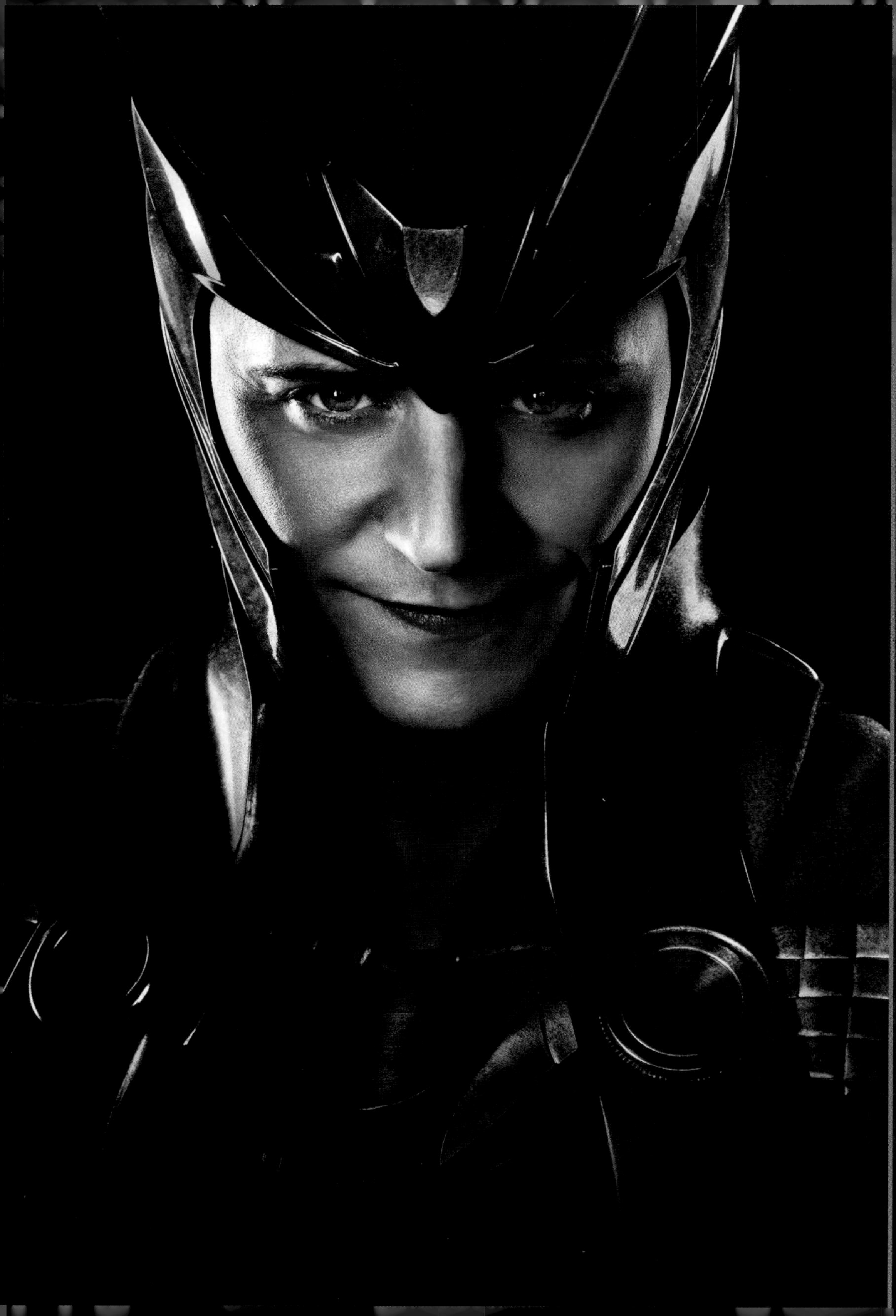

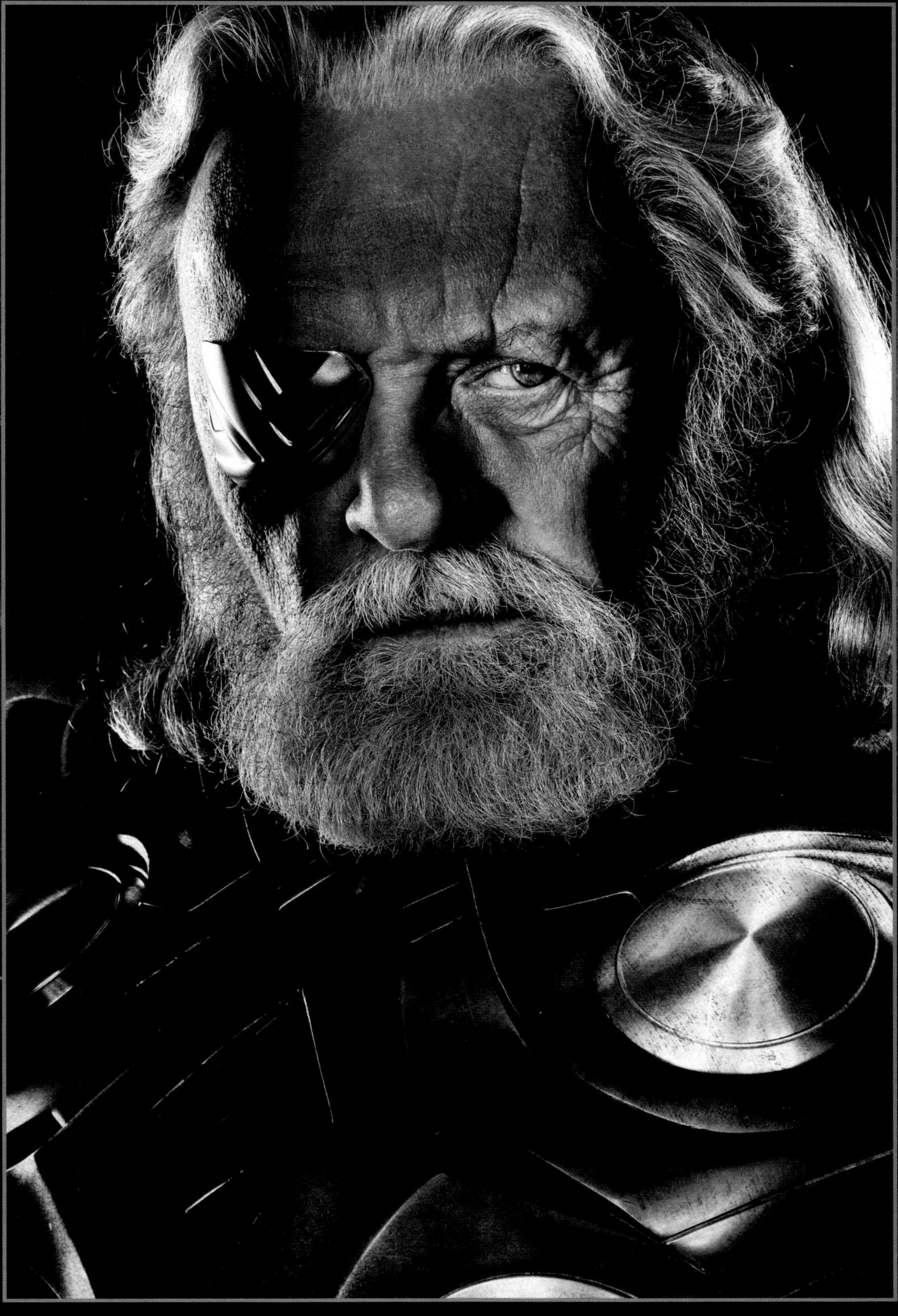

JOURNEY INTO MYSTERY #623 2ND PRINTING VARIANT

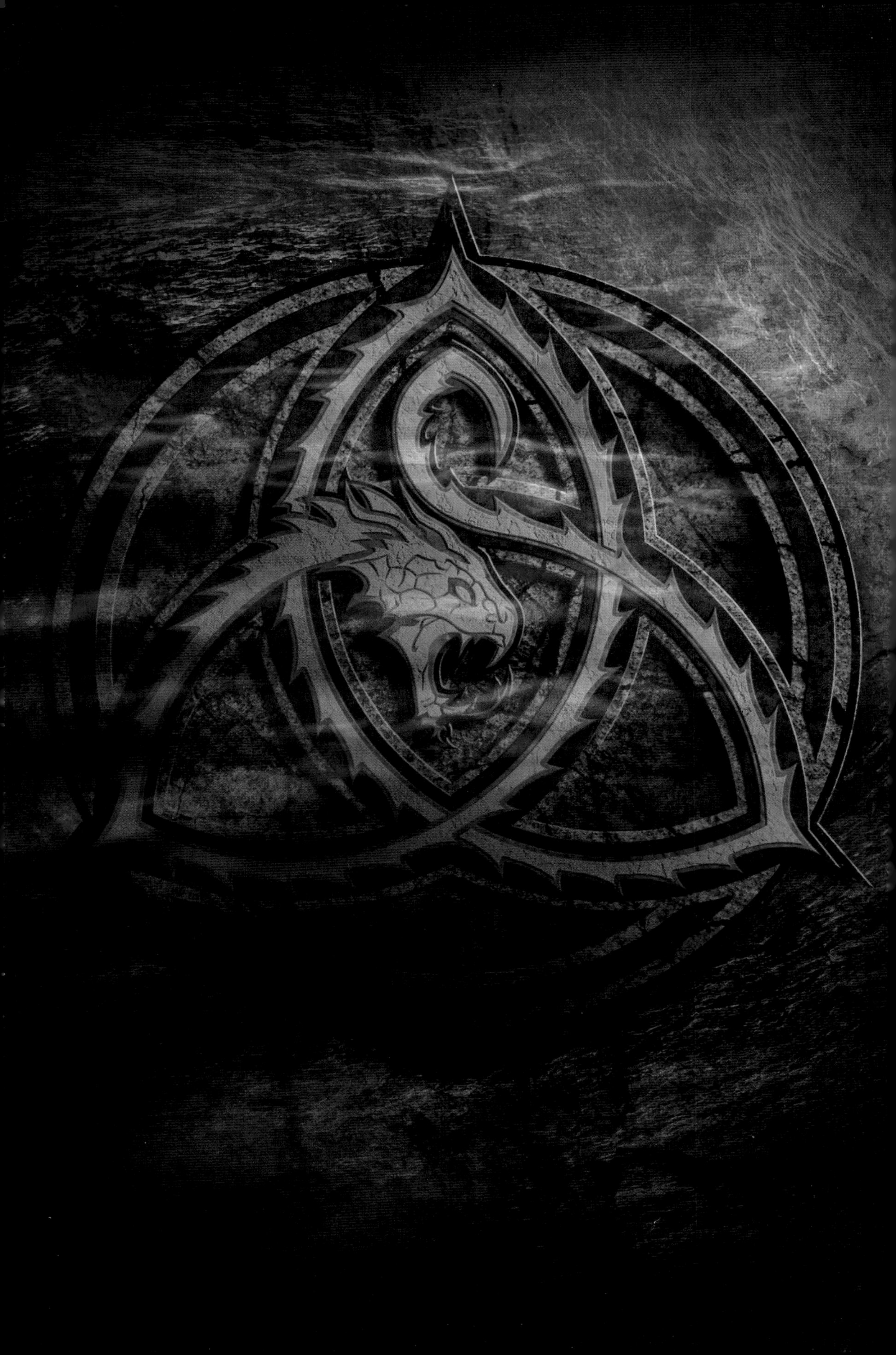